RIVER

West Boston Bridge

Charles Street

Pinkney St.

(Olive St.)
Mount Vernon St.

Parkman Market

Nos. 87, 89
Otis

29A

13-17

Walnut St.

Perkins
Joy

Mason
Nos. 43-57
Belknap St.

16,8

Cambridge St.

Sumner St.

STATE HOUSE

3

Memorial Column
Middlecot St.

Coolidge Sr.
Bulfinch Pl.

1

Green St.

Otis

Blake~Tuckerman
Bulfinch Homestead
Bulfinch St.

Bulfinch

Amory

Park St.

Nos. 1-8

Somerset St.

Southacks Ct.

Coolidge Jr.

Hawkins St.
School

Merrimack St.

MILL POND

CANAL

Canal St.

Leverett St.

Bridge

Alms House

Charlestown St.

Charles River Bridge

Latin School

School St.

County Court House

Cornhill

Tremont St.

Court St.

Concert Hall

Old State House
Manufacturers and Mechanics Bank
Boston Marine
New England Marine

Milk St.

Pearl St.

Oliver St.

Broad St.

Street

India St.

Suffolk Insurance
Union Bank
Boston Bank
Massachusetts Bank

State St.

Faneuil Hall

Ann St.

Union St.

Hanover St.

Fish St.

North Sq.

New North Church

Lynn St.

Ship St.

4

Fort Hill

India Wharf

Long Wharf

The T Wharf

HARBOR

BULFINCH'S BOSTON 1787-1817

A Dinner Party in the Tontine Crescent. Painting by Henry Sargent, c. 1816. *Courtesy of the Museum of Fine Arts, Boston.*

Bulfinch's Boston

1787-1817

HAROLD & JAMES KIRKER

NEW YORK
OXFORD UNIVERSITY PRESS
1964

For Our Parents

Preface

CHARLES BULFINCH occupied a unique and vital position in Boston for the three decades between the Constitutional Convention and the end of the War of 1812. During this period, he was much more than the architect of Federal Boston, although it is in this capacity that he is generally associated with the city's history. Bulfinch was best known to his contemporaries as the chairman of Boston's Board of Selectmen and Chief of Police. In his total involvement in local affairs—politics, society, reform, education, town improvements, town planning, architecture—Bulfinch was a major force in the life of Boston. This book is the story of that involvement.

WE WISH TO ACKNOWLEDGE the generous assistance given us by members of the Bulfinch family, especially the architect's great, great grandson, Commander Charles Bulfinch. We wish also to express our gratitude to Mr. John Alden of the Boston Public Library, Professor Howard R. Bartlett of Massachusetts Institute of Technology, Professor Carl Bridenbaugh of Brown University, Mrs. Yves Buhler of the Boston Museum of Fine Arts, Mrs. Harriet Ropes Cabot of the Bostonian Society, Mr. J. P. Carlhian of Sheply Bulfinch Richardson & Abbott, Mr. Abbott Lowell Cummings of the Society for the Preservation of New England

Antiquities, Professor Richard M. Douglas and Mrs. Ruth Dubois of Massachusetts Institute of Technology, Mr. George T. Goodspeed of Boston, Mr. Sinclair Hitchings of the Boston Public Library, Father James J. Manning of Holy Cross Cathedral, Mr. David McKibbin of the Boston Athenæum, Miss Carolyn E. Jakeman of the Houghton Library, Mrs. Langdon Marvin of New York, Mrs. Alice D. Maraspin of the Bostonian Society, Mr. William B. Osgood of Boston, Miss Rosemary E. Phelan of Boston, Mr. Stephen T. Riley of the Massachusetts Historical Society, Mr. Charles F. Rowley of Chestnut Hill, Mrs. Marjorie Drake Ross of Boston, Miss Caroline Shillaber of the Harvard Graduate School of Design, Mr. Nathan C. Shiverick of Cambridge, Mr. George B. Vaughan of Boothbay, Maine, Mr. Walter Muir Whitehill of the Boston Athenæum, Miss Helen D. Willard of the Harvard Theatre Collection, Mrs. Elizabeth Wright of the Boston Public Library, and Miss Barbara Wriston of the Chicago Art Institute.

H.K.
J.K.

Cambridge, Massachusetts
August 1964

Contents

BULFINCH'S BOSTON 1787-1817

I

RETURN TO BOSTON

THE BOSTON to which Charles Bulfinch returned in 1787 was still very much a colonial town. After a year and a half traveling between London, Paris, and Rome, it must have seemed to him incredibly small and provincial. By comparison the older cities of Europe were certainly over-whelming. London in particular made a tremendous im-pression upon the young Bostonian. Her Neo-classical architecture, then almost unknown in the New World, captured his imagination and burst through his notebooks. He was never again free from these memories. In a quiet, persistent way they changed his life, and the life of his town. For these impressions were not secretly hoarded or squandered in dilettantism; they were the stuff of his dream for rebuilding Boston in the image of mid-Georgian England. But London-insired building schemes were only part of an experiment in which the English model was evoked in every aspect of the town's life. This experiment, here called Bulfinch's Boston, began in 1787, the year a sensitive and enthusiastic young man arrived home from the Grand Tour with a collection of architectural books and a portfolio of drawings.

Bulfinch had gone to Europe on a legacy left by an exiled relative. He had not traveled abroad, however, in order to return an architect. On the contrary, he resumed a life of disinterested public service in the leisurely tradition of an eighteenth-century gentleman. That Bulfinch was very much a gentleman is evident in the portrait painted during his visit in England by Mather Brown (*Plate 1*). Writing home to his mother at this time, he shyly characterized the delineation as a "very dull, unmeaning face."[1] There is, undoubtedly, little in the portrait to suggest that the European experience would find important expression or that there were untried talents awaiting the test of adversity. The outstanding impressions conveyed by the portrait are breeding and withdrawal. The artist caught the somewhat complacent stare of a young man reared in the protective atmosphere of one of Boston's richest families; of the "sensible, well educated young gentleman" recommended to Benjamin Franklin by Governor James Bowdoin when, at the age of twenty-two, he set off on the journey that was to alter the course of his life.[2]

The English portrait is an accurate one, remarkably similar to the miniature of Bulfinch in the Boston Museum of Fine Arts done two years later in 1788 and attributed to Joseph Dunkerley. The miniature depicts the same thin, oval face with indecisive mouth and strongly marked eyebrows. The hair is dark brown and the quizzical eyes a lighter shade of the same color. Bulfinch had the ruddy complexion and slender build that visitors to Boston in the post-Revolutionary period were so fond of ascribing to its inhabitants. His physique was never robust but, again like so many of his townsmen, his carriage was erect and his deportment grave. He was not without moral and physical courage, although his disposition was retiring and timid.[3] When the time came to consider a profession, Dr. Thomas Bulfinch opposed the idea of his son following him into the practice of medicine, believing the duties of a physician too arduous and demanding. And even several years after his return, the matter of a profession remained unresolved; the town directory of 1789 lists Charles Bulfinch merely as "gentleman."

The powdered wig and ruffled stock in the Mather Brown portrait suggest a European sophistication that belies the provincial background of both Bulfinch and his town. For in 1787 Boston trailed far behind London in style, notwithstanding it was the fourth largest English city at the outbreak of the Revolution. Practically nothing in Boston had changed since then; mementos of the old regime were everywhere. During the previous quarter-century the population remained stationary and little building was undertaken. There was nothing to hint of the order and elegance Bulfinch would bring to the New England capital. Boston retained the appearance of a prosperous English town of the late Elizabethan period. The settled parts were crowded and their development helter-skelter; streets and lanes, twisting and turning, showed obvious departures from the original order of the town's seventeenth-century planners. Lining these byways, in some cases overtopping them, were buildings reflecting the somber heritage of the Puritans or the rustic grandeur of the royalists. Gothic utility jostled Stuart pretension along every street without creating too startling a contrast, the differences in time obliterated by the indeterminate nature of the architecture. The earlier tradition, however, was giving way, helped as much by frequent fires as any conscious endeavor by the townsfolk to create a modern city. But if brick and slate occasionally replaced wood and thatch, and sash windows and Ionic pilasters superseded leaded casements and carved pendants, the character of Boston building remained unsophisticated and undistinguished. What passed for Georgian architecture in the New England capital at the time of Bulfinch's return was already several generations out of date in London.[4]

Boston was the most conservative of the major colonial cities of the Atlantic seaboard, and its population was the most homogeneous. Until the War of 1812, the town was not subject to the immigration that kept New York and Philadelphia in a state of flux. The early settlers had come mainly from villages and towns in southeastern England scarcely affected by Renaissance building forms lately introduced from Italy, France, and the Low Countries. Artisans, fishermen, traders, and farmers by profession, they brought all their ancient ways to the New World. In the mythology of the frontier the colonist is portrayed as adventurous, original, anxious to kick over all traces of the past. Actually the opposite is a truer picture. And the English colonists in America were no different in this sense than Greeks in Italy, Romans in Britain, Spaniards in Peru, or Americans themselves as they moved westward. To survive in a strange and lonely wilderness the immigrant falls back more than ever upon old, proven ways. This natural conservatism was intensified in Boston by the parochial character and religion of the Puritans. Boston's growth was most spectacular in the first decade of settlement, in the eleven years after 1629 when England was without a Parliament. And though not all the settlers were Puritans or from East Anglia, they managed to control the colony until Massachusetts became a royal province in 1691. With important exceptions, the Puritan ascendancy supported a spirit of suspicion and exclusiveness that survived three-quarters of a century of royal rule and continued into the American period.

The oldest parts of the town—the areas facing the water or the lanes straying reluctantly toward the hinterland— were filled with wooden structures of Old World character. Only one of them, the Revere house, remains today. Erected in 1680, at the twilight of Puritan rule, and considerably enlarged in the eighteenth century, this lone survivor is not an especially good example of Boston's early building. The dwelling originally occupying the site, that of the Reverend Increase Mather, would tell a more interesting tale. A few years before Mather's house burned in 1676, the town passed an ordinance requiring overhanging stories to be at least eight feet off the ground. This restriction gives some idea of the low, sunless, and crowded streets of the Puritan settlement. There was plenty of space and light a short distance inland; but the inhabitants remained in protective knots long after external danger had passed. The emphasis in building was on the massing of vertical forms through steep gables and clusters of chimneys. Paul Revere's house lacks the angular silhouette so distinctive of Elizabethan dwellings in both Old and New England. And it hardly suggests the gaunt, indrawn nature of the Puritan capital: a place of unpainted wooden buildings, stocks and pillory, sober activity, and long hours

[7]

in the meetinghouse. But the original floor plan of the Revere house was typical, and the exterior of clapboards with overhanging story, leaded glass windows, and massive chimney reveal the general character of Boston's seventeenth-century building.[5]

Eight years after the Revere house was erected on the ruins of his own dwelling, the Reverend Increase Mather went to London as Boston's representative in her struggles with Governor Andros. In his descent from New England divines, his profession, and his house, Mather epitomized the vanishing rulers of the Old Colony. Edmund Andros, on the other hand, foretold by his Cavalier family, his knighthood, and his Episcopal religion the future leaders of the royal province. The people who counted most in Boston from 1700 to 1775 were crown officials and the local merchants who allied themselves with this ruling clique. Their rallying point was the Province House in Marlborough Street. Erected as a private mansion in 1679, the future Province House was one of only two known dwellings constructed of brick in Boston during the seventeenth century. The original structure, considered ostentatious by Puritan standards, possessed really only the simplest features of the English Jacobean manor. The transformation of this house into a quasi-Georgian mansion took place in 1716 when it was singled out as headquarters for the royal governors. An extra story, a new roof with dormers and cupola, sash instead of casement windows, and a classical porch attempted to bring the building into the modern age. In this remodeled mansion appeared most of the features of the Georgian house in Boston before Bulfinch. They were usually assembled in a simple, even crude, manner that mocked the formal and academic spirit of contemporary English building. Nevertheless, even in the New England adaptation, the authoritative character of Georgian architecture came through: it was manifestly the model for a Court party aping the London of the Georges.

Everything in Boston was in sight or sound of the sea (*Plate 2*). The town's 15,000 or so inhabitants continued to live and work close to the arching coves which gave the place the appearance of a pinwheel adrift in the harbor. Boston was then almost an island, its only land connection being the long, narrow neck at the southwest corner leading into Roxbury. The Neck was a forlorn place, dreaded in winter or in time of storm. For the intemperate person who tarried too long in the taverns, a journey across this narrow strip in the blackness of night was tantamount to suicide; and even after the road was fenced in 1724, the Neck remained a forbidding place where travelers, hounded by wind, seaspray, or darkness, stumbled into the mud flats and marshes to the west. These marshes, a part of the Back Bay, were the teeming habitat of wild fowl. Shooting on the Neck was prohibited early in the eighteenth century, but some of the old townspeople remembered fathers and brothers going off with guns on their shoulders to scout the marshes separating the Back Bay from the Charles River. The eastern side of the Neck faced the sea. Here began the line of docks which jutted out from the meandering coast like the teeth of a shark and culminated in Long Wharf at the foot of State Street.

The road traversing the Neck also intersected State Street. Beginning at the fortified gate separating Boston from Roxbury, this thoroughfare wound for a mile and a half northward under the aegis of four names: Orange, Newbury, Marlborough, and Cornhill. Eventually the many-named avenue became Washington Street. In Bulfinch's time this simplification had not taken place and Cornhill, the last lap of the highroad, crossed State Street to form the most prominent intersection in the provincial capital. This crossroad was the history-laden center of Boston, famous since earliest times when the road from the Neck was designated the High Street and State Street the Great Street. At their intersection stood the original symbols of church and state—the first meetinghouse and the first town house. In 1787, a century and a half after John Winthrop led the Puritans to the Shawmut peninsula, the ghosts of these buildings still dominated the scene. The Town House of Puritan rule was superseded by the State House of royal charter and the wooden First Meetinghouse by a brick church of respectable Georgian design. The rebuilding of these structures followed two significant events in the town's history: the naming of the Great Street as King Street in an attempt to establish the power of British crown over Puritan meetinghouse, and the fire of 1711. At the same time the third force in colonial Boston—commerce—was dramatically emphasized by the construction of Long Wharf at the foot of King (State) Street.

Viewed from Long Wharf, Boston described an arc of warehouses and steeples which followed the contour of the Town Cove stretching south to Fort Hill and north to Copp's Hill. Although both hills were familiar sighting points for mariners, the chief landmark of old Boston was the three-domed mountain rising precipitously behind State Street and falling away westward to the marshes of the Back Bay. This range gave the town its original name Trimountain (Tramount or Trimontaine). The highest peak was Beacon Hill, a remote pastoral region dominated by the wooden signal pole set up in the first years of Puritan rule. The peak closest to State Street, Cotton Hill, was occupied by a few country estates; the third summit, Mount Whoredom, supported a disreputable community along its sunless northern slope. When Bulfinch returned from Europe only a fraction of the land between Trimountain and the sea was utilized. This narrow belt between the wharves and the highroad to the Neck, with a fringe of waterfront shops and houses, masked the empty spaces trailing away in pasture, orchard, and garden. The underpopulated Shawmut peninsula was divided into three sections: the North, South, and West Ends. The West End lay between Trimountain, the Charles River, and the Mill Pond; the North and South Ends were mainly contained within the commerce-haunted basin of the Town Cove.[6]

Within the peninsula of Boston was another peninsula, the North End. This section too was almost an island, separated from the rest of the town by the Mill Creek, and its inhabitants were proudly conscious of their isolation from the comparatively empty stretches of the South and West Ends. Long before the Puritans lost their charter, the North End was the teeming, thriving part of Boston. The shoreline from Dock Square to the Charlestown ferry was a cluster of shipyards, wharves, and shops whose owners and workers dwelt within the shadow of their places of occupation. It was an area of prodigious activity, where the great and insignificant lived side by side in a maze of alleys and lanes. North Square, the heart of the quarter, exemplified this tradition. Ringed by modest shops and houses, and more substantial dwellings like those of the artisan Paul Revere and his shipbuilder cousin Nathaniel Hitchbourn, it also contained two of the grandest private structures in Boston, the Hutchinson and the Clark-Frankland mansions. The latter was a massive example of colonial Georgian architecture whose unadorned exterior concealed the handsomest rooms in town. The Hutchinson family home was an even more important building, sometimes considered the first classical house in America and the second of the two known brick dwellings constructed in seventeenth-century Boston. The mansion was badly damaged in a raid by the Sons of Liberty ten years before its owner left in the loyalist exodus of 1776. The fame of the North End waned with the Revolutionary phase in Boston and the area never recovered. The mobs that milled through the streets in the wild days of the Tea Party and the Massacre received little encouragement from the new rulers of post-Revolutionary Boston. And the area itself was too crowded and limited in space to appeal to the merchants and speculators who utilized Bulfinch's talents to transform the neighboring South End.

The South End was the oldest and most famous quarter in the town. Yet it was sparsely settled except for a few streets in the vicinity of Long Wharf and around the highroad to Roxbury. The area lying between this historic avenue and the sea was a sequestered place of country estates, farms, and scattered houses. Higher up, toward the Common and Trimountain, the concentration of building be-

gan again along the many-named thoroughfare to the
Neck. This was always a favored residential street; Bulfinch lived in the section called Marlborough in the first
years of his marriage. At the northern end, where Marlborough became Cornhill, and around the corner from
each other, stood the opposing citadels of religion in the
colonial town: the rebuilt First Meetinghouse of Puritan
rule and King's Chapel of the royalist heyday. The latter
was a fine stone structure erected largely through the generosity of Bulfinch's grandfather and probably the only
building in Boston designed by what could be called an
architect. Beacon Street began in front of King's Chapel,
sloped uphill past the beacon for which the highest of Trimountain's peaks was named, and then descended westward in front of the Hancock mansion. This house was perhaps the best example of Georgian domestic architecture
in Boston prior to Bulfinich, and it enjoyed a country prospect denied the rival mansions of North Square. The view
from the entrance porch of Hancock's house was completely rural: straggling westward down the wide ridge of
Trimountain were a few farmhouses belonging to the
painter John Singleton Copley, while to the south an almost treeless Common rolled away toward marsh and
river.

The steep northern side of Trimountain formed one
boundary of the underpopulated and scraggly settlement
of the West End. Most of the respectable life of this quarter
converged in a few streets along the southern rim of the
Mill Pond. The social center was Bowdoin Square, where
the Bulfinch homestead stood. With its white-painted clapboards and wide gambrel roof (*Plate 3*), the old-fashioned

dwelling was much more typical of better-class houses of colonial Boston than the uncertain Georgian creations in the North End. The homestead in Bowdoin Square was built by Bulfinch's grandfather, the first Doctor Thomas Bulfinch, on land acquired in 1737 from his father-in-law John Colmen. It was to this house that the second Doctor Thomas Bulfinch brought his bride, Susan Apthorp, in 1759, and here, four years later, Charles Bulfinch was born. Bowdoin Square remained a distinguished area throughout the Federal period, a stronghold of old families like the Bulfinches who figured prominently in the Province House set. But although a secluded and desirable place to live, the West End lagged far behind the South End in growth. For one thing it was a spotty quarter containing some sections of a very questionable nature, such as the tumble-down region called North Slope Village at the base of Mount Whoredom. At the time Bulfinch and his friends were trying to make Beacon Hill a splendid residential area, the suggestive name of this peak was dropped from the town's cartography and Mount Vernon substituted.

As yet, however, the ridges of Trimountain were practically uninhabited; the older sections along the waterfront easily absorbed the town's slight growth during the post-Revolutionary period. But in 1787 there was a great stirring, for this was the year of the Constitutional Convention that led to the creation of a Federal Union. And while there was anything but unanimity as to what this extraordinary moment foretold, it was generally assumed the period of warfare and division was over. Everyone held high hopes for the future of the new nation. Though it is

impossible to know how fully he shared it, Charles Bulfinch certainly sensed this feeling of optimism. His background and earliest associations had their basis in the
Province House aristocracy that ended with the British
evacuation. Yet his father was a patriot, and Bulfinch as a
child watched the Battle of Bunker Hill from the roof of
the family homestead in Bowdoin Square. He grew to
manhood with at least an awareness of the new social and
political ideas, and although his roots were deep in Boston's royal past, he believed the successful War for Independence would surely bring a promising future to his
town.

It is typical of Bulfinch that he left no account of his
emotions upon returning to Boston at so exciting a moment. This phase of his life is veiled by a personal reticence
that deepened with time and disappointment into quiet
bitterness. But the moment was romantically described
by Jean Brissot, a young Frenchman who arrived in Boston some months later:[7]

With what joy, my good friend, did I leap to this shore of liberty.
. . . I flew from despotism, and came at last to enjoy the spectacle of liberty, among a people, where nature, education, and
habit had engraved the equality of rights, which everywhere else
is treated as a chimera. With what pleasure did I contemplate
this town, which first shook off the English yoke. . . . How I
delighted to wander up and down that long street, whose simple
houses of wood border the magnificent channel of Boston, and
whose full stores offer me all the productions of the continent
which I have quitted! How I enjoy the activity of the merchants,
the artizans, and the sailors . . . the simple, dignified air of
men, who are conscious of liberty, and who see in all men their
brothers and their equals.

[15]

This description could not have been written, especially by a Frenchman, at the high tide of New England Federalism. And it was exaggerated even in 1787, reflecting the legend of pre-Revolutionary Boston rather than conditions as they were when Bulfinch returned home. For by that year a counterrevolution, which began after the British evacuation, had already brought the town well on the way back to the spirit of royalist rule.

The counterrevolution was engineered by a group of patriot merchants from the seaports north of Boston who migrated to the capital and became the town's new rulers. These men, the Country party, as one of their descendants characterized them, did not interpret the Revolution in the same light as its instigators.[8] For them the War for Independence signaled little change; the direct political domination of New by Old England was ended but the economic domination was retained, as were all the other ancient dominations: class distinction, privilege, distrust of democracy, hatred of France, and the supremacy of property. It took a while for the new rulers to play down the rebellion and patch up the old milieu. The Sons of Liberty were dispersed and the leaders of the patriotic cult gradually silenced. James Otis was confined to country seclusion, periodically insane; Samuel Adams and John Hancock held out, but they, too, were brought to check and exercised little influence in the dawning world of the Federalist merchant. Bulfinch's Boston was decidedly not the place the Revolutionary triumvirate conjured up in the electrifying days of the Tea Party, the Massacre, and the Liberty Tree.

After Massachusetts ratified the Constitution, Boston's new rulers paid only lip service to the superannuated men of violence, for they based their political and economic philosophy upon the federalism of Hamilton, not the republicanism of Hancock. The future Federalists became supreme in Boston after the British evacuation because of the continued domination of commerce and the town's susceptibility to English institutions. Representative of the post-Revolutionary age was James Otis's nephew, Harrison Gray Otis, who used the family gift of oratory in the cause of the few not the many. While the old uncle was adored by the mob and lived violently in a stormy time, the nephew served the new men of property motivated by the conservative goals of peace and prosperity. But unfortunately this was not a period of peace and only partially one of prosperity; the men who ruled Federal Boston were as much out of their time as the old radicals who lived impotently on into the counterrevolution. It was an age of paradox, not the least being the triumph of reaction following the British exodus of 1776. The new men who hurried in from country towns outside Boston to fill the power vacuum took over in a literal sense. Identifying themselves with the departed regime, they opposed all who cast a democratic eye in their direction. They believed the Revolution was waged for commercial, not individual, freedom. The new movements abroad in the land growing out of the War for Independence were inexplicable and unnecessary to them. Harrison Gray Otis expressed their sentiments in a letter written half a century later to another aged Federalist: "You and I did not imagine, when the first war with Britain was over, that revolution had just begun."[9]

The new rulers of Boston were blind or unsympathetic

to the forces that transformed America from colonial to national status, but they were swift and effective in realizing the advantages at hand. And the moment in eastern Massachusetts offered many opportunities to the newcomers from the wind-blown seaports of Essex County. These opportunists were neither the instigators of the War for Independence nor, in most cases, its fighters. They typified the men who often come to power when the immediate goals of revolution are achieved and the revolutionists, resourceful in tearing down the old order, are incapable of constructing a new one. These sometime-heirs of revolution do not look with indulgence upon other innovators. Their ambition is to assume the vacated places of authority with as little change as possible; their aim is to enjoy the fruits of revolution in the setting of the old milieu.

But the old milieu in Boston was gone, disappearing irrevocably on that fateful Sunday in March, eleven years earlier, when the British army evacuated the town. Until then, political and social power was held by the Province House set, with its amalgam of British officials and local Bostonians who had inherited or earned a place among them. The Province House survived the War of Independence only as a symbol of rejected grandeur, of an authority and exclusiveness guaranteed by a government based on inequality and privilege. The triumph of the American Revolution in the middle and southern colonies, in an aggressively republican form, made the Province House a highly questionably symbol. Quite understandably, Boston's reactionary new rulers wanted to maintain the English structure of power and privilege. But the military force sent to defend this structure in America had been defeated and had withdrawn. Further, their own fortunes and positions stemmed from privateering activities which contributed to the defeat of royal prerogative and privilege. Finally, the new men were neither of the Province House set nor capable of assuming its traditions. The exiled loyalist Samuel Curwen described the transference of power in Boston from a prejudiced but not inaccurate view when he wrote: "Those who five years ago were the *'meaner people'* are now, by a strange revolution, become almost the only men of power, riches and influence; those who, on the contrary, were leaders and in the highest line of life, are glad at this time to be unknown and unnoticed."[10]

Most of the Bostonians in the Province House set remained loyal to England in 1775 when the patriots sealed off the town by land. The ruling loyalists were of course committed to the British colonial system. Many represented generations of service to the crown, and it was impossible for them to conceive of any allegiance other than the established monarchy. Not that the loyalists were unaware of the commercial advantages of a looser connection with England. Such considerations, which weighed heavily with the patriots, were keenly felt by the prominent Tory families in Boston who participated in the commercial life of the town. But unlike their Whig counterparts they were not solely merchants. As administrators of the crown they saw things in a wider sense regardless of the side they were forced to take in the conflict. This was the distinguishing characteristic between the Province House leaders and the newcomers who attempted to emulate them. The future Federalists were overridingly merchants; they considered every problem, local or national, in terms of commerce. The counterrevolutionists knew nothing of the tolerance and compromise which made English rule so lenient and enduring. This proved especially fatal in the years following the ratification of the Constitution, when the interests of the New England Federalists were no longer those in which the country as a whole was absorbed. The disturbing paradox of Boston's new rulers was that though children of the Revolution in place, time, and opportunity, they either misunderstood or repudiated the upheaval in society and politics that accompanied independence.

There was considerable division among the people of Massachusetts during the brawling years preceding the Revolution. It is believed the population was equally divided into thirds: one third actively urging independence, a third avowedly loyal to the crown, and the other third undecided. Among those definitely committed to England was the Province House group, who defied the patriots as long as possible. When the British forces marched away the loyalists reluctantly went with them. The undecided third of the population survived intact, relying heavily upon the quality of discretion. The patriot third, the Whigs of pre-Revolution days, was composed largely of mechanics and workers of Boston and farmers from the neighboring counties. But their leaders were often of a higher social position. Some of them were rich merchants from Boston; a few, like John Hancock and his brother-in-law Josiah Quincy, Jr., had powerful Province House connections. Most of them, however, were the elite of the surrounding counties. With the assumption of privateering,

the patriot ranks were broadened to include the lawyers
and merchants from the seaboard towns of Salem, Newburyport, Beverly, and Marblehead. In fact, so many of
the new leaders after 1776 were from Essex County, and
so strong was their discipline in maintaining their recently
acquired power, that the ruling group in Boston for the
next forty years was known as the Essex Junto. With the
exception of Fisher Ames from Norfolk County and James
Sullivan from New Hampshire, practically all the leaders
who were not already established in the capital town before the Revolution came from the rocky strip of land running along the coast north of Boston to where the Merrimack meets the sea at Newburyport. The most important
of these were the Higginson, Cabot, Jackson, Pickering,
Parsons, and Lowell families. They contributed the new
men in Boston who represented the counterrevolution in
its most successful and tenacious aspects.

The evacuation of Boston by the British occasioned a fortuitous transfer of power for those capable of taking advantage of it. All the places of authority were vacated
while physical damage was minor. There was some destruction from bombardments and a number of houses, including the ancient Winthrop homestead, were pulled
down to provide firewood during the siege. On the whole,
however, the capital remained little changed and much
fine property as well as political and business leadership
fell to the victorious patriots. The patriot families who
lived in Boston before the siege returned and were soon
joined by the people from Essex County, who made their
strong and lasting bid for the places of the departed loyalists. The time was ripe in every sense for the new men

from the country. The shifting of warfare from the area around Boston to the middle and southern colonies created a situation in which the merchants of the nearby seaboard towns amassed great fortunes while acting in a patriotic capacity. With the principal ports below Narragansett Bay blockaded by the British, New England was, for the duration of the war, the *entrepôt* for most foreign goods. The merchants of Salem, Marblehead, Beverly, and Newburyport fitted out their ships as privateers or armed merchantmen and established commercial relations with England's old enemies, Spain and Holland, and with America's new ally, France. There were many hazards in this adventure but profits were enormous.

The victory of the country and conservative branch of the patriot party over the Boston radicals was inevitable. The future rulers from Essex County required a few years in which to work out the problems of privateering and move their center of operation from the towns of the North Shore into the capital. By 1779, however, they had all settled in Boston and were harvesting the rewards of wartime prosperity in Massachusetts. George Cabot and Stephen Higginson represent spectacular but not untypical examples of the rise of the new men who were related both by blood and common interest. Higginson, who operated as a shipmaster out of Salem in his youth, turned to privateering in the first years of the war and amassed a fortune. His cousin George Cabot of Beverly emerged from similar experiences as probably the richest man in New England. Higginson left Salem in 1778 to settle in Boston, where he entered into partnership with yet another kinsman, Jonathan Jackson, lately of Newburyport. These three enterprising merchants, along with Theophilus Parsons and John Lowell of Newburyport, and Timothy Pickering of Salem, formed the inner sanctum of the Essex Junto.

Bulfinch was trapped between the opportunism of the Essex Junto and his own debilitating heritage from the old order. He was the fourth generation on his paternal side of a Boston family that became rich in the time of its first American ancestor, and his mother was a daughter of Charles Apthorp, the head of a family powerfully entrenched in the Province House. Bulfinch's maternal grandfather, reputedly the richest Bostonian of his day, earned this enviable position through long and faithful service in the interest of Governor William Shirley. He was an outstanding example of how local merchants acquired wealth through close association with royalist rule. As paymaster and commissary to the British land and naval forces in the New England capital, Bulfinch's grandfather shared in the lucrative contracts arising from the Louisburg expedition and the French and Indian wars. But he was not content with political and social primacy among Province House magnates. The fame of Charles Apthorp owes to his crusade to strengthen the Episcopal Church in Boston. To this end he contributed over a thousand pounds to the building of King's Chapel in 1749 from plans drawn up by his friend Peter Harrison. Harrison, an amateur architect in Newport and later a crown official in New Haven, designed the most sophisticated buildings in New England before Bulfinch. The church he planned for the Anglicans of Boston was around the corner from the First Meetinghouse and reduced that edifice, architecturally at least, to insignificance.

But that was about as far as the contest went. For while few disputed the change in secular authority late in the seventeenth century when the Puritan charter was replaced by a royal one, religion was a different matter. So monolithic was the Congregational Church in the Old Colony that royal officials were hard pressed from the start even to get the Anglican Church established. Nor were the stormy years preceding the Revolution especially promising ones in which to extend the power of the English Church. Yet an attempt was made by the Anglicans of Boston, in conjunction with the Society for the Propagation of the Gospel in Foreign Parts, to break the Congregational stranglehold on the religious life of Massachusetts. In this unequal struggle Bulfinch's uncle, the Reverend East Apthorp, played the leading role. Apthorp was outwardly well-endowed for the contest: son of the richest man in the Province House set, educated at Cambridge University, and married to a granddaughter of Governor Shirley and a niece of Governor Hutchinson. The attack was commenced with one other promising weapon—Peter Harrison was again called upon to design a church, this time in Cambridge. The location of the proselytizing agency within sight of Harvard College suggests the naïve optimism of Apthorp and his London backers, for at this time there were scarcely ten Episcopal families in all of Cambridge.

The venture was doomed from the start. When the Reverend East Apthorp took up his missionary post in 1765, rebellion was pitched to a fury in Boston not equaled even while the War for Independence was actually fought. The mansion of his wife's uncle, Thomas Hutchinson, was sacked by a mob that year and the governor's library, the greatest in New England, trampled under foot. Nor were the lords spiritual spared. Mitre and sceptre were inseparably linked in the minds of the rampaging Sons of Liberty, and within little more than a decade all who played a part in the "Anglican plot" to convert the students of Harvard were driven from the local scene. The Reverend East Apthorp himself fled to England long before the British evacuation ended the power of his relatives and friends. By then the Hutchinsons were gone forever, the Apthorps badly depleted, and Peter Harrison had died soon after a mob destroyed his house in New Haven. But two important buildings remain in Cambridge to commemorate the venture: Christ Church and the mansion built at the same time for the Reverend East Apthorp. This fine dwelling, now the master's lodge of Harvard's Adams House, was immediately dubbed the "Bishop's Palace" following widespread circulation of a letter by Boston's patriot minister Jonathan Mayhew, which claimed "that a certain *superb edifice* in a neighboring town, was even from the foundation designed for the *Palace* of one of the *humble successors* of the apostles."[11] Much speculation surrounds the possible architect of the Apthorp house. Peter Harrison seems the most likely candidate, although it was conceivably the work of Bulfinch's uncle, Charles Ward Apthorp, also a talented amateur architect.[12] At any rate, the "Bishop's Palace" was one of the many badges of power and wealth devolving upon Bulfinch's maternal family. Another Apthorp brother married a daughter of Stephen Greenleaf, the last royal high sheriff of Suffolk County. The children of this marriage were orphaned at an early age and one of them, Hannah Apthorp, later married her architect cousin Charles Bulfinch.[13]

Bulfinch descended through his mother from a family interested in architecture to an extent unmatched in America. His grandfather Charles Apthorp, described by a contemporary as "very proficient in and a great admirer of the Fine Arts, especially painting and architecture," began the building tradition that survives to this day in Boston in the seventh generation of direct descent from the first Charles Apthorp.[14] The oldest son, Charles Ward Apthorp, who may have designed the "Bishop's Palace," is known to have built a house for himself in New York that was one of the most interesting of America's pre-Revolutionary buildings. Another son, John Apthorp—the father of Hannah Apthorp Bulfinch—was something of a dilettante in the arts. He and his first wife, a sister of Sir Horace Mann, lived in Florence, where Sir Horace was a celebrated figure. When another of Charles Apthorp's sons, George, left a legacy to his sister Mrs. Thomas Bulfinch of Boston in 1785, it was in keeping with a family tradition that the money should be used to send her only son, Charles, off to Europe in the footsteps of her brothers. And to follow in the footsteps, too, of his own father and his father's father, for both these gentlemen studied medicine abroad. Bulfinch remained in Europe for a year and a half, making the Grand Tour in the spirit of an English gentleman fascinated by buildings. And though he did not then consider architecture other than as a disinterested study, his letters written home to Bowdoin Square foretell a life that was to receive its rewards in this profession.

Bulfinch was always interested in architecture; his trip

to Europe simply sealed a fate long before determined. The Bulfinch family still possesses the school book given Charles when he was but ten years old, on the inside cover of which are pen-and-ink drawings of a fluted Corinthian column and a capital of indeterminate order. This boyhood interest continued after graduation from Harvard College when Bulfinch was placed in the counting house of Joseph Barrell. Because of an impasse in trade negotiations with England there was little business to employ the apprentice merchant. Late in life Bulfinch judged this to have been a fortunate circumstance, for it enabled him to spend his time in the counting room studying architectural books and practicing drawing. But there was another side too. "These pursuits," he concluded in a rare attempt at personal reminiscence, "did not confirm me in any business habits of buying and selling, on the contrary, they had a powerful adverse influence on my whole after life."[15] The gentlemanly diversion of architecture was indeed the poorest preparation for a competitive career in a business world dominated by the new men from Essex County.

In their pursuit of property and power, the new rulers of Boston were uninhibited either by their own past or that of their adopted town. For them the Revolution was merely fortuitous. But for Charles Bulfinch and Hannah Apthorp, children of old Boston families that included both loyalists and patriots, the Revolution was a sobering and even an incapacitating experience. Certainly it was a sorrowful time for Bulfinch's mother, who helplessly watched the banishment of her brothers and the confiscation of their property. In some of her most charming letters, written years later to these exiles, Mrs. Thomas Bulfinch tells

[27]

of the changes made by her son in the town to which none of them would ever return. Bulfinch's father, however, was mildly committed to the patriot side and the household in Bowdoin Square survived the British evacuation. This somewhat equivocal position was shared by a number of other Boston households with connections in both the loyalist and patriot camps. The future for these divided families could never be as bright as that which lay ahead for the newcomers from the seaboard towns. Bulfinch and his relatives and friends, haunted by a disruptive past, knew the sorrow of revolution. And as it was impossible for them to be really victorious, they formed a distinct group between the old royalist Boston of their ancestors and the new town ruled by the commercial urgency of the Country party.

II

Neo-classicism

When Bulfinch embarked for Europe in the summer of 1785, not a single important building had been constructed in Boston in twenty-five years. In this cultural hiatus an old order disappeared and a new one was entrenched. The crown officials and allied merchants who made up the Province House set—and the only people in royalist Boston seriously interested in architecture—were now gone, for the most part dead or in exile. Among them had been a handful of amateur designers like Governor Sir Francis Bernard, Bulfinch's uncle Charles Ward Apthorp, and the tax collector Joseph Harrison. Together they had been mainly responsible for the little that was excellent in Boston building during the period of the royal charter. But they concerned themselves with architecture only as part of a gentlemen's education and responsibilities and were wholly unaffected by the controversies raging in professional circles in the mother country. Their idea of correct taste corresponded to the Palladian revival that dominated the early building of Georgian England.

The original Palladian movement was the most significant phase of the renaissance in architecture that began in

England in the reign of Elizabeth I. In its initial stage, the English Renaissance was fantastic and exuberant; a product both of Elizabethan vitality and the extraordinary mingling of Italian, French, and Flemish decorative sources. With the advent of the Stuarts, however, and particularly the appointment in 1615 of Inigo Jones as court designer, architecture became austerely classical. In basing his work upon the writings of Marcus Vitruvius Pollio of Rome's Augustan age and Andrea Palladio of the late Renaissance, Jones established a precedent that survived one hundred and forty years in England and almost two hundred in New England. The Palladian style was characterized by simplicity achieved through symmetry with a minimum of ornamentation, the latter usually confined to a rusticated ground story, an Ionic portico or a range of giant pilasters, and a "Venetian Window." Although there was a movement at the end of the seventeenth century toward the Baroque forms first introduced by Christopher Wren, the traditionalists initiated a Palladian revival that became the official style of early Georgian England. In New England, the authority of Vitruvius and Palladio was unchallenged until after the Revolution, and every gentleman aspired to have their folios in his library. Among the treasures in the Bulfinch homestead in Bowdoin Square when the town's future architect was growing up were a French adaptation of Vitruvius and Palladio's work in an English edition.

The time lag between the building styles of Old and New England was approximately two generations. Though Palladian architecture was firmly established in England by the first half of the seventeenth century, New England craftsmen continued to follow Elizabethan models until well into the eighteenth. The period of classical building in Boston was limited to the last fifty years of royal rule. Houses constructed during this time reflected the authoritarian taste of the merchant-official, or more usually, the unenlightened conservatism of local carpenters. Occasionally a royal official like Peter Harrison or an artist with a penchant for architecture like John Smibert appeared on the local scene and the results were a King's Chapel and a Faneuil Hall. On the whole, however, Boston building before Bulfinch was the uncultivated domain of carpenters whose knowledge stemmed from pattern books.[1] Their field was only rarely contested, as when an itinerant surveyor arrived in 1768 and represented himself in the local press as "a Person lately from England, and well acquainted with the present *London* Method of Building."[2] The "method" referred to was undoubtedly acquired through the books of an army of popularizers of Vitruvius and Palladio. But unlike the Province House gentlemen who knew them in their original source, Boston carpenters had very imperfect impressions of these masters. They built heavy dull houses indistinguishable from English models of half a century earlier.

Bulfinch, who grew up among these somber, four-square dwellings, never entirely shook off colonial or Palladian traditions. But he had traveled to England and discovered the work of the Neo-classicists and henceforth counted himself among the adherents of Robert Adam. English Neo-classicism was a revolt against the increasing sterility of the Palladian revival as practiced by a second generation of Whig architects. The Neo-classicists sought to replace what they held to be the artificial vocabulary of Renaissance design with what they took to be the rational principles of pre-Roman building. Their sources were the new archaeological findings in southern Italy, Greece, and Asia Minor, which brought to light little-known or forgotten buildings that differed considerably from the temples and villas hitherto the patterns for the English Palladians. The high priest of Neo-classicism, Robert Adam, made the Grand Tour thirty years before Bulfinch. But unlike the Bostonian, who did not venture south of Rome, Adam crossed over to Spalato to draw the ruins of Diocletian's palace, saw the sporadic diggings at Herculaneum, surveyed the first breaches into Pompeii, and journeyed to Greece and Syria. These discoveries formed the basis for the new architectural style in England to which the young visitor from New England succumbed.[3]

Bulfinch returned home eager to introduce into the architecture of his native town the attenuated proportions of the Erechtheum and the delicate wall decorations of Pompeii that the Neo-classicists had by then reduced to pattern-book formula. But the task was not so simple. The town was esthetically unprepared for a wave of building in a new style. In fact, Bostonians were hardly aware of any changes in architecture since the days of Inigo Jones. Nonetheless, Bulfinch's lessons in Neo-classicism bore first fruit in 1792 when his sister's father-in-law, Joseph Coolidge, asked him for the design of a house for Bowdoin Square. Coolidge was a member of the intermediary group of Province House descendants, and the mansion Bulfinch designed across the square from the family homestead gave Boston her initial example of the prevailing English style. The central portion of Coolidge's house (*Plate 4*) was copied from Adam's building for the Society of Arts in the Adelphi—a section Bulfinch knew intimately both as the haunt of exiled Boston loyalists and the center of Adam building in London. But Bowdoin Square was not the Adelphi; the heavy hand of colonial building tradition haunted the area, exerting the force of past things cherished and respected. Above the delicate façade Bulfinch placed the massive hipped roof with widow's walk common to most Boston mansions. The Adam design all but disappeared under the old-fashioned roof. He did not, however, repeat this error. When he designed a neighboring house for Coolidge's son three years later, the low roof was masked by a balustrade and urns in the proper Neo-classical manner. The second Coolidge mansion shows the maturing of Bulfinch's London impressions.[4]

Stephen Greenleaf Bulfinch is the authority for the belief that his father never studied with a master but was entirely self-taught.[5] Although there is no positive evidence to dispute this, the family connection with Peter and Joseph Harrison remains, as does the professional relationship with Thomas Dawes. Dawes was an established builder in Boston before Bulfinch was born and certainly influenced him in his youthful, dilettante years. Bulfinch's copy of *The Builder's Dictionary: or Architect's Companion* bears Dawes's signature, and he is believed to have collaborated in the early planning of the State House.[6] Essentially, however, Stephen Greenleaf Bulfinch is right. His father made the Grand Tour in the English upper-class tradition of an amateur and not as the prelude to a profession. But Bulfinch returned to America at that wonderful

moment when the Constitution was about to be ratified
and a new nation established. It was a time when the best
citizens responded to the demands and opportunities the
moment evoked. Farmers became generals, schoolteachers
became statesmen, and a young Bostonian without precon-
ceived intent or professional training became an architect.
Under these circumstances it is too much to expect that
Bulfinch should have been daringly original. It was
enough that he understood and appreciated the new movement in England sufficiently to bring the refinements of
Neo-classical design to the blunt, sea-faring town of his
ancestors. For though artistic taste in the royalist period
was impressive compared to the vacuum of the Puritan
ascendancy, it hardly produced a milieu for exciting or
radical architecture. Bulfinch was exactly the right person
to guide Boston from her dull and stiff colonial building
traditions into the charming and flexible style that in
America is called Federal. And during the thirty years he
worked and fought to accomplish this feat, his lack of professional training was the least of obstacles.

When Charles Bulfinch returned from Europe in 1787
he already knew more about architecture than any of his
townsmen. Aside from traveling abroad, he came from a
family with a tradition for building and grew up in a
house containing as good an architectural library as any
in Massachusetts. Actually there was nothing in Boston at
this time like the collection assembled by the Library Company of Philadelphia and available to Bulfinch's contemporary William Thornton. Nor did any compare with the
private libraries of Peter Harrison or William Byrd. The
latter, dispersed in 1779, was the nucleus of Jefferson's col-

lection at Monticello. Harrison's books were scattered a
few years earlier when Connecticut's equivalent to the
Sons of Liberty wrecked his house in New Haven. His
brother Joseph, also an amateur architect and crown official, was badly mauled by the mobs in Boston and forced
to flee the town. It is not known if any books belonging to
the Harrisons reached their friend's house in Bowdoin
Square, but at least one title from the library of another
royalist and amateur designer did. This was a copy of Se-
bastien LeClerc's *A Treatise of Architecture* bearing the
signature of Bulfinch's uncle Charles Ward Apthorp and
the date 1759. Apthorp was proscribed as a Tory and never
returned to Boston after the evacuation, the event which
undoubtedly brought the book to the Bulfinch homestead.
The future architect was thirteen years old at the time and
perhaps just beginning to pore over the volumes which
were to influence his later life.[7]

Until his visit to England and the continent of Europe in
1785 and 1786, books from the library in Bowdoin Square
and visual impressions of Boston's colonial buildings comprised the limits of Bulfinch's architectural education.
When he returned home, he again relied on books as the
means of furthering his professional knowledge. The library originating in Bowdoin Square fluctuated during
the architect's lifetime, so it is impossible to define the con-
tents at any particular point. His granddaughter, Ellen
Susan Bulfinch, recalls the moments in her childhood
when she was "indulged with the privilege and delight" of
looking over her grandfather's books "with numerous
plates of the plans and elevations of country seats, hunting
lodges, farmhouses."[8] But some titles she designates as

being in the old homestead at the time Bulfinch was growing up—Vitruvius and LeClerc—are missing from the Bulfinch collection presently housed at Massachusetts Institute of Technology. Considering the vicissitudes of Bulfinch's fortune, it seems likely the more valuable of his books were sacrificed to creditors along with the property and other possessions of the once powerful family.

Entirely missing are any French titles, although Bulfinch wrote to his friend James Cutler in Paris in 1791 ordering half a dozen architectural books.[9] Equally conspicuous is the absence of books depicting the works of Robert Adam, James Wyatt, and William Chambers, the men who with John Soane most decisively influenced Charles Bulfinch. However, some of their designs are included in the copper plates inserted in his much-thumbed copy of *A Tour Through London;* and among the architect's papers deposited in the Library of Congress are several plates torn from English and French books as well as drawings of well-known buildings. Another surprising omission are the titles of William and James Pain, the best-selling popularizers of the Neo-classical style in America: *The Practical Builder* appeared in Boston bookstores a few years after Bulfinch returned from Europe and *The Practical House Carpenter* was on the local market at the time the second Coolidge mansion was erected in Bowdoin Square. The most influential works in the collection are those of John Plaw, William Thomas, and John Soane. Apparently Bulfinch procured Soane's *Plans, Elevations, and Sections of Buildings* shortly after he arrived back in Boston; his copy of Soane's *Sketches in Architecture,* recently discovered in the library of the late Francis Vaughan Bulfinch, probably reached the young dilettante about the time he designed the State House.[10]

As limited as Bulfinch's library seems by present-day standards, it was sufficient for the task at hand; as was his proficiency in drawing, which was apparently self-acquired. A teacher of architectural drawing appeared in Boston during the Federal period in the person of a Mr. Worrall. Worrall's talents, described in a press notice of 1808 as "too generally known to need elucidation," came too late to benefit Bulfinch.[11] Yet Bulfinch made the first architectural perspectives in America, a feat attesting to the skill and diligence with which he pursued the subject.[12] And he pursued the subject all his life: the margins of some of his papers in the Library of Congress are scrawled with architectural figures, and a card inviting the Bulfinches to dinner at the White House with President and Mrs. Monroe bears a rough plan of the Capitol sketched across it.[13] The drawing table used by Bulfinch remains in the family, and it testifies to his granddaughter's description of the architect's office as "a small table with a drawer containing his box of mathematical instruments, colorbox, and a few rulers."[14] This equipment was adequate for the slight elevations and rudimentary ground plans which survive as typical examples of his working designs.

The rewards of his profession appear equally startling by modern standards. Although Mrs. Thomas Bulfinch wrote to an exiled brother in 1803 that her son's "employment in the architectural line," supplemented by his salary as the town's manager, "enables him to support a very excellent wife and [family] tho' with economy, yet in a very pretty style," there seems to have been little monetary gain from the architectural line.[15] Bulfinch's early work was done in the tradition of his Province House ancestors, as a service owed by a gentleman to his community. Later, he did receive payment for some of his public designs, but what this amounted to is impossible to determine. In 1814 the town offered him a "premium" of $50 for the plans of a workhouse to be built next to the Almshouse. There is no record of any payment to Bulfinch for the latter project even though the Almshouse was one of his important designs. The $50 premium compares poorly with the £45 paid half a century earlier to Peter Harrison for his plans for Christ Church in nearby Cambridge, but it was on a par with the £10 William Thornton received in 1789 for his design for the Library Company of Philadelphia.[16]

Bulfinch carried out his design for Federal Boston in a manner remote from the modern expert. But his lack of professional training was only a minor obstacle; the main stumbling block was simply that the Federalist merchant did not occupy the milieu of the London Whig. Money for one thing, was much more a problem in New England than in Old. Because of this Bulfinch was never free to experiment with the building materials used by his English mentors. Some of Adam's and Wyatt's clients spent more on a single country house than was involved in all the Bulfinch houses put together. Bulfinch had to work both with restricted budgets and traditional building materials. Yet his determination to bring at least the appearance of Neo-classicism to Boston led to important innovations. One was the use of stucco scored to imitate hewn or squared stone, a variation on the provincial expedient of plastering over boards to achieve surface refinement. The technique was never popular in colonial New England, although Peter Harrison specified its use in the designs for Christ Church and the "Bishop's Palace" in Cambridge. After the American Revolution, however, stucco was fashionable in England, and when Bulfinch arrived there in 1785 Robert Adam and his brothers held important patents for its manufacture and sale. But though Bulfinch was sympathetic to the prevailing English sentiment that "a mere brick-face . . . makes a mean appearance," he was unsuccessful in converting his fellow townsmen.[17] Excepting the Brimmer house, whose sophisticated design demanded stucco facing, he usually had to sacrifice his preference for simulated masonry to the slimmer budgets and less elegant demands of local builders.[18]

Bulfinch met these conditions by substituting the painted-brick façade. Perhaps his feeling for this device derived from childhood impressions of the Hutchinson mansion in North Square, alleged to have been painted a "neutral tint." Or possibly it derived from the white and yellow brick used in the early, small country houses of John Soane. At any rate, this inexpensive substitute for stone was widely used by Bulfinch, though modern restorations disavow it. Contemporary paintings suggest the bright red fronts of today were more common on Beacon Hill than in other quarters of the town. A fireboard of about 1812 in the Bostonian Society shows the row of brick houses in Park Street painted yellow and the State House gray with white trim.[19] The Tontine Crescent, Bulfinch's ambitious London-inspired building scheme, was apparently originally painted gray, as were the double houses in Franklin Place.[20] The painted-brick technique generally did not prevail in the country, where the tradition of wooden construction was sacrosanct. But even there Bulfinch tried to give the effect of dressed stone essential to his lighter and more delicate designs. Whenever possible he designated smooth, closely joined boards instead of clapboards. The entrance bay of the country house for Perez Morton in Roxbury utilized this device beautifully. Unfortunately, the famous Republican and his poet wife did not let their achitect cousin complete the entire façade in this manner. The use of clapboards on either side of the central bay weakened the effect Bulfinch wanted to achieve.[21]

Boston in 1787 was predominantly constructed of wood; when Bulfinch left thirty years later it was a city of brick. At the beginning of the Federal period Jeremy Belknap and Thomas Pemberton described the houses in identical terms: wooden structures of three stories roofed with shingles.[22] This description was obsolete after 1803, when the selectmen passed an ordinance requiring buildings exceeding ten feet in height to be erected in brick or stone with roofs of slate or noncombustible material. Bulfinch had already designed several notable wooden mansions, but henceforth everything he built in Boston was of brick or stone and roofed with slate. Unlike dozens of fire restrictions going back to the days of the Puritan settlement, the ordinance of 1803 was enforced by Bulfinch, who by then was chief of police and head of the selectmen as well as town architect.

Bricks for Boston buildings came mainly from Charlestown, particularly the yard of the energetic manufacturer John Wait. For roofing, the architect favored native slate from Lancaster and employed the British master John Gilbreath, who may have been associated in some of the later building projects of the Adam brothers before migrating to the New World. The domestic production of bricks was encouraged by a 10 per cent importation duty, while similar tariffs protected other local building materials such as glass, marble, wallpaper, and iron.[23]

Stone rarely appeared in the architect's domestic work but was liberally used in important public structures. The stone Boston builders preferred was Chelmsford granite, which was floated into town via the Middlesex Canal. This was the material designated by Bulfinch in his designs for the New South Church, the county court house, and the state prison at Charlestown. Marble was never used except in the houses of opulent patrons, where it was substituted for stone in architectural details. Occasionally such refinements were of artificial stone manufactured in England by the Coades; usually they were rendered in wood by native craftsmen, such as the extant swag panel from Bulfinch's own house. There was no iron frame construction of any kind in America before 1820, but Bulfinch did use cast iron decorations which Bostonians believed gave the town a "Florentine look." Some of it in Chinese fretwork design can still be seen in the balconies of the two Harrison Gray Otis houses on Beacon Hill. The iron work specified by Bulfinch, often painted bright green after the English fashion, was entirely free of the dreary uniformity prevailing after the War of 1812. The availability of machined nails since the beginning of the Revolution, and the introduction of the circular saw near the close of the Federal period, gave builders an immense advantage over colonial craftsmen. Although the best nails were made from Swedish steel, iron for Bulfinch buildings was manufactured locally by Paul Revere and several rivals who operated foundries in the North End, where Revere's father had opened a goldsmith's shop in 1730. Despite the expansion of these foundries to produce a limited quantity of copper pipes, plumbing remained primitive and the old pipeless privy continued its dominance. No Bulfinch house had a bathroom; the more sensitive of his clients used commode chairs in their bed or dressing rooms—one of the reasons for introducing the service staircase into Boston interior planning.

Bulfinch's interior plans show a freedom in organization and a concern for convenience unknown in colonial times. The typical pre-Federal Boston mansion was a square with a stair hall dividing two more or less equal-sized rooms on either side. In one of his first commissions, the country house for Joseph Barrell in Charlestown, Bulfinch ignored tradition and designed a house carefully planned for function and comfort (*Plate 5*). The central feature of the plan was an elliptical salon arranged *en suite* on the garden front, the forerunner of many oval rooms created by the architect for his Boston friends. This concept of free planning, introduced into France early in the eighteenth century, was enthusiastically taken up by Bulfinch's English mentors William Chambers and Robert Adam. Adam acknowledged this in the preface of the edition of his works published in 1778: "To understand thoroughly the art of living, it is necessary perhaps to have spent some time in France." Bulfinch satisfied this qualification, arriving in Paris with letters of introduction to Lafayette and Jefferson. There the New Englander saw at first hand the French method of arranging rooms for function and convenience. Very likely Jefferson planned Bulfinch's architectural pilgrimage through southern France, for it was the same itinerary the Virginian himself followed.[24] Jefferson was already an old hand at architectural sight-seeing, going almost daily to watch the construction of the Hôtel de Salm, a single-story dwelling that influenced the remodeling of Monticello and probably inspired Bulfinch's scheme for Mrs. Swan's country place at Dorchester.[25]

The past, however, proved an obstinate force in Bulfinch's town. And the building style that evolved in this period of political retrogression was necessarily a compromise between the old and the new. The social arbiters of Federal Boston were delighted with the arrangement of rooms their architect introduced from Europe, but innovation could not be carried too far nor tradition by-passed entirely. To be quite correct, Mrs. Swan's country house should have been one story surmounted by a dome in the manner of a French pavilion; instead it followed English tradition, with the coved ceiling of the drawing room masked in a second story with dummy windows. Also Bulfinch should have used stucco or even painted brick instead of compromising his advanced interior plan with a clapboard exterior in the colonial tradition. But no Boston Federalist dared flaunt the Parisian influence in architecture evident in similar circles in New York and Philadelphia. Worlds apart were the French-inspired design for New York's City Hall submitted by Mangin and McComb and Bulfinch's contemporary plan for the remodeling of Faneuil Hall, seat of the town government. The people who counted in Federal Boston clung to the ways of the past, when ruling merchant-officials were content with a sampling of the latest London fashion strongly laced with local traditions. In this provincial climate Bulfinch's dream of re-creating Adam and Wyatt mansions was inevitably curtailed.

For working models Bulfinch turned to his recollections of less spectacular English country houses like Robert Mitchell's Moor Place in Hertfordshire and Robert Mylne's The Wick at Richmond. And they were excellent examples: Neo-classical but not radical; small, manageable, and constructed of brick. In evolving a style so satisfactory to the requirements of the Boston Federalists, Bulfinch also drew—as two of the books remaining in his library indicate—upon the works of John Miller and John Soane. The garden elevation of the Barrell house was suggested by Plate 16 in Miller's *The Country Gentleman's Architect* and from several designs for Letton Hall in Soane's *Plans, Elevations, and Sections of Buildings.*

The country mansion of Joseph Barrell was epochal in New England. Barrell was the family friend in whose counting house Bulfinch studied architectural books instead of commercials ledgers, and his tolerance was rewarded by the design of a house with a suite of three rooms strung along the principal side that startled and enchanted visitors. Bulfinch was one of the first Americans to consider rooms in relation to function, and those fortunate enough to live in houses from his design were not restricted to the colonial plan of two rectangular rooms on each side of a transverse stair hall. They could lead their guests through a suite of three connecting rooms, an ideal arrangement for public entertaining and private living made more exciting by shaping the middle room into a circle or ellipse. Bulfinch shares with James Hoban, the designer of the White House, the distinction of introducing the elliptical salon on axis into American architecture. The President's house in Washington and Barrell's country seat, Pleasant Hill, were both designed in 1792. Two elliptical rooms appeared four years earlier in the remodeling of Woodland, an estate in Philadelphia, but here they were isolated in corners of the plan. The concept of the elliptical salon on axis introduced at the White House and Pleasant Hill was to make this the principal room opening directly from the hall and flanked by rooms at either end to form a suite.[26]

The planning of country seats is generally more flexible than town dwellings, yet Bulfinch showed an equal concern for orientation and exposure in the case of Boston houses. When the street front faced north, he placed the main rooms at the back, as in Thomas Perkins's mansion on Beacon Hill with a rear view over the Common. This arrangement necessitated the elimination of the conventional hall with staircase ascending the wall at the opposite end from the entrance door. The architect solved the problem in his own house in Bulfinch Place with a small entrance lobby at the front and an elliptical stairway tucked into the wall. He used a free hung staircase in the Thomas Russell house in Charlestown and a double staircase in the Barrell mansion.[27] For town lots with the best exposure toward the street, the hall was planned so as to leave the front free to contain the principal rooms. This scheme appeared in all the Park Street houses, where the important rooms were grouped on the second floor front for the view across the Common to the Charles River. The mansions of his Beacon Hill patrons in Olive (Mount Vernon) Street had entrances at the side to allow connecting drawing rooms across the front. In a narrow lot he turned the end of the house toward the street and had the main rooms face a garden side, as in the surviving house at 29A Chestnut Street.

When it came to planning the interiors of his houses, Bulfinch disregarded the folios of Vitruvius and Palladio and forgot the lessons of a youth spent among carved paneling, scroll pediments, and bulging cornices. He followed the Neo-classical goal—movement through contrast—as fully as Federal budgets allowed. As this goal was best expressed in rooms with bare walls and decoration concentrated in ceiling and mantlepiece, he was far less curtailed by local restrictions than in exterior planning. In Bulfinch houses high, airy chambers with walls covered with plain paper or painted a solid color replaced colonial rooms whose form was sometimes lost in carving and paneling. Particularly favored were "Adam green" rooms with white stucco borders. These are known from contemporary accounts and by a reconstruction in the headquarters of the Society for the Preservation of New England Antiquities in the house Bulfinch designed for Harrison Gray Otis in Cambridge Street. Because of the emphasis on plain walls, the architectural focus of Federal houses was generally the ceiling, and here New England economy did play a role. Stucco details were rarely picked out in gilt paint, nor were the surfaces painted with classical motifs and arabesques in the English fashion. By comparison, the ceilings in Bulfinch houses were extremely simple. Those in the Amory manion in Park Street, the most expensive house he designed in Boston, are unadorned except for a garland centerpiece. Yet Bulfinch did create some fine examples when given a free hand, as in the country place of his cousin Perez Morton. This house contained an elliptical salon with a coved ceiling in which festoons and ribands were worked in stucco with the same design repeated in the door frames. The decorations in Morton's house were probably executed by Daniel Raynerd, the stucco worker who collaborated with Asher Benjamin in the production of architectural books.[28]

The other important decorative feature of Federal rooms was the chimney piece. Although many of the mantles in extant Bulfinch houses are of dubious authenticity, evidence suggests the architect used simple imitations of English models unless his patrons imported them from Europe. Several of the mantles surviving from the Barrell house are apparently English; those in the reception rooms in Thomas Perkins's Beacon Hill mansion were ordered from Italy. Before the War of 1812 newspaper advertisements for imported mantles from Europe, or even Philadelphia, were fairly common. Robert Hope, who worked for Bulfinch as a stone cutter, possibly provided mantles for the more extravagant clients like Perez Morton and Mrs. James Swan. The stucco and plaster composition chimney pieces developed by the Adam brothers were widely reproduced in America, and examples decorated with mythological figures mingled with garlands and husks in the Wedgwood tradition survive in the first Harrison Gray Otis house in Cambridge Street.

Bulfinch also borrowed from the English Neo-classicists the use of the alcove as an architectural component. The houses of Joseph Coolidge and Ezekiel Derby had niches designed to accommodate sideboards; those of Joseph Barrell and Thomas Amory contained shallow recesses for sofas and other drawing-room furniture. This sophisticated adaptation occurred because the Federal house, for the first time in New England, was planned with an eye for differentiation in the function of rooms. The oval or circular salon was indubitably a drawing room, balanced on one side by a dining room and on the other by a library or parlor. No longer was the kitchen banished to ells or outbuildings but incorporated into the main design and connected to the dining room by a pantry. Dressing rooms, sometimes with fireplaces, were liberally provided in Bulfinch houses. Harrison Gray Otis's Beacon Street mansion had three principal chambers, each connected with a dressing room lighted by a large window.

The innovations Bulfinch introduced from England appeared chiefly in houses commissioned by the lucky few comprising the circle of Province House descendants who ruled the social world of post-Revolutionary Boston. But the Essex County men were also interested in English mannerisms. As counterrevolutionists they were fascinated with every tradition of the vanished world of the royal charter. Forgotten were the days when they complimented visiting foreigners on their ability to "speak American." And while the Country party rarely patronized Bulfinch directly, its members did marry into the intermediary families and sometimes bought or leased houses originally designed by the architect for his friends and relatives. In the craze for building country houses, however, the new people took no part. And even the participants themselves could hardly be compared with their English prototypes. Federalist grandees did not survey thousands of acres from Grecian porticos or idle away afternoons in white and gold libraries containing half as many titles as could be found in all of Boston. But with the aid of their architect they did indulge in this pleasant British institution if only on a small scale.

A country house designed by Bulfinch represented the final extravagance of the really rabid imitators of Whig elegance. Created for entertainment, it was a luxury usually reserved for families already possessing Bulfinch town houses. The lead was taken by Joseph Barrell when he built Pleasant Hill, and soon those who could afford to follow his example were begging plans from their architect friend or kinsman. In 1796 Bulfinch supplied the design for Mrs. James Swan's country house at Dorchester and Perez Morton's at Roxbury; twelve years later he rebuilt Oakley at Watertown for Harrison Gray Otis.[29] Gore Place in Waltham is not documented as coming from the drawing board of Charles Bulfinch. Considerations of time, style, and circumstance, however, raise at least the possibility of his authorship. The garden front, with central block, corridors, and flanking pavilions, is similar in concept to Heaton Hall, probably the most talked-about country house in England when Bulfinch arrived there; it also resembles Soane's designs for Saxlingham Rectory and Chilton Lodge, both included in this architect's work in Bulfinch's library. Gore Place is noteworthy too as being the only country house in which the architect, whoever he was, used brick painted white to simulate stone. In this he followed the rule of the English landscapist Lancelot "Capability" Brown, who decried the use of red brick because it clashed with the green of nature.[30]

The country mansion Bulfinch designed for Joseph Barrell in Charlestown revolutionized the New England house. The owner's friends, and even strangers, swarmed out to see the place. Samuel McIntire came all the way from Salem to sketch the house and he used many of its innovations in subsequent buildings of his own, especially in the important commissions from George Lyman and Elias Derby. Lyman was a Boston Federalist who departed from pattern by passing over the town's architect in favor of McIntire. The faithfulness with which the Salem builder copied Bulfinch is evident in the garden front of Lyman's country house at Waltham, where three rooms are arranged *en suite* around an oval salon. The only other time McIntire used this sophisticated floor plan was when he took over Bulfinch's design for the Salem house of Elias Derby, the plans for which he slightly altered and executed. In fact the Derby family twice employed Boston's greatest architect for their ambitious Salem projects and on each occasion famous models were used: the design for Elias Derby's house was taken from a drawing of the Provost's lodge in Bulfinch's copy of James Malton's *A Picturesque View of the City of Dublin;* the façade of the house for Ezekiel Hersey Derby reproduced the London mansion Robert Adam designed for Sir William Watkins Wynn.[31]

McIntire was not the only local craftsman influenced by the Neo-classical style Bulfinch introduced into Boston.

Although a contemporary observed that Bulfinch went his modest way "without the stimulus of competition or the encouragement of good fellowship," the architect's isolation was not as complete as is generally assumed.[32] Beginning in 1803 a small fraternity of builders came together to study and work under his influence. The most distinguished were Asher Benjamin, Peter Banner, Alexander Parris, and Solomon Willard.[33] With the exception of Banner, all were Massachusetts country lads who learned the carpenter's trade in their native villages. Attracted to the capital town, they copied the architect's style and so industriously filled Boston with replicas of his work that today there are dozens of buildings innocently attributed to Bulfinch. While he was not a teacher, a "school of Bulfinch" sprang up among the men irresistibly imitating his work. They undoubtedly knew more about the practice of building than the master himself. And it was a good thing they did; Bulfinch was generally too busy as the town's chief civic officer to do more than draw up conceptual studies for builders to execute. Parris made the working drawings for the Massachusetts General Hospital from Bulfinch's plan and Willard did much of the interior design for the Federal Street Church.[34] The freedom and responsibility under which the Boston builder operated is seen in the experience of Thomas Hearsey, sent to Lancaster, Massachusetts in 1816 to execute the design of Bulfinch's most beautiful church. The architect's design was carried out by a master builder who did not need detailed specifications or explanations. As far as can be known, Bulfinch never saw the finished church at Lancaster, although he certainly read flattering accounts of it in the local press.[35]

Builders of high caliber were numerous in Federal Boston; the directory of 1789 lists more than one hundred of them. The number increased rapidly, augmented by men coming from the country with a knowledge of the building trades. This increase produced price slashing and cutthroat competition which continued until the summer of 1800, when a published list of prices was accepted by the Boston building fraternity.[36] But even this measure did not restore full order within the ranks; shortly afterwards a rash of "absconded apprentices" notices appeared in the newspapers. The return of one runaway, described as "a true Epicurean and no enemy to Bacchus," was not encouraged—the reward was sixpence.[37] But by and large the men who climbed the carpenters ranks to become architects in the post-Revolutionary age were hardworking, studious, and talented. They mastered the building trades during long working hours and learned architecture by reading in their spare time. One of them, Asher Benjamin, took to writing books himself and became important as a disseminator of Bulfinch's version of Neo-classicism. Benjamin acknowledged this debt in the preface to *The Practice of Architecture:*[38]

The time has been within my own recollection when New England did not contain a single professed Architect. The first individual who laid claim to that character was Charles Bulfinch, Esq., of this city; to whose classical taste we are indebted for many fine buildings. The construction of the Franklin Street houses, of which that gentleman was the Architect, gave the first impulse to good taste; and Architecture, in this part of the country.

III

CHALLENGE AND FAILURE

THE FIRST OPPORTUNITY to challenge the architectural monotony of old Boston came when the Hollis Street Church burned down shortly after Bulfinch returned home in 1787. No attempt was made to rebuild the church in Boston's historic meetinghouse style. Instead the architect struck a forward note by combining the classical traditions of England and New England. The resulting design (*Plate 6*) won the enthusiastic approval of Bostonians, who sensed in this blending of the old and the new the role Bulfinch was to play in the transformation of their town. The *Columbian Magazine* of April 1788 commented on the "elegant building which is now rapidly advancing to completion, under the direction of Charles Bulfinch. It is with pleasure that we mention the name of the young architect, whose genius, aided by a liberal education, and improved by a tour through Europe, has rendered him an ornament to the place of his nativity."[1] For the Hollis Street project Bulfinch consulted his sketches of St. Stephen's, Walbrook, the London church designed by Christopher Wren more than a century before. But Bulfinch drew as well upon the craft of Peter Harrison, the family friend whose life had ended sadly in the first months of the Revolution. The porch and twin cupolas of the Hollis Street edifice are identical to those used by Harrison in designs executed for Abraham Redwood in Newport. Bulfinch also had to tailor his memory of European grandeur to the realities of local budgets, and not even General Lafayette's generous gift of 300 gold louis enabled the church proprietors to build in stone.[2]

As Bulfinch's earliest public work, the Hollis Street Church was necessarily tentative and amateurish. A few years later, however, he began a group of related buildings in the South End which made that area the most exciting in Boston. Comprising the Franklin Place scheme, this group included the first architectural crescent in the New World as well as the town's first theater and first Roman Catholic church (*Plates 7, 8, and 21*). In every sense these three buildings represented daring innovations: the crescent was revolutionary as an isolated example of disciplined planning in America; the idea of a theater or a Catholic church was equally revolutionary in the town still struggling with its Puritan background. The theater was, in fact, the first wedge Bulfinch and his friends drove between the new people and the stern past they inherited both from their Essex County ancestors and the town they took over after the Revolution. In their mutual aversion to theatrical performances, the Country party and the Boston radicals met on common ground. Samuel Adams, prime mover among the destroyers of the old regime, was no exception to the rule that revolutionists are generally puritanical. How much his plans for the future of the town differed from those of Charles Bulfinch is reflected in his plaintive cry: "I love the people of Boston; I once thought that city would be the Christian Sparta."[3] This vision was not offensive to the new men from the North Shore; they also suffered from a deep-rooted Puritanism more compatible with Sparta than Athens. Henry Cabot Lodge, in the biography of his ancestor George Cabot, describes them:[4]

The men of Essex were descendants of those who, in the dark days of 1629 followed Endicott into the wilderness. They were of the oldest Puritan stock; and, after all the modifications of a century and a half, they still retained the marks of their ancestry . . . their intellectual vigor and clear perceptions were in many instances combined with great mental narrowness and rigidity.

The new rulers of Boston were morally and esthetically Spartan, but in their devotion to commerce they were Athenian. And even with the narrowest-minded, commerce has a broadening effect. Furthermore, the Essex people who stepped into the shoes of the Province House set as the business and political leaders of the town aspired ultimately to the social primacy enjoyed by that departed order. This objective was not attained in Bulfinch's period; but in the early years of Federalism the new people leaned heavily on the intermediary families for social guidance. Accordingly, the more enlightened members of the Country party joined the descendants of the old elite in their struggle to set up a theater. It was not an easy task, the acting of plays in Boston having long been restricted by unwritten agreement to household performances. Despite Cotton Mather's warning in the dying years of Puritan rule that "there is much discourse now of beginning stage plays in New England," no effort was made to perform publicly until 1750, when two Englishmen came to Boston and staged a production of Otway's *Orphan, or Unhappy Marriage* in the British Coffee House.[5] This foredoomed attempt was immediately suppressed and a law enacted banning stage plays and theatricals. Entirely amateur productions staged as family diversions continued to be tolerated so long as money was not exchanged. These were particularly popular with the Province House people, and many in the group pressing for a theater in Bulfinch's time had acted out roles as children behind closed blinds in their parents' houses. The Revolution changed all this. Faneuil Hall was fitted up by the British as a theater, and General John Burgoyne, who took an interest in theatricals disproportionate to his occupation duties, produced his own play, *The Blockade of Boston,* in the winter of 1775. The first scheduled performance of this play was interrupted by the bombardment of Charlestown, and with the British evacuation theatricals of all kind were again prohibited.

But the theater was a stronghold of the social leaders of New York and Philadelphia, who in turn exercised an influence on their counterparts in Boston. When Charles and Hannah Bulfinch were in New York for Washington's inauguration in 1789, the theater was their chief diversion. The young dilettante witnessed many theatrical performances during his travels in Europe; for his wife and their Boston companions, however, the experience was entirely novel. In the course of this trip, Bulfinch wrote from New York to his mother on the subject:[6]

Among the pleasures my companions promised themselves in this journey, you know that the seeing of a play was not reckoned among the least; I have the pleasure to inform you that although their expectations were highly raised, they have been *more* than gratified. We attended three plays in Philadelphia, and have already seen two here; and I suppose it will be thought *absolutely* necessary by our party to see every one that shall be performed during our stay; . . . You must expect our ladies to form a party in Boston for establishing a Theatre there, and they are pretty sure of success.

But it was the gentlemen rather than their ladies who took the lead in agitating for a theater in Boston. And fortunately for the success of the project, they were joined by the more liberal and ambitious members of the Essex party. Samuel Cabot, for example, was among the committee of seven chosen at a town meeting in October 1791 to draft a petition to the legislature for the repeal of the law of 1750. This alliance of interest, power, and taste was responsible for establishing eventually a theater in the face of public apathy and suspicion.

Despite a negative reaction by the General Court to the petition of 1791, the alliance held together, and in the following summer a theater was founded and given the disarming name New Exhibition Room. The name indicated a desire to arouse as little comment as possible. The same hope determined the selection of a site for the theater in one of the stables off Board Alley. It was not an auspicious place, and women, whether by rule or inclination, were excluded. The director of the theater, Joseph Harper, further disguised the enterprise in his advertising. In this he was aided by Benjamin Russell, leader of the Boston press and one of the moving forces in the establishment of a theater. Through the summer and autumn of 1792 discreet notices appeared weekly in the newspapers commenting upon the highly respectable nature of the performances in

Board Alley. *The London Merchant* was billed as "a moral lecture in five parts wherein the pernicious tendency of libertinism will be exemplified in the tragic story of George Barnwell," and *Beaux Stratagem* was cited as a lesson in "the different methods of procuring a fortune." In his editorials, "Good Ben" Russell unflinchingly presented the theater as "a school of virtue." In this the Boston Federalists were merely following the line of their party chief George Washington, who justified the theater as a means to "advance the interest of private and public virtue . . . to polish the manners and habits of society."[7] It was not possible, yet, to justify the theater on the grounds of pleasure.

Regardless of apparent subterfuge, the theater in Board Alley was set up as a test case. The crisis came in December after five flourishing months of what the wits called *teatro incognito*. A production of *The School for Scandal* progressed through the first act when authority intervened in the person of Sheriff Allen, who arrested Director Harper in a scene far more dramatic than the play at hand. The audience reacted in the same spirit; a riot ensued. The portrait of Governor Hancock was flung from its place of honor and trampled, and the arms of the Commonwealth were pulled down to suffer a similar fate. The audience poured into nearby streets where they staged a demonstration. Harper was released the following day and two weeks later a resolution calling for another petition to the legislature for repeal of the ban against theatrical performances passed in town meeting. In the following spring a committee was formed to open subscriptions for "an ele-

[58]

gant *House* for Theatrical Exhibitions" and one hundred and twenty shares at £50 each were immediately subscribed. By the end of the year the Boston (or Federal Street) Theatre was practically completed and an opening night scheduled for February 1794.

In spite of public approval for repeal of the Act of 1750, the theater remained the preserve of the liberal-minded, London-oriented descendants of the Province House set and the country families who imitated them. The status of the theatergoer during this period is revealed in the pomp and elegance which distinguished the building Bulfinch designed and erected on an open area where the eastern tip of the Tontine Crescent met Federal Street. Gone was subterfuge, mud, and the smell of livery stables. Women were welcomed and the most privileged subscribers escorted to their boxes by a footman in powdered wig. For a picture of the theater there is no better source than Thomas Pemberton's memoir of 1794, written especially for the newly founded Massachusetts Historical Society. "We are obliged," writes Pemberton, "to Charles Bulfinch, Esq., the architect, a gentleman of taste and ingenuity, for the following accurate description of this building":[8]

The theatre in Federal Street, is a lofty and spacious edifice, substantially built of brick, with stone fascias, imposts, etc. It is one hundred and forty feet long, sixty-one feet wide, and forty feet high. As it stands in a conspicuous situation, it has been thought necessary to observe a strict symmetry on the outside. It has the appearance of two stories in height; the lower a basement, with three arches in the front and five on each side, the windows square. The second story is more lofty, with large arched windows. The front and rear are decorated with Corinthian columns and pilasters; and in front a projecting arcade gives the convenience of carriages landing their company under cover.

. . . . .

The back walls are painted of a light blue, and the front of the boxes, the columns, etc. are of straw and lilach colour: the mouldings, balustrades, and fret work are gilded: a crimson silk drapery suspended from the second boxes, and twelve elegant brass chandeliers of five lights each, complete the decoration . . . The stage opening is thirty-one feet wide. It is ornamented on each side with two columns; and between them, a stage door and projecting iron balcony. Over the columns, a cornice and balustrade is carried across the opening; and above is painted a flow of crimson drapery, and the arms of the Union and of the State of Massachusetts, blended with tragick and comick attributes. A ribband depending from the arms bears the motto, "All the World's a Stage."

Bulfinch's design was taken from Plate 35 in John Crunden's *Convenient and Ornamental Architecture* and modified by the memory of two theaters he knew from firsthand knowledge: the one at Birmingham, which he sketched on his architectural pilgrimage abroad, and the Chestnut Street Theatre in Philadelphia. The Birmingham theater was allegedly the work of the Neo-classicist William Wyatt and reflected the current movement in England to which the young Bostonian proved so susceptible. The Philadelphia theater was constructed in 1792, and this suggests Bulfinch made at least one trip to that city between his journey in 1789 and completion of the Boston edifice five years later. The detailed description of the Chestnut Street Theatre in the *Massachusetts* (formerly *Columbian*) *Magazine* for September 1792 was probably supplied by Bulfinch himself, for he was their architectural commentator and contributed drawings of Federal Hall, the Hollis Street Church, and the Tontine Crescent. The Philadelphia theater was the work of a trio of English scene-painters: Charles Catton, John Richards, and Robert Smirke. From their design Bulfinch borrowed a number of motifs for the exterior of the Boston project, and these he combined with elements from the theater in Birmingham. But as a hand-colored lithograph of the Philadelphia building in the Harvard Theatre Collection shows, he relied almost entirely upon the work of the visiting English scene-painters for the interior design.[9]

The Boston Theatre opened in February 1794 with a performance of the tragedy of Gustavus Vasa Erickson, "the Deliverer of Sweden." The patriotic note struck by the choice of this drama was emphasized in the playing of "Yankee Doodle" and "General Washington's march." With the exception of a lengthy and dull prologue by the manager Charles Powell, the performance was acclaimed by local critics. Benjamin Russell, who for two years championed the cause of the theater in its changing fortunes from the mud of Board Alley to the glitter of Bulfinch's edifice, found the gala occasion well worth the long struggle. After reporting on the virtue and respectability of the enterprise, he turned his attention to the ladies in the boxes, who confirmed him in the observation that "beauty needs not the aid of ornament but is when unadorned, adorned the most."[10] To the wives of Federalist grandees, decked out in furs, plumed bonnets, and feathered muffs, this observation was perhaps gratuitous. But Mr. and Mrs. Charles Bulfinch were immensely pleased. The architect was of course conspicuous among the opening night audience and modestly showed the gold medal presented to him by the proprietors of the theater, "for his unremitted and Liberal Attention in the Plan and Execution of that Buildings [sic] The Elegance of which is the best evidence of his Taste and Talents." The obverse side of the medal contained an engraving of the theater and bore the pleasant inscription: "This medal entitles Charles Bulfinch, Esq., to a seat in the Boston Theatre for life."[11]

Life in this case proved to be unfortunately short. The first Boston Theatre burned down on a February afternoon in 1798—after barely weathering a disastrous season that entailed a loss of $8000. The archives of the theater reveal the melancholy history of this last full season, which ended with the principal actors absconding to New York with most of the theater's portable property.[12] But neither theft nor fire deterred Bulfinch and his friends; the theater was rebuilt and opened in October of the same year. The acoustics were much improved and the interior as handsome as before; the façade, however, was very plain. The colonnaded portico, Corinthian pilasters, and Palladian windows were not replaced. Gone too were the small card and tea rooms which previously served as lingering symbols of the colonial society identified with the Province House. There was instead a "spacious ballroom with a cuisine beneath," where the wives and daughters of the Federalist merchants overwhelmed by numbers and wealth the war-thinned ranks of the old aristocracy. The importance of the theater to the country people who controlled Boston is confirmed in their refusal to permit either popular or religious questions to stand in the way of social gains.

The burning of the first theater on Federal Street was the cause of a renewed outburst against theatrical perform- ances. But the proprietors not only crushed the opposition, they showed their strength by disregarding an unwritten agreement with the congregation of the Federal Street Church to refrain from giving performances in the theater on the evenings of weekday meetings. As an added insult, the newspapers began printing theatrical notices in the columns devoted to local news ahead of those announcing ordinations of Congregational clergy. By 1798 the police power of the Boston ministry was gone. Henceforth the clergy had to accept the fact their congregations would entertain themselves in this world even though they had to suffer for it in the next.[13]

The rebuilding of the Boston Theatre signaled the com- pletion of the alliance between the new people and what remained of colonial society. Bulfinch and his friends and relatives had social and cultural precedence, but political and economic control of the town was securely in the hands of the Country party. The theater presented an early opportunity for the Essex County families to compete in social equality with the descendants of the Province House set. It superseded the church as the arena where the accouterments of wealth and fashion were displayed. The ostentatious décor of the interior of the theater showed how determined the new group was to establish a social center with the prestige and style of the old Province House. The Boston Theatre was never a financial success; it went into the red each year. Yet the shrewd merchants from Essex County accepted its liabilities because the in- tangible assets were so great.

Nevertheless, there was a certain amount of grumbling about maintaining such a costly gesture. Henry Jackson, one of the proprietors of the theater, wrote to his friend General Henry Knox:[14]

Mr. Charles Bulfinch . . . calculated the cost of our Theatre to a Brick, a foot of boards, and every other material to compleat the workmanship, and to his calculations added ten per cent:—the whole expense did not amount to *twenty thousand* dollars—Altho every article has been purchased with cash, at the cheapest rates, and the work performed on the most reasonable terms, the Theatre will cost *Forty thousand* . . . double the sum contemplated.

This letter was apparently written in response to one from General Knox complaining about the cost of his new mansion, Montpellier, in Thomaston, Maine. The authorship of Knox's house is disputed although evidence strongly points to Charles Bulfinch. The plan of Montpellier is similar to that of Pleasant Hill, the country house of Joseph Barrell that astounded Federalist magnates and revolutionized domestic architecture in New England. Furthermore, the general's daughter was married to the son of Mrs. James Swan, one of Bulfinch's most opulent patrons, and Knox, who was very much *persona grata* in Federal Boston, certainly appreciated the esteem in which the town's architect was held. The letter from Jackson, so pointedly referring to Bulfinch, appears to be part of a commiseration between the proprietor of a Bulfinch building and the owner of a Bulfinch house over the high cost involved in such a privilege.

One reason Bulfinch gave little attention to the exterior of the second Boston Theatre was his absorption in the Tontine Crescent. Architecturally, the Crescent was the most interesting building he designed, legendary, even, as the only thing of its kind in Boston. In fact there was nothing like it anywhere in America. The first attempt to copy the scheme, in Philadelphia almost a decade later, resulted in a dull arrangement of houses inexpertly tied together. The Tontine Crescent doubtless owes something to the plan Robert Adam devised for two half circles of connecting houses as an extension to Portland Place in London. But even more influential was the memory of earlier crescents Bulfinch saw in Bath; a memory reinforced by a folio of pictures of that town, which is preserved among the books from his library. The opportunity for Bulfinch to put this building scheme into practice came in 1793 when Joseph Barrell moved from a large tract of land in the South End to the country house his former apprentice designed for him in Charlestown. The vacated Barrell property was bought by Bulfinch in association with his wife's brother-in-law Charles Vaughan and the merchant William Scollay. Bulfinch drew up plans for an ellipse in the form of two crescents separated by an enclosed park. But like many designs he created for Boston, this suffered change between the stages of conception and completion. Only one-half of the ellipse was erected—the Tontine Crescent. It was strung along the southern side of Franklin Place with the western tip intersecting Hawley Street and the eastern end approaching Federal Street. The specter of the Crescent still haunts this site, explaining the otherwise unaccountable curve along present-day Franklin Street.

The Tontine Crescent took its name from the proposed financing on a tontine principle in the form of an annuity, the shares of which pass upon the death of each beneficiary to the surviving partners until all are held by a single shareholder. A year before Bulfinch began his project, a coffee house in New York City and a water works in Rochester were successfully financed on this basis. And even earlier, in the autumn of 1791, two of Bulfinch's kinsmen, Joseph Coolidge and Ebenezer Storer, organized a tontine venture in Boston. Although supported by the clergy, their plan was lampooned in the press, and the General Court, reflecting public suspicion, withheld articles of incorporation.[15] Bulfinch refused to heed the warning of this earlier venture and on July 6, 1793, published the following announcement: "The public are hereby informed that a plan is proposed for building a number of convenient and elegent Houses, in a central situation, in a scheme of tontine association." The foundation stone of the first house was laid one month later.[16]

It was an ambitious project undertaken at a time unfavorable to the building of several dozen expensive houses, a fact recognized by the legislature, which, acting on precedent, refused to pass a bill of incorporation. But the Crescent was so much a part of Bulfinch's dream for improving Boston that only financial ruin prevented him from pushing the scheme to completion. Business activity was at a standstill by the necessity of signing a commercial treaty with England. Unfortunately, the British negotiations with the American emissary John Jay were prolonged just enough to ruin Charles Bulfinch. For it was in this uncertain atmosphere, and with less than 50 per cent of the shares taken up, that he began building in Franklin Place. In 1794, at the critical moment when half the houses in the

Crescent were completed, Charles Vaughan retired from the venture and Bulfinch was forced to take over his interest. Vaughan was related to the architect through marriage with Frances Apthorp, a sister of Hannah Bulfinch. He withdrew from the Franklin Place project at the instigation of his brother Benjamin, who resided in London and saw little hope for improvement in commercial relations between Old and New England. Though Bulfinch lost a business associate by the intervention of Benjamin Vaughan, he later secured several important commissions through this old champion in Parliament of American rights who, in 1795, went into voluntary exile and settled in Hallowell, Maine. Tradition assigns Bulfinch the architect of the belfrey of Old South Church in Hallowell, and Vaughan's influence was significant in getting him the commission to design the Maine state capitol in Augusta.[17]

Bulfinch completed the Tontine Crescent in 1794. Four hundred feet in length, it included sixteen brick houses whose entrances were grouped within eight porches with identical doorways. The project was influenced by the architect's memories of two building schemes he admired when visiting friends in Bath, England. The semi-elliptical form is taken from the Circus, completed shortly before Bulfinch's visit by John Wood II; the façade, with central and secondary end pavilions, suggests Queen's Square, constructed more than half a century earlier by the senior John Wood. In style the Tontine Crescent was Neo-classical rather than Palladian, depending for ornament upon attenuated pilasters, swag panels, and delicate fanlights and lunettes. The entire structure was painted to simulate masonry. Contemporaries were unanimous in their praise of the Crescent: Asher Benjamin claimed it "gave the first impulse to good taste; and to architecture, in this part of the country," the *Massachusetts Magazine*, from which plate 8 is taken, called the style "the most approved of modern elegance" and was particularly impressed by the spacious rooms and the attention given household conveniences.[18] The architect's concern for utility and comfort in interior planning was also appreciated by the public; within the year every house in the Crescent was occupied. The list of residents and owners is a representative roster of Federal society: William Tudor lived in the first house; Number 3 was owned by Thomas Handasyd Perkins; 6 and 7 were occupied by Stephen Higginson and Edward Tuckerman; William Payne owned 9; William Welch and Ebenezer Preble lived in 14 and 15; Samuel Parkman owned Number 16.

This concentration of wealth, however, did not save Charles Bulfinch. His financial ship, sinking fast in the winter of 1795, went down completely the following year. First the architect was forced to abandon his original plan for a corresponding crescent on the north side of Franklin Place; finally he had to sell his interest in the four large unfinished double houses which replaced the projected crescent. Bulfinch was ruined in the period between the signing and ratification of Jay's commercial treaty with England. Although not particularly beneficial to American interests, it represented the maximum concessions Washington's negotiators could wring from the British. The Boston Federalists, after first denouncing the treaty, came to a more reasonable appraisal as a result of an ugly riot in September 1796, when demonstrators massed in

Liberty Square to hang Jay in effigy. Sheriff Allen, the representative of authority, appeared cautiously on the scene. Finding the multitude more dangerous than the gentlemen who trampled Hancock's portrait over the closing of the New Exhibition Room in Board Alley three years before, he retired from the field and appealed to the merchants of Boston to defend the treaty negotiated by a Federalist administration for their benefit. The Essex Junto threw its most impassioned orator, young Fisher Ames, into the battle raging in Congress, and Jay's treaty was forced through the legislature. This seemingly unpromising agreement between England and her former colonies ushered in a prosperous era of trade for Boston. But it came too late for Bulfinch. All of Franklin Place and the remnants of the Bulfinch and Apthorp fortunes passed into the hands of his creditors. When the disaster was behind him, and the life of his family irreparably altered, the architect bitterly reproached himself: "With what remorse have I looked back on these events, when blindly gratifying a taste for a favorite pursuit, I envolved for life myself and wife with our children."[19]

A park was set up in the middle of Franklin Place following in pattern the curved and straight lines of the buildings it separated. Here Bulfinch placed an urn as a memorial to Benjamin Franklin.[20] After the buildings in Franklin Place were demolished in 1858, the urn was moved to Bulfinch's grave in Mount Auburn Cemetery. In the architect's lifetime, however, the urn stood below the great Palladian window in the central block of the Crescent; a window associated with the generosity of Charles Bulfinch. For just prior to relinquishing the last of his

rights in Franklin Place, and completely ruined, he presented the large room behind the Palladian window to the
Boston Library Society. Bulfinch was among the secular
minority of the dozen or so gentlemen who organized the
library in 1792 and one of the seven trustees when it
opened in the old Massachusetts Bank building with a collection of nearly one thousand volumes. He was still a
trustee in 1796 when he presented the room in the Crescent. Two years earlier, Bulfinch, along with Scollay and
Vaughan, offered space in the central pavilion of the Tontine Crescent to the newly founded Massachusetts Historical Society, then lodged temporarily in an attic of Faneuil
Hall. The president of the Society, James Sullivan, accepted this gift in a letter noting that the members derived
"no small degree of pleasure from the consideration . . .
the donation is made by gentlemen whose feelings for the
public interest and taste for architecture have ornamented
the capital with buildings so exceedingly elegant as the
Crescent."[21] The Historical Society occupied these quarters
for almost forty years; the Library Society remained in the
Palladian room until the building was destroyed.

Bulfinch's generous and public-spirited nature found an
even wider expression in the part he played in the building
of Boston's first Roman Catholic church. The fortunes of
this faith had improved in the New England capital since
pre-Revolution days when the pope and the devil were
burned in effigy annually. Yet when the Reverend John
Thayer returned to his native town in 1790 as the first
resident priest, the one hundred or so Roman Catholics in
Boston had no place of worship. Thayer, formerly a Con-

gregational minister converted to the Catholic faith while traveling in Europe, was a member of a Massachusetts family with another prominent connection with the church architecture of Charles Bulfinch. For the Reverend Nathaniel Thayer of Lancaster commissioned Bulfinch to design the Church of Christ over which he presided. The church in Lancaster is Bulfinch's finest ecclesiastical building and is still standing, as beautiful as ever in unaltered condition.[22] Father John Thayer was not destined to preside over a fine Bulfinch building. But he did lay the ground work leading to the erection of Holy Cross at the eastern end of Franklin Place.

Father Thayer was ordined in Paris and called by Bishop Carroll of Baltimore to the mission in Boston. It was not a happy choice. While Thayer's former associations and his sincerity mitigated in part the inherent suspicions of the town, he proved a controversial figure. Further, he was indiscriminate in his highly publicized quarrels. On a single day in 1791, two challenges appeared in the newspapers under his signature. One offered to meet "in combat" any of the local clergy in regard to "genuine Popery which is taught in all council, catechisms and schools of the Universal Church," and urged all those who "sincerely desire salvation" to witness the struggle. The other proclaimed war on "a Priest, by name Mr. Louis Rousselet, who styles himself Pastor of the *Catholick Congregation of Boston* [and] is carrying about a subscription for the education of two Indians."[23] The Boston clergy refused to be drawn into quarrels with Thayer, nor did they interfere with the services held in the small and dilapidated meetinghouse lately

transformed into a chapel on the south side of School
Street. Charles Breck in his *Recollections* describes the im-
provised chapel:[24]

A subscription put the sacristy or vestry-room in order, erected
a pulpit and purchased a few benches. A little additional furniture and plate was borrowed. At length everything was prepared
to solemnize the first public mass that was ever said in Boston
. . . I attended the mass and carried around the begging box.

Thayer remained in charge of his small congregation
until 1792 when he was replaced by Abbé François Matignon. Matignon in turn relinquished his command in 1796
to his former pupil at the Sorbonne, the Reverend John de
Cheverus. Father Cheverus was exactly the man to win
the respect and confidence of the leading Bostonians. If
nothing else, the fact he was the last priest to be or-
dained in France before the Revolution and had fled
to England in disguise endeared him to the Federalists
with their hatred of Napoleon and his French adherents
in America. But Cheverus brought much more to Boston
than an exciting past. He performed his duties discreetly,
helped to found the Boston Athenæum, and was one of
Bulfinch's staunchest supporters in the promotion of civic
and artistic improvements. The first Roman Catholic
bishop of Boston was also the architect's intimate friend.
He remained at his post for twenty-seven years and, according to Breck, was "so attached to his flock, his diocese
and his place of residence that he refused to comply with
Louis XVIII's summons which called him to the diocese
of Montauban in Languedoc, and that king had to lay his
commands upon him before he would consent to leave the

United States." From Bishop of Montauban, Cheverus went on to the archbishopric of Bordeaux and received a cardinal's hat in 1835, the year of his death.[25]

The little church in School Street, rented to the Roman Catholics by Bulfinch's Beacon Hill patron Thomas Perkins, soon became inadequate. In 1799 a committee was organized to raise funds for the purchase of a building site for a larger edifice. The chairman was Don Juan Stoughton, the Spanish Consul, who lived in one of the Bulfinch houses in Franklin Place, and the site chosen was opposite his house and across from the theater. The property belonged to the theater proprietors and Bulfinch, who was a member of the corporation, obtained the land for the Catholics at a modest figure. He then submitted plans for the church to Bishop Cheverus without fee. The architect also assisted in the subscription taken for the erection of the building. About sixteen thousand dollars were collected, more than one-fifth donated by the Protestants of Boston, who seem generally to have agreed with Shubael Bell, senior warden of Christ Church, that "no circumstance has contributed more to the peace and good order of the town, than the establishment of a Catholic Church."[26] John Adams, then President of the United States, headed the list of non-Catholic subscribers with the gift of one hundred dollars, a sum matched by other leading Federalists of the town. Bulfinch was present at the ground-breaking ceremonies and devoted much time and assistance to the construction of the building. His concern for the interior decorations stimulated the interest of a number of his Protestant friends, particularly the artist Henry Sargent, who painted an altarpiece representing the Crucifixion. Holy Cross was consecrated as a parish church in September 1803.

Contemporary sources describe the church, whose model Bulfinch found among the works of his English mentor William Chambers, as being in the "Italian Renaissance" style. This designation was prompted by the architect's placement of the cupola on a line with the front elevation and his use of a pair of Baroque consoles to conceal the pitch of the roof.[27] Although the first Roman Catholic church in Boston was razed almost a century ago, its physical appearance can be recaptured by a visit to St. Stephen's Church (*Plate 24*) on Hanover Street, designed by Bulfinch in a similar style only a year after the consecration of Holy Cross. St. Stephen's was originally built for the New North Religious Society and became a Roman Catholic church in 1862, when it was decided to locate the new Cathedral on Washington Street near Union Park.[28] The sincere and unremitted efforts Bulfinch made in the Holy Cross project—purchase of the land, raising of the money, design of the church, and continuous help in the building—received recognition in the gift of a silver tea urn bearing the inscription: To Charles Bulfinch, Esq., Presented by the Catholics of Boston.[29]

Holy Cross was completed at a time when the Federalist experiment was in its halcyon stage and Bulfinch deeply involved in more ambitious projects. Yet none of the later building schemes gave him a greater sense of achievement than the three structures he designed for Franklin Place. Despite the fact he was ruined over the building of the Tontine Crescent, it was still an object of unfailing pleasure. No subsequent grouping of houses—the mansions for

Beacon Hill proprietors, "Bulfinch Row" in Park Street, or the Colonnade in Tremont Street—could bring back so forcibly the memory of the London he loved in the carefree days of his architectural pilgrimage. And he was entirely satisfied with the results of the designs he submitted for the theater and the Catholic church. The buildings in Franklin Place were epochal. Each of them—the Boston Theatre, the Tontine Crescent, and Holy Cross Church— were "firsts" in Boston. In their varied purposes, they represented an advancement in pleasure, taste, and tolerance undreamed of a few decades earlier in the old Puritan capital. No other spot in Boston attested so eloquently to the new and broader life Bulfinch brought to his native town. Franklin Place was the microcosm of what he dreamed Boston might be.

I V

THE GREAT SELECTMAN

BULFINCH RETURNED from Europe eager to take the lead in rebuilding Boston in the image of Neo-classical London. In this pursuit, however, he did not expect to immerse himself completely in town affairs. But when his financial ship went down in 1796, with it disappeared the optimistic dilettante. The man who emerged from the economic wreckage of Franklin Place was drastically altered; the affluent and fashionable dreamer vanished overnight. As if by some delayed action, the promising heir was made to suffer the fate of the other recipients of the once-great Apthorp heritage. But, unlike his mother's loyalist relatives, he was not forced to leave Boston. On the contrary, he was bound more firmly than ever to his native place. And, as the stimulant in the development of Bulfinch's life from leisured amateurism to professional achievement, financial ruin was the proverbial blessing in disguise.

Nevertheless, it was still an awful period for Bulfinch and his family. They followed the pattern usual in bankruptcy, moving from one small house to another. Hannah Bulfinch recorded the migration in terms of a saga: "Read, my children, the wanderings of your mother, who once thought herself plac'd by fortune far above these vicissitudes."[1] When the blow fell, the Bulfinches were living in the house he built for them in Bulfinch Place. Begun in 1794, and occupied by the family the following year, this house was similar in style and proportion to the neighboring mansion Bulfinch designed for Joseph Coolidge Jr., in Bowdoin Square. Ellen Susan Bulfinch described the dwelling as "a large brick house, painted white, with a very handsome spiral staircase and a good-sized garden in the rear."[2] But Miss Bulfinch erred in supposing this the house to which the family fled after the Crescent disaster. All but four of the succeeding nineteen years were passed in the so-called Clap-Bulfinch house in Bulfinch Street.

These years of distress and achievement began in the spring of 1796 when the architect moved his family into a small dwelling on Middlecott (Bowdoin) Street close to the ancestral homestead. This exodus closed the period of prosperity begun seven years before with a listing in the town directory of "Charles Bulfinch, gentleman, Marlborough street." Of the architect's personal reaction to the disaster in Franklin Place there is little record. But Hannah Bulfinch, in a letter written to her son Thomas twenty-one years after the event, tells something of the sadness: *"Your birth took place when heavy misfortune oppressed the hearts of your parents, nor did we look upon even your existence with cheerfulness, yet it has been to us a bless-ing."*[3] This son, the second to be named Thomas, was born in a modest house whose rent was paid by a relative. For though Bulfinch arranged his affairs so that the workmen employed on the Crescent suffered little loss, his failure engulfed his wife's fortune and involved his father and his brother-in-law, George Storer, both of whom acted as his endorsers. Storer was also Bulfinch's intimate friend and a member of the intermediary family group that comprised most of the architect's relatives and patrons. He was the son of Ebenezer Storer, Boston merchant, treasurer of Harvard College, and owner of an historic mansion around the corner from Bowdoin Square. This old-fashioned house was not far from Southack's Court (Howard Street), where George and Anna Bulfinch Storer lived. In 1797 the Charles Bulfinches moved into the younger Storer's house, recalled by one of the family as "a quaint old wooden building with many gables." The two families shared the house for financial reasons, but it was a mutually satisfactory arrangement. The childless Storers enjoyed the young Bulfinches, whose number was tragically reduced by the death of four of the six sons born, up to this time, to Hannah Bulfinch. In 1799 the family moved back to the little house on Middlecott Street to which they fled in the first months after the Tontine failure. They moved again the following year into a pleasant house purchased from William Clap that stood on the southeast corner of Bulfinch and Howard streets. Mrs. Bulfinch noted the family's satisfaction with this change: "At last we find ourselves established in a comfortable house, with a moderate income." The architect-administrator lived in this house until 1815, when the family was caught up once more in a financial disaster. In October of that year Mrs. Bulfinch writes: "The pressure of creditors has oblig'd us to remove into a smaller house." This house, Number 5 Tremont Street, sheltered the wanderers until they left Boston in 1817.[4]

Doctor and Mrs. Thomas Bulfinch anxiously watched

their son's financial difficulties from the family mansion on the north side of Bowdoin Square. And when the crash came, only the marriage of their daughter Elizabeth to Joseph Coolidge, Jr., saved them from the migratory fate of their son's family. Elizabeth Bulfinch Coolidge's father-in-law purchased the threatened homestead from creditors and presented it to his son and daughter-in-law, an appropriate gesture since Coolidge was also a descendant of Adino Bulfinch, the founder of the family in America. The young Coolidges remodeled the mansion as a home for themselves and the distinguished old doctor and his wife. Dr. Bulfinch died a few years later but his wife lived until 1815. She was an intelligent and accomplished woman whose long life spanned three distinct phases of Boston's history. Blackburn's portrait of her as a young woman shows beauty and the self-possession of the daughter of the richest man in Boston; her letters reveal a faithful wife, devoted sister, and comforting mother.[5] She was a valued link between the old Province House set and the up-and-coming society of the Essex County families. This role was emphasized in the eulogy delivered at her funeral service in King's Chapel. "In her," said Mrs. Thomas Bulfinch's friend and minister, the Reverend James Freeman, "might be seen what is sometimes styled the manner of the old school: her deportment was erect and dignified; it inspired respect, and frequently awe."[6]

Joseph Coolidge prevented the Bulfinch homestead from falling into the hands of creditors but nothing could save the remaining Bulfinch properties. The most important of these was a pasture of four acres purchased by the architect's grandfather, the first Dr. Thomas Bulfinch, in 1754.[7]

That part of the pasture fronting on Bowdoin Square was sold to Kirk Boott, who almost certainly commissioned Bulfinch to design the well-known house built on this land in 1803.[8] The Bulfinch pasture extended up Beacon Hill to the present-day boundaries of Bulfinch Street and Ashburton Place. Beacon Hill was then mainly a pasturage for cows and horses. Of the three peaks that towered over the Common, the highest, Beacon, was a rugged and steep eminence about twice the present height. Originally called Sentry Hill, it was renamed for the beacon existing there since the earliest days of the town's history. The beacon blew down shortly after Bulfinch's return home and he suggested replacing it with a column commemorating the Revolution. The monument symbolized Boston's consciousness of her famous past as the instigator of the War for Independence and Bulfinch's determination to introduce into the former Puritan capital some of the objects of grandeur he admired in the cities of Europe. The Reverend Jeremy Belknap, who with Bulfinch composed the inscription carved on the base of the column, described the project as a "pillar to be sixty feet high; over its capital, the American eagle, which is to perform the office of a weathercock. The arrows are to serve for points, and a conductor is to be added for the lightning. The designer is Mr. Charles Bulfinch, a very ingenious and accomplished gentleman, and as modest as ingenious."[9] The young amateur architect personally managed the subscription to finance the project and before long a column in the Doric order was erected on the summit of Beacon Hill (*Plate 10*).[10]

It is difficult to envisage the state of Beacon Hill in 1790 from any present-day associations, for at that time the summit still soared over Hancock's garden and pasture—a strange looking, cone-shaped mound sloping down to the site of the future State House. The Massachusetts State House, designed two years later by Charles Bulfinch, established the enduring character of Beacon Hill, and this building with its great dome became the signature of Boston. But the memorial column continued to dominate the skyline until 1811, when it was pulled down and the crest of the hill made level with the ground on which the State House stands. A replica of the monument was constructed at the end of the nineteenth century on what was then the east lawn of the capitol and is today a parking lot. Viewed from this position, one finds it hard to believe Bulfinch's column was once one of the sights of the town, ranging proudly over the dome of the State House.

Yet even in the Federalist heyday the site of the memorial column was not too inviting a place. Bulfinch planned to convert the area immediately surrounding the monument into a mall or pleasure ground such as he had seen on his Grand Tour. Charles Shaw, whose history was published six years after the monument was pulled down, says the base of the pillar was surrounded by a railing in the form of benches "for the accommodation of those who ascended the hill."[11] These conveniences, however, are not shown in contemporary representations of the column, and whatever the designer's original hopes, the summit remained during its allotted existence a barren and rocky wilderness. From the north there was a flight of a dozen or so steps taking the adventurer a little way up the slope. The rest of the route was by foot holes worn into the earth and probably needed the assistance of the vigorous shrubs which overran the place. On the south side, there was a similar combination of dirt path and wooden planks leading into Sumner Street, which then ran perpendicular to Beacon Street along the east side of the State House before sloping down hill to join present-day Mount Vernon Street. It is doubtful if all the town's inhabitants were able to get up to the summit and read the inscriptions the Reverend Jeremy Belknap and Charles Bulfinch took such pains to prepare.

A few years before the Bulfinch pasture was sacrificed, another grazing field on Beacon Hill was sold for a building site. The two-acre plot east of John Hancock's mansion, traditionally known as "the Governor's pasture," was purchased by the town as the location for a new State House. For more than a decade there was talk of building a new capitol, and Bulfinch supplied his first plan for the project the year he returned from Europe. Eight years later, in 1795, he was appointed to a committee charged with constructing the State House from his revised design. The corner stone was laid on the Fourth of July the same year at a ceremony in which most of the surviving local heroes of the Revolutionary period were displayed. Samuel Adams assisted Paul Revere in placing the corner stone, which was drawn to the site by fifteen white horses representing the current number of states in the Union.

In its original form, the State House was considerably smaller and simpler in construction than the present-day edifice. The crude but authentic water color reproduced in Plate 10 shows the State House before the addition of a basement above ground but after the dome was covered with copper by Paul Revere.[12] Bulfinch's plan suggests the north façade corresponded exactly with the front facing the Common excepting for the elimination of the central portico. The origin of the design in the Neo-classical architecture of London is obvious. Bulfinch himself admitted it was "in the style of a building celebrated all over Europe."[13] He referred to Somerset House, the government building William Chambers began a decade before Bulfinch arrived in England. The Massachusetts State House was much admired by contemporaries, especially southerners. But there were flaws. Visitor Elias Boudinot, who risked an attack of gout in climbing to the upper story in the summer of 1809, found the ceiling of the House of Representatives "too high for the members being heard, they have effectually remedied the evil by a kind of large Umbrella suspended from the Ceiling, over the Heads of the members." The House of Representatives is now the Senate chamber with improved acoustics.[14]

The Massachusetts legislature met for the last time in the old State House in January 1798 and then joined in a ceremonial parade up Beacon Hill to open the capitol building. Bulfinch occupied a prominent place in this procession. The evacuation of the old State House as the seat of government put to rest one of the famous ghosts of Boston's past. Located on the town's "political" street, the building was redolent with history: the scene of Royalist pomp, Revolutionary ardor, Federalist defiance. Although clinging to the past in politics and commerce, Boston was geographically moving into the future. The location of the seat of government at the top of Beacon Hill focused all eyes in a new direction—to the largely deserted site of Bulfinch's memorial column. At the time the architect guided the procession up the hill from the old State House he had designed only one dwelling on the sunny slope between the summits of Beacon Hill and Mount Whoredom. This dwelling, the yellow frame country house built for Dr. John Joy in 1791, was separated from the new capitol by the Hancock mansion.

The Bostonians, observed Governor Oliver Wolcott of Connecticut in 1802, "like the Romans, may boast of their Capitol and their triumphal column."[15] Though his townsmen preferred comparison with the Athenians, Bulfinch received the compliment with satisfaction. For by this time the architect was a member of the Board of Selectmen and completely identified with the civic life of Boston. The selectmen were the town's highest administrative body and almost the only source of authority. The people of Boston resisted every attempt to turn the town government into a city with mayor and elected officials; all important matters were still settled at town meeting in Faneuil Hall. Early in her history, however, the town relegated some executive power to the "seven men" or "selectmen" and time raised the number to nine annually elected. Bulfinch turned increasingly to his duties as selectman in the years following the Tontine disaster. At first this was mainly a means of solace. But as a large part of the selectmen's duties were concerned with town building and its dependencies, he naturally came to shoulder the bulk of the work.

Bulfinch himself is authority for the belief he was first elected selectman in 1789. He was, indeed, a member of the town government that year, serving as Clerk of the Market. However, the memorandum he made late in life describing himself a "junior member" of the Board of Selectmen in

1789 and chairman in 1797 seems to be inaccurate in both instances. Actually, Bulfinch was first elected to the Board of Selectmen in 1791. He was re-elected each year until 1795, when he resigned to devote himself entirely to private affairs. Four years later, he successfully returned to active public life and was chosen chairman of the Board of Selectmen. And he held this position without interruption for nineteen years.[16]

The reason for Bulfinch's return to political life is evident in the "Appeal to A Generous Public" published in the *Columbian Centinel* January 27, 1796:

The feelings of our fellow-citizens of this town, are arrested by the recent, and unhappy embarrassments of one of its best supporters. To effect a relief from his present perplexity, should be the first object of this community, which, by his generous and spirited exertions, have been greatly benefited. Could not some methods be devised, which might extricate, from immediate difficulty, that liberal protector, that noble patron of the fine arts? Mr. B. (we all know) has sacrificed the best part of his time, nay, his interest also, in ornamenting and beautifying the town —and shall he be suffered to remain in this involved situation, without receiving from *that town*, a helping hand? Since he fails in a *public cause*, shall he not from the public find redress?

Despite this plea by the leading Federalist newspaper, four years passed before the architect received tangible evidence of the town's good will.

Bulfinch's election to the entirely honorific chairmanship of the Board of Selectmen came only after several attempts to secure a salaried post at both town and county levels. His defeats in campaigns for town notary and county treasurer show how poorly he was equipped by na-

ture or background for the rough-and-tumble life of post-
Revolutionary politics. In each of the nineteen years Bulfinch was chairman of the Board of Selectmen he seems to
have received the least number of votes of any elected official. His place on the board was clearly secured for him by
the party chiefs who, despite a lack of political vision, at
least appreciated the versatility of their architect and understood his importance to Boston. Yet Bulfinch was not
paid until 1799, when the selectmen created the post of
superintendent of police and he was unanimously elected
to fill the office. The salary was six hundred dollars a year,
later raised to one thousand.

Although Bulfinch owed to his party his appointments
as chairman of selectmen and chief of police, the positions
were not sinecures. One newspaper account of the unsuccessful attempt in 1815 to dislodge him from office estimated that, in addition to devoting one hundred and thirty
days a year to his duties as selectman, Bulfinch, as permanent chairman and head of police, was never free from
town responsibilities.[17] Furthermore, the architect's long
experience in public affairs qualified him uniquely for the
position of chief town officer. The records show that in his
first year in office as selectman Bulfinch served on general
committees charged with the collection of taxes, examina-
tion of town books, supervision of the poor, making of laws
relative to scavengers, and regulation of the market area.
That same year he served the city as an architect when
he was directed to investigate "a dangerous situation of a
House at the corner of Merchants Row," contract for the
painting of Faneuil Hall, and supervise the repair of the
town watch houses and hospital building. The min-

utes of the town meeting of December 30, 1791, report him among the twenty-one "most influential citizens" appointed to consider "the want of a more efficient police." Their recommendations were rejected and a decade elapsed before the police function encompassed much more than the inspection of wells and the supervision of a night watch. It remained for Bulfinch to transform the rudimentary police office into the town's most efficient administrative agency.

Bulfinch administered the affairs of Boston for two decades following the business failure in Franklin Place. Purely architectural pursuits continued to be a part of his life, the most important and rewarding in a personal sense. "My husband," wrote Hannah Bulfinch, "made Architecture his business, as it had been his pleasure."[18] But most of his time, talent, and energy was expended in the multiplying duties of Boston's principal official. As chairman of the selectmen and chief of police, he was directly responsible for the safety, health, and harmony of the town. He concerned himself with politics only on the local level; as a conscientious administrator, he avoided taking sides in the rivalries between Federalists and Republicans which divided Boston in his age. Bulfinch was personally unambitious, neurotically self-effacing, disinclined to engage in controversy; but he was ambitious for his town. And almost everything accomplished in this period that was worthy of Boston's splendid natural site and famous past was planned, designed, or implemented by Bulfinch. Patient, hard-working, conscientious, he was also imaginative and intelligent and possessed the best taste of anyone in post-Revolutionary Boston.

The problems confronting Bulfinch as the town's chief officer were diffuse. Although Boston lost primacy in America to New York and Philadelphia before the Revolution, her population rose to 20,000 in 1797, to 30,000 in 1807, and 40,000 in 1817. The need for new and wider streets, public buildings, wharves, bridges, the draining and filling of marsh lands, the leveling of hills, the extension of street lighting, sewers, water pipes—these and a thousand other demands taxed Bulfinch's time and patience and his architectural and engineering knowledge. A considerable part of the population lived in the crowded North End, where wooden buildings and narrow streets provided special problems in safety and sanitation. Fire regulations were vigorously enforced and town ordinances decreed that public and large private buildings be constructed of brick or stone and roofed with noncombustible materials. A law passed in 1803 prohibiting the erection of wooden buildings over ten feet wide augmented previous ones requiring the largest side or both ends of private houses to be of brick or stone. The enforcement of fire laws led to the use of brick in most of the new buildings constructed during Bulfinch's time, an important esthetic point, as the Neo-classical English models used by Bulfinch required brick or stone facing.[19]

Some of the fire and safety laws of Federal Boston were excessive by today's standards, such as one prohibiting "lighted segars" in the streets. Chimneys had to be swept by licensed sweepers and pumps inspected four times a year to ensure proper functioning in case of fire. Bulfinch's first official act as chief of police was to draft regulations regarding the responsibilities of licensed sweepers, and the act was published in the town papers a day after his appointment. Wood, the only means of fuel, was cut in the street and taken in before dark so that inhabitants would not stumble over it. Open drains and pitfalls had to be lighted by lamps until midnight. Citizens were encouraged to maintain street lights, and severe fines were imposed on those who broke or extinguished them. Sanitary laws were primitive, but attempts were made to maintain the public health by regulations prohibiting the sale or storage of fish in any receptacle not standing over salt water. Oystermen were required to carry their empty shells to places especially designated by the selectmen. The oystermen and lobstermen, chanting their wares through the evening streets, were an unforgettable sight and sound of old Boston. Long afterwards an "Old School Boy" described the cries which rang through the town at dusk:[20]

Oysterman carried a well-fitted sack, and with sonorous voice pitched to a minor key, yet musical withal, sent out his cry of "Oise, buy-ni'-oise; here's oise." Lobsterman had a nicely painted barrow, always red within and blue without, and as he walked his evening rounds like a watchman called: "Lob, buy Lob."

Various regulations attempted to restrict the herds of cows exercising their primordial rights on the Common. These rights were hedged about with qualifications, like the ordinance of 1646 restricting the number of cows to seventy. But on the whole they enjoyed a sacred inviolability, and the only creatures seriously contesting their priority were sheep. A piece of Staffordshire china made in 1818 shows a group of Bulfinch buildings on upper Beacon and Park Streets with three cows in guarded possession of the best portion of the Common; farther down the hill, in front of Dr. Joy's house, a flock of small black-faced sheep graze alertly in the shade.[21] Still, many cows wandered off and eventually found their way into the pages of the local press, like the one who "Strayed away from the Common, on Tuesday last, a large red Milch COW. Whoever will give information to the Printer, so that she may be recovered again, shall be rewarded for their kindness."[22] Perhaps they fled such raids as that carried out by Madam Hancock, who, when she found insufficient butter for the preparation of one of the Governor's feasts, dispatched her servants to the Common with orders to milk all the cows indiscriminately.

Bulfinch was also responsible for the enforcement of Boston's extraordinary Sunday or "blue laws." Sunday was quietly observed throughout the United States, but hardly anywhere with the same intensity and vigilance as in Boston. The Sabbath lasted from midnight Saturday until six o'clock Sunday evening. All travel in and out of the town other than emergency was suspended. The driver of a hack or carriage had to secure permission for himself and each passenger in order to leave or enter Boston, and no vehicle could travel faster than a walk during church hours. Horses could not be washed or publicly watered on Sunday nor could they be ridden or driven through the Common. Boston's chief of police found town boys more difficult to bend to Sabbath obedience than hackney coach drivers. At a meeting of the selectmen in December 1807, Bulfinch was charged "To employ a Constable to attend on the Common" Sundays to prevent boys from skating on the Frog Pond. In the same month six years later, the chief of police himself tried "on two Sundays passed" to clear the pond of youthful skaters. Summer was equally troublesome for watch and wards. In June 1802 the selectmen observed disapprovingly "That great numbers of Children & young Men have lately adopted the practise of going into Water on the Lord's Day . . . to the encouragement of idle habits & the offence of the seriously disposed part of the Community." But neither Bulfinch's constables nor his fines (in this case four dollars) had much effect. Twelve years later, in the midst of "Mr. Madison's War," swimming was so common on Sunday that a town memorial was framed calling upon the chief of police to arrest all offenders.

Bulfinch administered the town's laws scrupulously free from the influence of the warring political factions. This is evident in a proclamation he published in both Federalist and Republican newspapers in March 1800:[23]

The Subscriber having been reappointed Superintendent of the police of this town for the year ensuing, solicits the concurrence of his fellow townsmen, in his endeavors to promote good order. He will be ready to hear complaints against all breaches of the law, which he will endeavor to enforce with mildness and impartiality.

As a public figure, Bulfinch was amazingly complete. In addition to his duties as chief of police, for example, he designed the State House, where law was promulgated, the Court House where it was administered, and county and state jails where the guilty were incarcerated. And he also designed many of the buildings, houses, streets, and wharves in which the crimes were committed. Yet the administration of the police alone was a big job, enough for any man less dedicated and conscientious than "the Great Selectman." Bulfinch was responsible for the functioning of a force that included two assistant police officers, seventeen constables, and thirty watchmen. He discharged his responsibilities with tact, tolerance, and understanding. Perhaps he was a little too understanding, if the following quotation from his granddaughter is applicable to all cases: "He was always incredulous, it is said, of tales of scandal, or, if forced to admit the facts, ingenious in explaining them away, or reconciling them with the innocence, or at least the good intentions, of the accused."[24]

Criminals nevertheless were apprehended by Bulfinch's police force and brought to judgment in buildings he designed. The old jails were overcrowded and antiquated when Bulfinch drew up the plans for the Massachusetts State Prison in 1803 and supervised its construction across the river in Charlestown. This was a formidable structure with a high central projection and two grim-looking wings of massive granite walls; its windows, mere elongated slits in the stone, ironically commanded a "rich and variegated prospect."[25] Bulfinch's mother visited the jail and described it in a letter to her exiled brother in England: "It is divided into solitary cells, lighted by small apertures in the wall, each cell just large eno' to contain a Bed, a small table and chair. . . [I] suppose a few hours in the day a person might read in them."[26] This description is verified in detail by the British visitor Thomas Hamilton, who, like Mrs. Thomas Bulfinch, viewed the new penal system of solitary confinement with mixed emotions. Hamilton was particularly interested in the method of security and surveillance devised by the architect, which included "a

safety watch-box, with an alarum bell" and stone galleries that commanded a wide view of the cell blocks.[27]

Post-Revolutionary Boston was hardly advanced over Puritan times in its penal system and inhuman punishments. In a single day in 1787, the year Bulfinch returned from Europe, the following sentences were passed by the Supreme Judicial Court: "One burglar to be hung; five female thieves to be whipped; four male thieves whipped; two big thieves to sit on the gallows; one counterfeiter to stand in the pillory, and have right ear cut off."[28] On October 22, 1799, the Boston *Gazette* reported that "several male and female rogues were publicly whipped and pilloried on Friday last." And added: "We are glad that the scene of their punishments has been removed from State street to the Common." It is not certain whether the *Gazette* was "glad" because the new site offered more room for spectators than the old whipping post or because, as stated in Samuel Breck's *Recollections:*[29]

The large whipping post, painted red, stood conspicuously in the most public street in town—State Street, directly under the windows of a great writing school which I frequented, and from them the scholars indulged in the spectacle of all kinds of punishment, suited to harden their hearts and brutalize their feelings. Here women were taken from a huge cage in which they were dragged on wheels from prison and tied to the post, with bare backs, on which thirty or forty lashes were bestowed; amid the screams of the culprits and the uproar of the mob.

The outraged Breck wrote his memoir after more than half a life spent among the Quakers of Philadelphia. But so indelible was his boyhood memory of the savagery of eighteenth-century punishment in Boston he could recall vividly the pillory, located further down State Street, where three or four lawbreakers usually stood for an hour or more exposed to the insults of the public and a barrage of rotten eggs and garbage.

Certainly more space for spectators was a practical necessity. In 1812, the last year executions were permitted on the Common, ten thousand people witnessed the hanging of the pirate Sam Tully. The spectacle of a public execution was not limited to the thousands on hand; they merely witnessed the final act of a drama begun many hours earlier. The unlucky actors, the condemned persons, were marched in a procession through the main streets over a route advertised well in advance. It was customary to suspend all work during the period of the procession so that even the most industrious might not miss the gruesome spectacle. Hawkers pushed through the crowds crying their wares, which included printed poems for the occasion. A few lines of verse survive from one written in reference to two sailors hanged in 1810:[30]

> And oh, the cruel murders! it was a dreadful sin,
> The one he took a loggerhead, another a rolling-pin.

After 1812 public executions took place at South Boston, where in 1817 a young Englishman was hanged in the presence of 20,000 spectators. On this occasion, they were rewarded by the novelty of the doomed man reading a poem to the edification of the mob. Public hanging came to an end about 1822, when the Leverett Street jail was completed and its rear courtyard became the place of execution. But sometimes the criminal was almost literally executed by the public itself. A pickpocket, caught in the act, was beaten just short of death by a mob in 1802 before he could be carried off to jail.

Malefactors were immured in the town jail on Court Street erected in 1794. It is not known whether Bulfinch was the architect, but he was destined to become intimately acquainted with the interior arrangement, for here, in the summer of 1811, the permanent chairman of Boston's Board of Selectmen and its chief of police was confined as a debtor. Mrs. Bulfinch sadly notes the event in a journal entry for July: "My Husband, disappointed in his reasonable hopes, has been obliged to submit himself to his creditors, and to go into confinement for a month. How gladly would he pay his engagements if it were in his power."[31] The chief of police could at least console himself with the knowledge that his temporary Court Street lodgings were "as commodious as the locked apartments appropriated to debtors in any gaol in the commonwealth."[32] Charles Shaw, who made this observation five years after Bulfinch's imprisonment, describes the debtors' cells as individual apartments equipped with glazed windows, plastered walls, and fireplaces. While it is disappointing to know the town's first citizen should have been allowed to suffer imprisonment, at least not all his creditors were determined to exact punishment in lieu of payment. Francis Cabot Lowell lent Bulfinch $500 in 1806 and canceled the unpaid debt eleven years later "in consideration of his regard for Mr. Bulfinch and on just estimate of the service he had rendered to the town of Boston."[33] The circumstances of Bulfinch's imprisonment remain unknown, although most of his creditors were personal friends or associated with him in town improvements. "The trial is over," writes Mrs. Bulfinch in

August 1811, "he is returned to the bosom of his family, and they once more enjoy serenity and content, soothed by the kindness of friends and acquitted by our consciences of intentional error."[34] And apparently his fellow citizens were undisturbed by their chief of police's brief sojourn in the Court Street jail; Bulfinch immediately returned to his civic duties.

The exercise of the town's police power was only one of the many responsibilities confronting the Board of Selectmen. Another was the inspection of Boston's free educational system, then unrivaled in America and extending back in time to 1642. A revision of the educational system adopted in town meeting in 1789 created a visiting committee composed of the selectmen and twelve interested citizens. Bulfinch not only served as committee chairman but also designed some of the buildings to which these duties pertained. The Latin School, best of Boston's seven schools and where the architect himself prepared for college, was enlarged by Bulfinch in the autumn of 1800. Twelve years later he designed a new building to house the classical scholars, using his earlier Court House as the model.[35] There were "writing" schools in the North, West, and South Ends as well as three "reading" schools for additional instruction in grammar. The Latin School was restricted to boys over ten years of age who had already attended a reading school; the six others were open to children of both sexes above seven years. Boys attended school all year round, while girls went from the end of April to the end of October. Bulfinch designed at least two of the reading and writing schools: one in Hawkins Street, just behind the old homestead in Bowdoin Square, and another in Mason Street, across from the former Greenleaf estate in the South End where Hannah Bulfinch passed her childhood.[36]

The selectmen were responsible for the care of the town poor, and again the chairman designed the buildings in which they were housed. The completion in 1801 of a new almshouse at the foot of Leverett Street had a favorable effect on the development of Beacon Hill. Prior to this time, the Almshouse and Bridewell formed an unsightly cluster at the top of Park and Beacon streets directly across from the new State House. Park Street, a part of the eastern boundary of the Common, was occupied by the town granary as well as the workhouse. When the new Almshouse was completed (*Plate 11*) and these buildings pulled down, Bulfinch replaced them with a row of fine houses, which made Park one of the most desirable residential streets in Boston, a fitting counterpoise to Beacon Street. Nathaniel Shurtleff describes the transition:[37]

The old dingy buildings and the broken fences have disappeared, and stately houses have succeeded in their places. No more will the staid townsman nor the jocund youth, proceeding to the Common in wonted manner on election and Independence days, be interrupted by the diminutive hands thrust through the holes in the almshouse fences, or stretched beneath the decaying gates, and by the small and forlorn voices of the children of the destitute inmates entreating for money; nor will the cries of the wretched poor in those miserable habitations be heard calling for bread, which often times the town had none to give.

The new almshouse, located at Barton's Point in the outermost section of the West End, was a handsome structure admired by the architect's contemporaries as second only to the State House among the buildings of Federal Boston.[38]

The dismantling of the ancient eyesores on Beacon and Park streets represented a particularly gratifying phase of the chief selectman's duties. Charles Bulfinch returned from Europe with the knowledge, taste, and enthusiasm to introduce a number of important architectural innovations. Now, as chairman of the Board of Selectmen and chief of police, he held the authority to make really substantial changes. And he exercised this authority with courage and discretion. Stephen Greenleaf Bulfinch, the architect's son, gives an idealistic example in reference to the law his father had enacted giving the selectmen the power to widen streets:[39]

I have heard on one occasion, when the removal of some protruding building had been ordered, and a ladder raised to begin the work, the owner appeared above, and armed with a musket, and threatened to shoot the first who should dare to climb. His object was to frighten off the workmen but Mr. Bulfinch, who probably knew that the man was not as violent as he appeared, mounted the ladder himself and thus dispelled the terror.

The problems involved in widening old streets and creating new ones, laying down sidewalks, arranging for street lights, sewers, and water pipes were enormous. At the time Bulfinch took over his civic duties, only one street, Cornhill, is credited with having a sidewalk. Twenty years later a visiting Englishman could write: "Boston is well paved, and has excellant foot paths of flag stones. The streets . . . are for the most part clean and in good order."[40] In the Federal period, however, everyone walked in the center of the street except when forced aside by carriages and carts or by cows who did not always limit their

perambulations to the Common. There was stiff opposition
to every effort made by the selectmen to bring order to the
bewildering web of streets, lanes, and alleys; interminable
law suits and political wrangling went on around the
seemingly unperturbed chairman. In all these controversies Bulfinch leaned heavily upon the Association for Town
Improvement, founded at the turn of the century largely
through his own effort. He and his kinsman Joseph Coolidge, Jr., were among the five trustees whose duty it was
"To invite and collect subscriptions; to devise and adopt
the best plans for general and permanent improvements;
and to execute the same in a manner most economical and
advantageous."[41] The Association for Town Improvement
did its most spectacular work in transforming the neglected Common into the finest urban park in post-Revolutionary America.

As the chief administrator on whom practically all town
problems devolved, Bulfinch traveled a long way from that
"season of leisure, pursuing no business, but giving gratuitous advice in Architecture" by which he characterized his
first year in Boston after returning from Europe.[42] His financial ruin proved, naturally, a terrible personal experience. The comparison between the portrait painted in London while on the Grand Tour and a sketch made after he
retired from civic life is devastating; the Bulfinch of the
latter sketch was a bitterly disappointed man.[43] Yet it was
a fortunate circumstance for Boston because it compelled
Bulfinch to involve himself in all the problems of the town
in the twenty-one years following his bankruptcy in 1796.
The Federalist merchants who ruled the New England
capital during this period were more powerful, in an ob-

vious sense, than Bulfinch. But not one of them can be recalled and made the symbol of his age as completely or as
meaningfully as the architect. "Few men," wrote Mayor
Josiah Quincy, referring to Bulfinch shortly before his
death in 1844, "deserve to be held by the citizens of Boston
in more grateful remembrance." And this not so much for
his architecture as for the totality of his achievement. "During the many years he presided over the town government," continued Quincy, "he improved its finances, executed the law with firmness, and was distinguished for
gentleness and urbanity of manners, integrity and purity
of character."[44]

V

POLITICS

THE THREE DECADES during which Bulfinch administered
the affairs of Boston were a time of violent political commit-
ment. Politics was the single consideration to which every
endeavor was subordinated. And as politics in Boston was
partisan, savage, and ultimately futile, the period of Federalist supremacy was a time of unrelieved tension. In this
atmosphere Bulfinch accomplished a great deal. But meas-
ured in terms of the vision revealed in Franklin Place, the
results were disappointing. Yet when the Federalist experiment began in Boston it seemed anything but a lost cause.
In fact, when President Washington visited the town in the
autumn of 1789, the future of New England Federalism
looked as promising as that of the new nation itself.

Thirteen years had passed since Washington led the Continental troops across the Neck on the heels of the evacuat-
ing British army, and Boston, mindful of its famous past,
gave the first president of the now United States a demonstration of affection worthy of the place that started the
Revolution. Although it was a bleak and chilly October day,
everyone was in the streets. A bitter wind blew northeast
from the harbor, and many in the patient crowds caught

colds which for years afterwards were referred to as "the Washington influenza." There were other mishaps, too, besides the weather. The President was kept waiting a long time before it was confirmed that Governor Hancock would not be on hand to greet him. In the meantime Hancock's representative, Sheriff Henderson, was wrangling with the selectmen of Boston over the disposition and precedence of the marchers in the ceremonial parade that would convey the General to the State House. The issue was settled in a summary manner when Henderson threatened "to make a hole" through the clamoring officials of the town. At last the parade started off, headed by Washington astride the white horse given him by Charles IV of Spain.

The procession ended at the old State House before a triumphal arch designed by Bulfinch, the first of many public commissions he was to receive from his native town. The arch was akin to one in a drawing made in Milan three years earlier and represents a rare instance of Bulfinch subordinating the lessons of England to the memory of Italy. As could be expected in so political an age, the project aroused heated controversy. The Republicans wanted to honor Washington by raising a public subscription to build a stone monument at the entrance to the town from Roxbury. They failed, and the resulting compromise was an arch some twenty feet high, adorned with a frieze of thirteen stars, and surmounted by an intricate canopy supporting the American eagle.[1] Although it fell short of the Italian model, no monument of antiquity welcomed a hero more beloved by his people than the little span through which Washington passed to enter a colonnade erected west of the State House. The colonnade was the work of Thomas Dawes, the housebuilder-statesman who served as Bulfinch's earliest collaborator.[2] Here the President reviewed the parade and gazed out upon a crowd of frozen faces. A chorus precariously placed on top of the triumphal arch brought the ceremonies to a close by shouting out a song written for the occasion by Oliver Holden, Boston's leading man of music:[3]

> General Washington, the hero's come,
>   Each heart exulting hears the sound;
> See, thousands their deliverer throng,
>   And shout him welcome all around.
> Now in full chorus bursts the song,
>   And shout the deeds of Washington.

This unsophisticated song expressed the simple and genuine admiration the people of Boston felt for Washington. He meant everything to the town in the past, coming up in 1775 to lead the militia in its hour of greatest peril. But the Revolutionary phase was over; forgotten, it was hoped, except as history. Boston's new leaders did not recall with enthusiasm the wild past of the Sons of Liberty. As counterrevolutionists they hoped to bind the town's future inflexibly to the Federalist party, which Washington represented as the first citizen of the new nation. They had worked hard to win the many enemies of a strong central government over to the side of the Constitution, and Washington's triumph was interpreted by them as a personal vindication. One event, though, hinted at the dangerous force of disunion never far from the surface of Bulfinch's Boston: Governor Hancock did not come forward to greet the President. This act betrayed the parochial character of the town lurking beneath a semblance of loyalty to central authority.

Washington planned, during his first day in Boston, to visit Governor Hancock at his stone mansion on Beacon Hill. But when the Governor failed to materialize at the public ceremonies, the hero of the Revolution went directly to his lodging at the Widow Ingersoll's on the corner of Tremont and Court streets. From these quarters Washington waited resolutely for Hancock to make the first move. The General was aware, as was most of the town, that Hancock insisted upon the precedence of the Governor of the Commonwealth over the President of the United States. It was one of the last great acts of public vanity indulged by John Hancock. Yet like everything surrounding the old Midas of the New England capital, the incident was not without drama. As that day and part of the next went by, Hancock feared he might not get a chance to see the President at all; there was nothing to do but capitulate. He wrote Washington, offering to call immediately, explaining that only the gout in its most painful stages prevented him from doing so earlier. Hancock went forth the loser in the battle but in full command of the situation from the point of histrionics: he was carried to the General's lodging swathed in flannel, borne on the shoulders of four men.[4]

Charles Bulfinch was among the town officials engaged in the wrangle over precedence while Washington stood by in the October cold. It is certain, however, that he was not one of those clamoring for a place above his fellow Bostonians. Nor was this the first time he had seen Washington in the role of President of the United States. In the spring of this same year Bulfinch and his bride Hannah Apthorp, together with several of their relatives and friends, journeyed to New York to witness Washington's inauguration. There Bulfinch executed his famous drawing of Federal Hall, transformed by the French engineer Major Pierre L'Enfant especially for the inaugural ceremonies. Bulfinch's drawing of Federal Hall was published in the *Massachusetts Magazine* a month after Washington's inauguration and widely reproduced. Appearing at the moment when the states were faced with the task of creating capitol buildings, it helped define the Federal style that distinguished the formative years of the Republic.[5]

The inaugural ceremonies were the chief objective of the trip. And Bulfinch, writing home to his parents, expressed the enthusiasm and hope of the well-connected Boston Federalist: "We expect not only to see General Washington, but to see *him* the favorite of this whole continent, the admiration of Europe—to see *him* publickly introduced to office and take an oath to preserve inviolate the constitution."[6] Boston Federalists expected a great deal from the new government they so conspiciously helped to establish. Bulfinch expressed one of their chief hopes when he emphasized Washington's obligation to uphold the Constitution. The thirteen states could no longer act exclusively as independent territories; they would have to relinquish a part of their sovereignty to the central government. This issue divided the parties for and against the Constitution and was decided in favor of Federalist principles by only the narrowest majority in Massachusetts. But it had been decided. The men who counted in Boston in 1789 knew Washington would uphold the central government committed and empowered to maintain law and order in the new United States; there would be no more episodes like Shays' Rebellion.

A business depression had followed on the heels of several years of great prosperity after the conclusion of the War for Independence. It had proved especially severe for the farmers of western Massachusetts who, when their farms were attached for debt, gathered in armed groups in the winter of 1786 to prevent the courts from meeting and carrying out orders of foreclosure and eviction. This kind of action, reminiscent of Boston a decade earlier, spread alarmingly toward the eastern section of the Commonwealth. Its suppression marked an important victory on the state level for the new men from Essex County who already controlled the capital town. As the storm gathered in the west, Governor Hancock wisely decided not to run for re-election, and James Bowdoin came in as the representative of the Country party who suppressed the rebellion. The manner of dealing with the captured rebels then became the main issue in the gubernatorial election of 1787. Bowdoin wanted them punished while Hancock came forward as the advocate of mercy; the public confirmed Hancock's judgment by defeating Bowdoin. But the tide had turned in favor of the Essex County leadership in its battle to extend control beyond Boston to the Commonwealth itself. Shays' Rebellion frightened conservative leaders throughout the thirteen states and was a contributing factor in bringing about the Constitutional Convention in 1787.

Nevertheless, the problem of getting the Constitution

ratified in Massachusetts was formidable. The majority of delegates, led by John Hancock and Samuel Adams, opposed it. But to the former North Shore merchants, now patently labeled Federalists, the problem was not unsurmountable. It was privately suggested to Hancock that the most powerful state, Virginia, would not ratify the Constitution and hence he, the governor of the second state, would qualify as first president. This appealing prospect brought the irresolute old man over to the side of ratification. Samuel Adams was secured through the co-operation of his companion of the Sons of Liberty days, Paul Revere, who organized a crucial meeting of the mechanics in favor of the Constitution. The Federalist then went to work on a lower level and, in one way or another, achieved the ratification of the Constitution in Massachusetts by a majority of nineteen votes.

It was a close call; but everything after that moved ahead in jubilant fashion. The Federalists expanded their control from Boston out into the rebellious countryside. Alive to the nature of their victory, the new rulers of Boston—and Massachusetts—set about securing the elevation of men absolutely devoted to their party. In the first election under the Constitution both senators from Massachusetts were country men. One of them, Tristram Dalton of Newburyport, journeyed to New York, the new seat of government, in a carriage whose panels were emblazoned with the Dalton arms and surrounded by a cloud of liveried servants. There was no question as to where the sentiments of the Boston Federalists lay; they were ineradicably lodged in the concept of property as the value of man. The victory of the Essex Junto was epitomized in the election of

Fisher Ames over Samuel Adams as congressman from Boston. No single event suggested the future more prophetically than the toppling of the old popular idol and the emergence of a man who fully represented the goals of the Country party.

The creation of a strong central government was linked to another problem close to the hearts of the Boston Federalists: the funding of the national and state debts, the origins of which went back to the first months of the Revolution. The system devised for funding the debt divided the American people more violently than any other problem of Washington's first administration. By 1789 few of the Revolutionary securities were still held by the people who originally exchanged goods and services for them, most having been bought up at great discount by Federalist men of property. They understood Alexander Hamilton's determination to have the central government assume payment at par of all national and state debts. Boston merchants were well represented in this creditor class. Furthermore, with the exception of Virginia, whose indebtedness was liquidated by the sale of western lands, Massachusetts had the largest state debt. Assumption of this obligation by the federal government was enormously satisfying to the Boston merchants who not only held the notes but also ruled the Commonwealth. Hamilton's fiscal policies were based on the machinations of Sir Robert Walpole, who secured a rich and powerful backing for the Whig government in England from the class holding the public debt. The idea of a government dependent upon the men of property, and vice versa, remained one of the cardinal principles of the Essex Junto.

Enterprising Boston Federalists looked to the presidency of Washington as portending, above all, a new era in trade. It was impossible under the Confederation to make commercial treaties with a foreign power or even to trade effectively among the several states. It was hoped this would change under a government safely in the hands of the Federalists. The leading men of Boston had not supported the Constitution on a basis of caprice or altruism. The powerful group of well-connected people Hamilton expected to weld into a ruling class were largely merchants or lawyers committed to commercial interests. They watched the bitter issue of the funding of state and national debts both from the immediate view of holders of the debt and for its future effect upon commerce. One of the aims of Hamilton's funding system was the establishment of American credit abroad, especially in England and Holland. The Federalist fiscal policies designed to perpetuate an elite backing a strong central government had their basis in commerce. It was a marriage of interests. Credit and a central government capable of negotiating and enforcing treaties were essential to commerce, and as custom duties were the principal source of national revenue, commerce was equally essential to the federal government.

As long as the Federalists had General Washington as their leader they were irrepressible. John Adams, however, lacked popular or party support. During his administration Federalist frustration bore fruit in the Alien and Sedition Laws, designed to gag Francophile politicians, journalists, and immigrants. In this legislation the Federalists copied the English laws instigated by the younger

Pitt. To a nation at war such repressive measures were plausible; in America they were simply vindictive. But the Federalists too were at war—they were battling against the democratic forces let loose by the American Revolution. Originally the *enfant terrible* of the New World, Boston made a quick about-face when British rule precipitously ended in the first year of the war. The transfer of power in Boston from one propertied class to another was swift and sensational; nothing like it occurred anywhere else in America. Even more significant was the rapidity with which the Country party took over the prejudices of the old ruling class. These prejudices, however, were based upon an established and legitimate aristocracy, and the Essex County oligarchy of "the rich" but not necessarily "the well born" proved a poor substitute for the fallen British model. It was natural for the Massachusetts Federalists to attempt to legalize their usurpation by taking on the English attitudes of the class they superseded. But the Province House outlook was fatally unrepresentative of the new nation whose center of power shifted away from New England, whose future lay westward, and whose mentor was France. Stubbornly and resourcefully the Massachusetts Federalists reverted to a past that threw them back into the lap of European intrigue; that made their adopted fortrees dependent upon Old World affairs in which New England commerce was but a minor counter. Furthermore, in siding so uncompromisingly with the enemy of France, the Bostonians were stricken with the same reactionary fever that gripped the English ruling class during the Napoleonic wars.[7]

The Boston Federalists were already conservative

enough. Their teacher was Judge Edmund Trowbridge, who had presided over the trials of the soldiers involved in the Boston Massacre. Although uncommitted in the Revolution, he wisely left the Boston area during the violent phase in Massachusetts for a sojourn in the Essex County home of future Federalist Theophilus Parsons. And just as wisely, during his absence, the Trowbridge family burned the full-length portrait of Governor Hutchinson that hung in the judge's Cambridge house. Trowbridge was the most learned lawyer in New England, with a galaxy of Federalist pupils that included Parsons, Harrison Gray Otis, and Christopher Gore. Parsons revealed the Boston Federalists' mentality when he commended their lawyer-like determination to consider every event or concept in the light of precedent. They were all good Lockeans in holding experience the basis of knowledge. Much of their spare time was spent reading history, and as merchants or lawyers concerned with maritime activities they knew the world and insisted what happened in the past would happen again. There was no place in their Boston for Jefferson's concept of a new kind of man and a new approach to government. Of course the Federalists were anti-democratic before the French Revolution. But in that lurid event they found the perfect red flag; it was so convenient to identify every democratic demand with the Paris mob and atheism. This argument was particularly effective in Massachusetts, where Federalist control was built on a solid alliance of business, bar, and pulpit.

The life-and-death struggle between England and France was refought in the United States along party lines. The pre-Revolutionary Whigs-turned-Federalists sided with England; the Republicans favored France, although their affection for that country was less constant than their rivals' hatred. This alignment developed back in the days of the Constitutional Convention when old radicals like Samuel Adams and Mercy Warren opposed the strong federal government demanded by the merchant class under Essex County leadership. The Constitution, accepted only after the radicals obtained the promise of a Bill of Rights, was the foundation of the new government in which opposing Federalist and Republican parties swiftly developed. Washington tried to restrain the warring factions but passions were much too alive in the aftermath of modern history's greatest revolutionary movement. Each party found in the Napoleonic wars the banner around which to rally. And they rallied with a vengeance; the period of Bulfinch's Boston was a furious age of party commitments.

American sympathy was generally with Paris in the battle between the two contemporary capitals of political philosophy. The London-worshipping Federalists were mainly restricted to New England, while the Republicans held the southern and middle states with the larger cities of New York and Philadelphia. The decline in English influence following the Revolution was accelerated by immigration and the westward movement. Although Boston's population rose steadily in the three decades of Federalist rule, the accretion was mainly a growth in the old stock predating the Revolution. Compared to the swarms descending weekly upon New York, Philadelphia, and Baltimore, few immigrants landed on the docks of Boston. The hostility to British traditions shared by most of the new arrivals complemented that already prevailing in the middle and southern states as a result of the long years of warfare with England. Democracy served as the fusing force in America, and everywhere outside of New England popular sympathy was with egalitarian France. Even Massachusetts rejoiced with the rest of the English-speaking world in the first stages of the French Revolution. And while more restrained in their admiration than the Republicans, Boston Federalists saw no threat in the formation of a local French Constitutional Society. But very soon the atmosphere changed. The execution of Louis XVI and the wave of violence and irreligion that followed filled Bostonians with horror. France became the Federalist scapegoat, the cause of every wrong, and Republicans were indiscriminately denounced as "Jacobins."[8]

The Federalists were motivated too exclusively by private interest in a period when the public interest was exalted. They clung to the idea the American Revolution was begun in Boston solely to protect New England's commercial advantage. But revolutions are seldom static; original grievances are buried in the unpredictable upheavals that follow. Unluckily for the Boston Federalists, their concept of the Revolution's meaning was not held by most of the former colonists. The larger populations in the middle and southern states, who sustained the struggle against the British long after the war receded from New England, generally gave their support to the Republican party. And after 1800 that was the winning side. Jefferson's belief in man was the future against which the Federalists waged a losing battle. They were victims of too much knowledge and too little faith. As Edmund Quincy writes in the biog-

raphy of his father, the Federalists "dreaded the renewal
of the scenes in ancient and modern republics without considering how much wider was the stage on which American drama enacted and how much broader the influences
which formed the actors in it."[9] The subject of this biography, Josiah Quincy, son of the patriot Josiah Quincy, Jr.,
and later mayor of Boston, was pathetically conscientious
about his election to Congress in 1804. Before going down
to Washington he studied not only ancient but contemporary history. When he arrived in Congress he found
power in the hands of the middle and southern states
whose representatives were busy making new history, especially in the west. Quincy was not a typical Federalist
of the Essex breed; he was a member of the intermediary
family group with a famous Boston past. But like his intimate friend Charles Bulfinch, he prepared for life along
English lines. And again, like all Bostonians overly sensitive to British ways, he saw America's future only in terms
of thirteen former colonies with New England leading in
the place of Old England. In spite of his fine approach to
politics, Quincy could not visualize the new nation apart
from the limitations of past and predictable history. Consequently, he voted against measures which, like the Louisiana Purchase, indicated the new or westward destiny of
the United States.

Quincy merely voted against the Louisiana Purchase; it
was Fisher Ames who grandly wrote: "Louisiana excites
less interest than our Thanksgiving."[10] This single remark
provides the key to the Essex Junto's exaggerated preoccu-
pation with old Massachusetts ways and their inability to
comprehend a new political orientation. This incapacity to

conceive of America as having a special and historically unrevealed future proved the Federalists' undoing. Within a dozen years after the founding of the United States they crashed from a position of national dominance to one of regional obscurantism. The Federalists performed a great service to the new nation in establishing the government on a stable basis. But the retirement of Washington and the death of Hamilton left them in a defensive and divided position. The second and last Federalist President, John Adams, coined the phrase "Essex Junto" when he acidly remarked on the scant support he received from the Essex County men who controlled the party in Massachusetts.[11] Adams pointedly referred to George Cabot, late of Beverly; Stephen Higginson, late of Salem; and Theophilus Parsons, late of Newburyport. To these three must be added Timothy Pickering of Salem, John Lowell of Newburyport, and Fisher Ames of Dedham—the latter the only member of the Junto not born in Essex County. Boston's intermediary-family politicians, men like Charles Bulfinch, Harrison Gray Otis, and Josiah Quincy, served the party's Essex leaders but were never admitted to the inner sanctum. The members of the Essex Junto were intelligent, well informed, and widely traveled. But they were also chillingly anti-democratic and pathologically obsessed by a fear of the people.

The men of Essex County proved in a number of ways to be very unlike the English Whigs whose politics, houses, and manners they copied. Almost without exception of Puritan stock, in contrast to the intermediary families of Boston, they had no viable contact with the Province House and little understanding of British ruling-class tolerance and compromise. Very un-English too was their disinterest in office and the outward signs of power. The Junto exerted a strong control on state politics from a be-hind-the-scenes position. The members generally refused public office, and most of them retired to the country when the going got rough. They lacked stamina and fight—the implements wielded by their Republican rivals. John Quincy Adams summed up the collapse of the Essex Junto with a classical allusion: "In the days of the Cato and Cae-sar, the men who had no affections but for their gardens and their statues and their palaces were destined to be van-quished, and were so."[12] Like his father before him, John Quincy Adams fought bitter battles with the Junto and un-derstood their peculiar physical and intellectual debility.

Though Boston Federalists raged impotently against the engulfing Jeffersonians in national affairs, they could still harry their Republican townsmen. Not that there were many to persecute. Yet some Republicans actually owned Bulfinch houses on Beacon Hill or in the garden areas of the South End and could not positively be excluded. The most extravagant was Perez Morton, who occupied two Bulfinch houses: a large dwelling in Franklin Place oppo-site the Tontine Crescent and a country house in Roxbury. But the most important Boston Republican was James Sul-livan, twice governor of Massachusetts and related to a number of prominent Bulfinch patrons through the mar-riages of his children into the families of Harrison Gray Otis, Thomas Amory, Thomas Russell, and Mrs. James Swan. Sullivan was one of the few new men to arrive in the capital via a route other than Essex County. Born and raised on a New Hampshire farm, he came to Boston after the Revolution and lived at first in Bowdoin Square in close intimacy with the Bulfinch family. Sullivan worked hard with Bulfinch in getting the Boston Theatre established, and the architect rewarded him with the design of an austere double house with tall windows cut in white-painted brick bow fronts. This Summer Street mansion was occupied after Sullivan's death by another Republican, William Gray.[13]

William Gray was a phenomenon—a newcomer from Essex County, the largest shipowner in America, and a Republican. He accepted Jefferson's embargo even though he was affected more directly than any person in the United States. Another great Massachusetts shipping family, the Crowninshields, was also Republican. Jacob Crowninshield defeated the Essex Juntoite Timothy Pickering for a seat in Congress in 1802 and was Jefferson's choice for Secretary of the Navy. He did not take the post but his brother held it under Madison. There were, however, few well-born or rich Republicans in Massachusetts. The extent of the estrangement between them and the Federalists is depicted by the son of Theophilus Parsons in his account of an incident that occurred when he was ten years old and an uncle, not known to him but reputed to be a "Jacobin," came to dinner. The meal progressed pleasantly and the host asked his guest to take a glass of wine with him. At this young Parsons blurted out:[14]

"Why he is not a Jacobin, after all!"

"No my young friend, I am not a Jacobin; at least, I hope not. Did you think I was?"

"Yes, sir," said I, "I have always heard so; but I see you are not, for I have heard father say, again and again, that nothing on earth would make him drink wine with a Jacobin."

Boston gentlemen in the Republican party were not Jacobins and often did not approve of Jefferson's measures. But this did not save them from abuse when the Embargo Act was passed in Congress over their objections. The Embargo Act of 1807 was resented in Boston by leaders of both political parties; to Republicans and Federalists alike, it seemed to be aimed principally at the destruction of New England shipping. The original act prohibited the sailing of any vessel from an American to a foreign port. Ships unable to clear before the embargo became law, or those returning after its enactment, were restricted to the coasting trade within the territorial waters of the United States. Deep-sea ships were required to sail under bond double the cargo value to ensure their compliance with the act; supplementary legislation extended the bond to fishing and coasting vessels. The climax came when a final supplement gave federal agents despotic power in carrying out the full measure of the law. Whatever the original justification, the partisan character of the embargo was betrayed in its excessive restrictions. The Embargo Act was the Republican complement to the Alien and Sedition Laws passed by the Federalists in the administration of John Adams. Both were ill-advised and revengeful, reflecting the hysterical nature of American politics in an age almost without literature, art, sports, or hobbies. Politics was the one subject in which everyone took a part. "My Son," wrote Mrs. Thomas Bulfinch in 1806, "is much engag'd in public business but contrives to see me every day. He usually calls about one o'clk with my Son, Mr. Storer, and when my third Son, Mr. C[oolidge] is at home, we settle the affairs of the Nation, and feel ourselves quite politicians."[15] The few Republicans received in the Bulfinch homestead in Bowdoin Square, relatives and friends like Perez Morton, James Sullivan, and Joseph Story, were as deeply disturbed by the embargo as their host, and their influence was instrumental in bringing about its repeal.[16]

The embargo was a blunder that worked only to the advantage of the European antagonists. As most of America's trade was with England, the embargo was a boon to Napoleon's continental blockade. But England, too, gained much from Jefferson's intransigence. She not only took over the carrying trade previously held by Americans but was unopposed in opening up the Spanish and Portuguese ports in South America in the wake of the Peninsular War. Completely disastrous to Boston was the ban on China trade. Of all the provisions in the embargo this seemed the most vindictive. English orders in council did not affect American commerce in the Orient and France never could enforce a decree in Far Eastern waters. To Bostonians dependent on the sea for their livelihood, the embargo was devastating: merchants, masters, mates, sailors, shipbuilders, stevedores—all who sailed the seas or served as purveyors to oceanic adventures were thrown out of work.[17] The resulting economic depression in the capital town was inevitably felt throughout the Commonwealth and temporarily checked Republican victories won in the gubernatorial elections of 1807 and 1808. In this general misery, Boston's Federalist leaders again became political rulers.

VI

COMMERCE

THE POLITICAL ACTIVITIES of the Federalists were motivated by their attempt to reunite Boston's economic life
with that of England. And it seemed possible, for a few decades, that the town which started the Revolution could
disavow the responsibilities of independence; that the ambitious country families who flocked to the capital after the
evacuation could have Boston as they found her—a rich ap-
pendage of the British mercantile system. Efforts in this
direction perpetuated the colonial town whose economic
basis was commerce on the seas. The Federalist merchant
has been characterized as truly approximating his profession as defined by Dr. Johnson: "One who traffics in remote
countries." Unlike his agrarian antagonists in the Republican party, the Federalist turned his gaze outward, along
the old sea-routes, into the entanglements and wars of
European nations. It was an impossible orientation, and
failure was foretold by no less a friend than President
Washington. Still, so long as Boston was controlled by an
alliance composed of former Essex County merchants and
lawyer-politicians and the sons of Province House families

engaged in shipping, the town's economic life was committed to foreign commerce.

It took a long time and much patience on the part of the Federalists before New England effected a reunion with her trans-oceanic parent. When the Revolution ended, the angry mother was in no mood to welcome back the prodigal son. New England was swamped with cheap British goods at the same time English colonies were barred to American shipping. The Boston merchant was forced to pay for English goods in specie, a rare item in the new states gathered together under the Articles of Confederation. To make matters worse, the drain on specie in Massachusetts coincided with the Commonwealth's attempts to collect its long outstanding debt. The farmer was ruined along with the merchant, and Shays' Rebellion underscored the dangers the Federalist party was quickly formed to check. Commerce was the chief consideration when the new government was launched under the administration of Washington. As the future Republican governor James Sullivan put it: "The merchants made the Constitution and they should name the candidate."[1] Boston's Republican leaders were as closely identified with commerce as their rivals. Inevitably the interests of Massachusetts, the birthplace of the ruling party, received preponderant consideration from the new central government. High tonnage duties drove foreign ships from American ports, the coasting trade was returned to national ships, and a system of drawbacks and fishing bounties was put into operation. But, above all, Massachusetts wanted a revival of trade with England on something like the pre-

Revolutionary basis. The ratification of Jay's treaty in 1796 brought about this result, and the reunion between Old and New England ushered in a dozen years of plenitude for the Federalist merchant.

The treaty also diminished the monetary problem plaguing Boston merchants from the days of independence. For though specie continued scarce, despite Hamilton's fiscal policies, notes drawn on London banking and mercantile houses were legal tender anywhere in the commercial world. To the Boston merchant English exchange was a necessity. The Federalist's lack of flexibility in politics was nowhere evident in the trading world, to which he was supersensitively attuned. Boston ships zigzagged over the oceans alert to every new opportunity and changing situation. The Essex County families were all interrelated and the necessity of keeping in touch by ship and letter intensified their clannishness. Trading opportunities were flashed from one to another over all the accessible world, and the swift little Boston ships went out like hounds on the scent of a fox. Under these conditions, English exchange was invaluable. A captain could sell his cargo for bills drawn on a London house and be off immediately on a new scent. The Boston shipmaster grabbed his profit where he saw it and hurried off in search of more. Ships out of Massachusetts would often be gone three or four years, moving all kinds of cargo, picking up commissions here and there. It was a brilliant system of trading but complicated and vulnerable. The success of the whole depended upon the smooth functioning of all the parts. The agrarian Republicans never understood this; when they arbitrarily tampered with one aspect they brought the whole structure down.

Boston's maritime resurgence was initiated during Washington's two terms in office, nurtured under the administration of Adams, and, surprisingly, brought to flower in the presidency of Jefferson. Despite Federalist foreboding, the Republicans continued all the beneficial Hamiltonian devices and even added some of their own. The first six years of Jefferson's administration were prosperous ones for Boston. But toward the end of the Virginian's second term, the waters upon which American commerce depended were dangerously agitated. England and France, locked in a life-and-death struggle, swept neutral shipping from the seas. The issue was drawn in America along party lines and dominated politics until the War of 1812. In the early stages of the French Revolution, most Bostonians tentatively approved the overthrow of an ancient tyranny. One important Boston merchant, James Swan, even published a book in Paris urging close commercial ties between revolutionary France and New England. The Reign of Terror and war with England eliminated this hope entirely. And while a great deal of money could be made trading with France, it was a risky business, and the problem of getting profits out of the country often proved insuperable. Many a Boston adventurer, including James Swan, found his way into French jails.

The Boston Federalist merchant was a paradox. Politically, he was narrow-minded, obstinate in the face of change, and short-sighted. Yet in business he was broad-minded, inventive, far-sighted, and possessed consummate judgment of people and places. Nothing illustrates this better than the role he played in capturing the China trade. This fabulous prize came to Boston just at the time when the old alignment with England seemed hopeless. English policy toward American shipping after Yorktown was vindictive, and it would have caused absolute havoc in New England were it not for two events which took place in 1784: the publication of Captain Cook's journals and the departure of the *Empress of China* for Canton. The *Empress* was entirely a New York venture. The supercargo, however, was Samuel Shaw of Boston, who did more than any other American to encourage the trade that brought such wealth to his native town. But it was Captain James Cook's fascinating account of the Russian-Chinese barter in otter skins that pointed the way for Boston's supremacy in the Canton trade. The short, luxurious, black fur of the otter had an idolatrous public in China. And China possessed a fabled array of items—silks, teas, lacquers, nankeens, porcelain—just as idolatrously demanded by American and European consumers. The merchants of Boston and New York seized upon this trading possibility. For them it was a blessing from heaven—a rich new trade completely free from English orders in council. The *New York Gazetteer* summed up the merchants' relief: "Thank God! The intrigues of a Christian court do not influence the wise decrees of the Eastern world."[2]

The *Empress of China* was the first American ship to penetrate the fantastic trading capital of Canton. She sailed along the old trade routes, reaching China via the Indian Ocean with a cargo of ginseng, the "dose for immortality." This once-precious root, gathered by Indians in New England and New York, was much desired by the Chinese and offered the most valuable commodity America then possessed in the Eastern trade. The epochal voyage of the Boston ship *Columbia* in 1787 changed all this by abandoning the traditional route to the Orient and instead sailed to China by way of Cape Horn, the Pacific Northwest, and Hawaii. The China trade was as simple as it was direct: otter skins were gathered along the coast of what later became Oregon Territory and provisions were secured in the Hawaiian Islands before sailing on to the Canton market; on the return, stops were usually made at Central and South American ports as well as the Pacific Islands. This new triangular trade seems to have been suggested by Joseph Barrell, who, like other far-sighted merchants of his town, knew of the fur trade between the Russians and Chinese from Cook's recently published journals. Accordingly, he organized an expedition financed by selling fourteen shares at $3500 each among seven gentlemen, including Doctor Thomas Bulfinch and his son Charles. A medal was struck to commemorate the project, and that given to Charles Bulfinch remains in the possession of his descendants, as does an early model of the ship that opened the Boston China trade.[3]

The expedition, commanded by Captain John Kendrick of the *Columbia* and seconded by Robert Gray of the *Lady Washington*, sailed from Boston in September 1787 on a three-year voyage. The *Columbia* logged over forty thousand miles—the first ship to carry the Stars and Stripes around the world. The financial profits were small compared to the achievement of the expedition. Yet while the first voyage of the *Columbia* only hinted at the riches

ahead for Boston, the future of the China trade was sufficiently comprehended at the time by the local press. In
announcing the ship's arrival home on August 11, 1790,
the *Columbian Centinel* added that "to Messrs. Barrell,
Brown, Bulfinch, Hatch, Derby, and Pintard, who planned
the voyage, their country is indebted for this experience in
a branch of Commerce before unassayed by Americans."
Charles Bulfinch and his father were among the ship's
owners and officers who paraded in a long procession
through cheering crowds to mark the occasion. Captain
Gray, who took command when the *Columbia* left the
Northwest for the Hawaiian Islands, walked arm in arm
with a brilliantly arrayed Pacific island chieftain, the first
of his race to be seen in the streets of Boston. But Gray did
not prolong his hero's welcome; he sailed a month later
in the *Columbia* on a second epic voyage in which he discovered the Columbia River, named a nearby port Bulfinch
Harbor, and planted the American flag on the Northwest
coast. Years later, Bulfinch wrote of the significance of this
voyage in regard to the current dispute with England over
Oregon Territory:[4]

I accordingly made a disposition before the Federal Judge . . .
stating the history of the voyage of the discovery of the Columbia
river by the commander of our ship *Columbia* . . . which may
become important in the future discussions with foreign powers
respecting priority of discovery or right of jurisdiction. This disposition was ordered by Congress to be put on file in the State
department.

The China trade meant a great deal more to Boston than
simply monetary profits. It was a totally new and thrilling
adventure. The wonder of it—the Pacific islands, the

brown-skinned people, the sudden appearance of pirates, the smell of a cargo of sandalwood, the river city of Canton —spread like wildfire through Massachusetts. The sea, traditionally the escape route for restless boys, was irresistible when coupled with the excitement of the China trade. And not only to boys. Even the most staid housekeepers schemed to get their hands on some fragment of the traffic. Matrons handed over their requests with maritime terseness: "Two Canton Crape shawls of the enclosed colors at $5 per shawl. Enclosed is $10." Or, "One Tureen 14 x 10 inches, China."[5] Officers and supercargo were allowed a specified amount of space on the return voyage for the rewards of their own private adventures in Canton; seamen carried on a more limited business for personal profit or on commission from friends. There was hardly a Bostonian who did not make some little bargain in the Chinese trading capital. And while shipowners preferred that private transactions be financed in currency or notes which could help defray the initial expense of sailing, every kind of commodity went out in lieu of cash. Those who could not surrender up silver dollars turned over whatever barter they had: a box of candles or nails, a barrel of cod, a dozen handkerchiefs, a bundle of lady's shoes.

The China trade was a wonderful, enriching tonic to the somber town. So general was the obsession with things Chinese that it even spilled over into architecture. Although the exteriors of the houses Bulfinch designed for Federalist merchants were generally untouched by the China fever, their Neo-classical interiors were sometimes adorned with Chinese wallpaper, rows of Canton porcelain, screens, and teakwood furniture. In one spectacular instance, the serenity of a Bulfinch exterior was actually altered. This occurred when John Cushing, returned to Boston from enriching years in the China trade, purchased the house designed for James Sullivan in the South End and enclosed it with a brilliantly colored Chinese porcelain fence. The same nabob startled Boston by dressing his Cantonese servants in native costume.[6]

Otter peltry formed the basis of the China trade. In bartering for them with the Indians of the Northwest, the crews of the Boston ships unrolled before the spellbound natives all the paraphernalia of the Yankee trader—scrap iron, buttons, looking-glasses, nails, red woolens, beads, rum, and even Indian slaves. Each step in the Northwest trade was exciting. Often a ship had to fight its way from anchorage to the sea once the bargain was completed and the hold stowed with otter skins. And the adventure had only begun. The Boston trader followed the sun across the Pacific to Hawaii, where provisions and sandalwood were taken on; a few weeks later the ship and its expectant crew passed between Formosa and Luzon into the South China Sea, sometimes the arena for skirmishes with pirate junks. Canton lay fifty miles up-river from the estuary flanked by Macao and Hong Kong. The armed and agile Boston merchantman usually had little trouble gaining the river and Whampoa, the anchorage for foreign vessels a dozen miles below Canton. Then cargo and crew were transported in small boats to the teeming city where so much of the population worked and lived on the water. The impact of Canton upon the young seamen from Bulfinch's town is unforgettably described by Samuel Eliot Morison in his *Maritime History of Massachusetts:*[7]

To Yankee seamen, fresh from the savage wilderness of the Northwest, how marvelous, bewildering was old Canton! Against a background of terraced hongs with their great go-downs or warehouses, which screened the forbidden City of Rams from foreign devils' gaze, flowed the river, bearing a city of boats the like of which he had never dreamed. Moored to the shore were flower-boats, their upper works cunningly carved into the shape of flowers and birds, and strange sounds issued from their painted windows. Mandarin boats decorated with gay silk pennants and propelled by double banks of oars, moved up and down in stately cadence. Great tea-deckers, with brightly lacquered topsides and square sail of brown matting, brought the Souchong, Young Hyson, and Bohea from upriver. In and out darted thousands of little sampans, housing entire families who plied their humble trades afloat . . . Twilight brought the boat people to their moorings, a bamboo pole thrust in oozy bottom, and paper lanterns diffused a soft light over the river. For color and exotic flavor there was no trade like the old China trade, no port like Canton.

The technicalities and rituals of the Canton transactions were highly stylized. Cargos from Boston ships were deposited in the warehouses or hongs of the Cantonese merchants allowed to do business with "foreign devils." There was also an American factor who guided the ship's captain and supercargo through the bewildering ceremony. When the *Columbia* anchored in Whampoa on its pioneer voyage from the Northwest, Captain Gray found a Boston agent already on hand to greet him. For Samuel Shaw had returned to Canton in 1786 as United States consul and established the first American agency there. Shaw and his fellow countrymen were aptly designated by the Chinese as the "New People." Although certainly new in the China trade, the Bostonians soon mastered its complexities. They were especially successful in the preliminary bargaining in the Northwest and along the routes in the homeward journey, the same kind of trading that had already made the Bostonian a legend in the West Indies and the Atlantic and Indian Oceans. They were ambitious, resourceful, active, well informed, often ruthless; the prototypes of one of modern history's great shibboleths: the "Yankee."

The seamen and the type of ship they manned accounted for much of the Bostonians' success at sea. Boston's deep-sea ships were small and modest, averaging only about two hundred tons. But many a vessel with tonnage alarmingly short of this sailed out of the Federalist capital for China. A seventy-two ton brig, the *Hope,* was one of the first Boston ships to clear for Canton after the return of the *Columbia;* and when Captain Richard Cleveland took a fifty-two-ton cutter to the Northwest he was undismayed at finding some of the Indian canoes larger than his own ship. In constructing these vessels, the Massachusetts builders followed the dictates of older times. Their ships were squat and wide at the water line, the length always less than four times the beam. The elegant prow of the *Columbia,* prominently shown in old drawings, was purely ornamental superstructure masking a sturdy bow of traditional dimensions. In spite of seemingly clumsy proportions, the Boston merchantmen maneuvered well, moved swiftly, and carried considerable arms. Most of the Federalist ships were built north of Essex County along the Merrimack River and the coast of Maine, or south of Boston in the shallow estuary of the North River. The *Columbia* was launched from one of the yards along the North

River where laborers worked for a dollar a day and a "rum-break" at mid-morning and afternoon. Low wages on land helped drive the best of New England lads to sea. Sailor's pay was not much lower, if lower at all, then land wages; there were no expenses on shipboard; and there was always the chance of making something extra in private trading.

As Samuel Eliot Morison has pointed out, New England seamen in this period did not form a disorderly or disaffected class. Unlike European seamen, they could generally read and write a little, very soon learned something about navigation and command, and caught on to the ways of commerce quickly. They were most distinguished by youth and daring. Boston boys sailed before the mast at thirteen and fourteen years and became officers while still in their teens. On one China passage the little ninety-five-ton *Betsy* carried a crew of thirty with not a man over twenty-eight years of age. The voyage of the *Benjamin* in 1792 was an act of unrivaled juvenility: the nineteen-year-old skipper, Nathaniel Silsbee, had already been to sea for five years; the first mate, Richard Cleveland, was exactly one year older; the only member of the crew over twenty-one was the second mate, a venerable twenty-four-year-old.[8] Boys who answered the hypnotic call of the sea wanted more than wages. In Bulfinch's Boston, foreign trade and its dependencies provided the path to social and political success as well as wealth. The sea was the route by which most of the important men of this period made their way unless they were lucky enough to be born into the intermediary families whose prominence pre-dated the

Revolution. Silsbee, the young commander of the *Benjamin,* was a model of the self-made man, climbing the ladder from seaman to United States senator.[9]

The unerring flow of ambitious boys into the sailor class gave Federalist skippers the bold and imaginative crews necessary for long and dangerous voyages. The sea was the place of romance for the young New England adventurer. Nothing compared with it, not even the West. Boston was geographically separated from the arteries leading westward, and lads who might have followed Boone into Kentucky and Missouri turned instead to the sea. The youngster who grew up among the narrow streets of the North End or the sleepy pastures of Trimountain was set adrift on legendary seaways. He followed the trail of Magellan up the coast of California and fought Indians in the coves of the Northwest; he sailed up the River Plate to penetrate the estuary opened to Boston shipping during the Napoleonic wars; he lay becalmed at dawn in the Hawaiian Islands awaiting an attack by natives; he ran the gauntlet of English and French ships into the Baltic Sea and the frozen ports of Russia; he retraced Vasco da Gama's route around Africa into the burning Indian Ocean; he sailed into Haiti, where a slave was crowned king; he rounded Cape Cod matured and jubilant and flew before the wind into Boston harbor, not young or unknowing any more.

Profits on the China trade were unpredictable. While the returns on the *Columbia*'s first voyage were relatively modest, on her second trip the ship exchanged pelts acquired for a few thousand dollars worth of trinkets for Canton goods valued at ninety thousand. Much depended upon the current value the Indians placed on trading commodities and the prevailing price of otter skins in Canton. Sometimes a trader who made a killing on an absolutely absurd barter, such as shoe buckles or brass-headed canes, would return a few years later hoping to repeat the performance only to find an equally capricious market in snuffboxes. When Captain Joseph Ingraham reached the Northwest in the *Hope*, he found the natives all running about in trousers and jackets. They were totally uninterested in the cloth he brought out from Boston until he hit upon the idea of sewing brass buttons on it. Success in the China trade depended on the combination of chance, intuition, and daring the Federalist so conspicuously embodied in commerce and so lamentably lacked in politics. When Captain William Sturgis heard rumors that the Northwest Indians used ermine pelts for currency, he obtained five thousand of these skins at Leipzig for thirty cents apiece and traded them for one thousand otter skins selling that year in Canton for fifty dollars each. After such a deal, Sturgis could maintain with conviction that excepting "a beautiful woman and a lovely infant, a prime sea-otter skin two feet by five, with its short, glossy jet-black fur, was the finest natural object in the world."[10]

Captains Sturgis and Ingraham were hatched in an unparalleled incubator of China traders, the Boston mercantile house of Thomas Handasyd Perkins. Perkins himself was reared under a no less interesting system: he learned the ways of commerce as a child toddling at his mother's heels. For his mother carried on the family business single-handedly after the death of her husband shortly before the Revolution. Mrs. Perkins discharged these affairs so adroitly that the question of her sex was never an issue.

At least not among non-Bostonians, who addressed their business correspondence to "Elizabeth Perkins, Esq." Thomas Handasyd Perkins was a splendid example of his profession. A member of the intermediary group of old Boston families, he prospered in the rough-and-tumble period of new men and new wealth. He supported the Federalist party with spirit and devotion without the corroding bitterness of the Essex Junto. Yet Perkins was completely alive to the matter of profits and sensitive to the complicated and fluctuating character of commerce as practiced by the Federalist merchant. A quotation from Thomas Cary's *Memoir of Thomas Handasyd Perkins* indicates the wide nature of Boston's commercial ventures as well as the kind of profits expected. It is a memorandum from Perkins to his agent in Canton, dated January 1, 1814:[11]

You say a cargo laid in at Canton would bring three for one in South America, and your copper would give two prices back. Thus, $30,000 laid out in China would give you $90,000 in South America, one half of which laid out in copper would give one hundred per cent, or $90,000,—making $135,000 for $30,000; 60,000 lbs. of indigo, even at 80 cts., $48,000; 120 tons of sugar at $60, $7,200; and cotton, or some other light freight, say skin tea, $20,000,—in all $75,000,—would be worth here $400,000, and not employ the profits of the voyage to South America. Manila sugar is worth $400 to $500 per ton, clear of duty. The ship should be flying light, her bottom in good order, the greatest vigilance used on the passage, and make any port north of New York.

The commerce of Bulfinch's town was extraordinarily interrelated in its far-flung parts. It was like a jigsaw puzzle whose final representation only emerges when the last pieces are fitted together. The pieces were diverse; it often took several years and the produce of many lands to make up the cargo for a single voyage to Canton and back. Iron was brought from the Baltic, colored cloth from India, specie from everywhere it could be gotten, hides from South America, wine from Madeira, cod from the New England fisheries. Ships out of Boston moved cargo from place to place all along a general destination which might never be reached at all because the vessel itself was sold for a large profit at some intervening port. Trading in the West Indies, and along the east and west coasts of South America, was perfunctory on voyages to the Northwest and Canton; Madeira and the Mediterranean were usually visited en route to the Indies. The East India trade was restricted to Salem just as the China trade was the preserve of Boston, although prior to the historic voyage of the *Columbia,* Salem vessels were actually in greater force in Canton. Thomas Handasyd Perkins was supercargo on the Salem ship *Astrea* bound for China in 1789—sailing, of course, the old route around Africa and the Indian Ocean. But the owners of the *Astrea,* the Derby family of Salem, withdrew almost entirely from the China trade a few years later. The fabled Salem East Indiamen sometimes reached Canton, although by way of Mauritius, the English stations in India, and Sumatra. Profits from the East Indies were even more fabulous than those from China. They enabled members of the Derby family to commission three of the grandest houses to come from the drawing board of Charles Bulfinch.[12]

The Federalist merchant of Boston, whether newly arrived from the North Shore or descended from old local stock, displayed eccentricities peculiar to his profession. For one thing, he was addicted to the colonial manner of dress. Lucius Manlius Sargent has left a detailed picture of the "cocked hats of enormous proportions, queues reaching to their middles, cloaks of scarlet broadcloth, lined with silk, and faced with velvet . . . doeskin or beaver gloves, and glossy, black Surinam walking canes, six feet in length," which greatly amused visitors from New York and Philadelphia.[13] Yet to the town's leaders it seemed quite fitting to cling to the costume of their Province House models. Furthermore, it showed their disdain for the French style in dress which was transforming the inhabitants, especially female, of the rival Republican cities south of New England. Another eccentricity, and a delightful one, was the habit of doing the family marketing on the way to work, a morning ritual observed by all leading townsmen whether they set forth from Bowdoin Square, Beacon Hill, or the South End. Determined mercantile figures, followed by a servant, turned down every respectable street to converge on Faneuil Hall. There they wandered among mountains of meat, fish, fowl, vegetables, fruits, and dairy products displayed in a confusion never entirely rectified by Bulfinch's market regulations. When all the makings of the early afternoon dinner were stowed away in a servant's basket, the merchants marched off to counting houses along the wharves or offices in State Street.

Although Boston Federalist merchants were resourceful, ambitious, and conscientious in their business, few could boast with Jefferson that the sun never caught them in bed. They were relatively late risers. Their opponents explained this as too much rum and Madeira the night before. The Republican merchant William Gray was up and ready to receive his barber between 4 and 5 o'clock in summer and 6:00 in winter; but the Federalist merchant Samuel Eliot was at least two hours behind him the year round. And the social lion Harrison Gray Otis, who appeared at breakfast between 8:00 and 8:30 in a silk dressing gown, slept even later. Otis's barber reported after breakfast, perhaps having finished "frizzing and powdering" one or two other merchants by that time. A number of Negroes living in North Slope Village on the wrong side of Beacon Hill performed the duties of barbers. These duties were performed in the merchant's dressing room if he lived in a Bulfinch house, for the architect popularized that English luxury in the New England capital. When his wig was neatly placed or his hair dressed and powdered, the merchant slipped into a costume reminiscent of royalist Boston and started off for Faneuil Hall.[14]

Federalist nabobs in Province House attire prolonged their morning marketing in the stalls of Faneuil Hall as long as possible. The surviving impression of the merchant's working day is that he really had little to do. Success came early in post-Revolutionary Boston, frequently through inheritances or particularly rewarding feats by young men in exotic ports. Samuel Eliot passed a part of his working day writing poems to his wife. One of these survives, and the opening lines throw some light on the affairs of this benevolent merchant:[15]

Katy, I send you this to tell
That I am better though not well,
And having little else to do,
Have set down to write to you. . . .

The labors of business were carried on by clerks while the master in wig or powdered hair dreamed of other things, usually of a political nature. His goods were on hand, his ships at sea; he could depend on New England seamen to deal with the Indians of the Northwest, and evade the savages of the South Seas and the pirates of China. But he had no such assurance on political matters, especially after the national capital fell to the Republicans. When his doubts got the better of him, the Federalist merchant jumped up, grabbed the symbols of his creed—scarlet cloak, cocked hat, walking stick—and dashed into State Street to talk the matter over with his fellow sufferers.

State Street, in the few hours before the merchant's early afternoon dinner, duplicated the morning scene at the market stalls of Faneuil Hall. The merchants insisted on conducting their business in the street despite the construction in 1808 of the Boston Exchange Coffee House, designed to reform this ancient custom. All the commercial leaders were on hand regardless of their political commitments. Of course most were Federalists, but the Republicans did count a number of powerful mercantile figures among their ranks. The latter were hard pressed by the Federalist majority to reconcile the town's economic life with their party's policies in Washington. Tempers were easily raised in Bulfinch's Boston, and the division among families over national issues was reminiscent of the rift

between patriot and loyalist households a half-century
earlier. In the Sullivan family, for example, James was a
Republican governor while his son William was a leading
Federalist politician. Both lived in houses designed by Bulfinch. The Bulfinches themselves were assenting Federalists, though one cousin, Perez Morton, was an important
Republican merchant. When it came to selecting an architect for his country house at Roxbury, Morton unhesitat-
ingly commissioned the leading Federalist designer for
the job. The political tension in State Street, intense at the
beginning of the mid-day session when the merchants met
to air their latest or particular grievance, subsided as anticipation of the forthcoming dinner asserted itself. At the
appointed time they all trooped off to their houses in the
South End, Bowdoin Square, or Beacon Hill.

They were not disappointed when they arrived home.
The dining room was the most frequented one in Federal
houses. Neo-classical architects borrowed interior planning and decorative devices from France, but English
builders stuck to the old supremacy of the "eating room."
By the time the merchant arrived, the cloth was laid on
the table, the plate warmer rested before the fire, and the
children were in a state of anticipation equal to their father's. The mistress of the house was busy in the kitchen
with elder daughters, unmarried aunts and cousins, and
the female servants who came from surrounding farm
areas and were practically accepted as members of the
family. In spite of all their financial troubles, the Bulfinches were never deserted by their faithful servants,
"Ma'am" Pollard and Eliza. The kitchen, even in Bulfinch

mansions, was a primitive affair with most of the activity around the open hearth. Meat was roasted on a jack turned by hand or sometimes by a little dog enclosed in a contraption similar to a squirrel cage. Perhaps these dogs were descended from those bred in Boston after 1728 when a town ordinance attempted to restrict the height of canines to ten inches. Plenty of meat and drink found its way to the table, but silver and glasses were used sparingly and napkins were unknown. The Charles Bulfinch family, which included a number of children, all drank from four silver cups strategically placed around the table. If the merchant dined alone with his family, he had a final glass of Madeira before retiring for a quiet hour in his library, pottering in his garden, or dozing in a chair by the fire. If there was a party, the ladies withdrew and the gentlemen settled down to the serious and time-consuming business of politics and wine. They would still be at it when the servant came in to light the candles, when it would be tea time and time to eat again.[16]

The course of life in a Boston merchant's household was relatively simple compared with that in the Republican strongholds of New York and Philadelphia, or even the Federalist sister city of Charleston. The merchants did not constitute a distinct class, as they did in the middle and southern states, separated by special interest from their fellow citizens. Everyone in Federal Boston was affected by the fluctuating course of commerce. An extraordinary unity of interest and purpose bound the Bostonians together and gave their town a distinct maritime flavor. It was a flavor retained from the past when Boston's commercial supremacy secured political dominance along the eastern seaboard. In reviving the seafaring spirit of the old town, the Federalist merchants believed they could perpetuate Boston's historic role in the new American age. And they succeeded, in the interval between Jay's treaty and Jefferson's embargo, in resurrecting the ghost of colonial Boston. But it proved to be, after all, only a phantom.

VII

BEACON HILL

CHARLES BULFINCH'S PLAN to transform the barrens of Beacon Hill into a dwelling place for merchant princes failed. Though the houses he designed there were for families whose wealth was gleaned from commerce on the seas, the Hill's real development belongs to the next age of mill and factory. The only serious attempt to improve Beacon Hill in the Federal period took place during the single decade in which the Federalist merchant was ascendant. Until then, the area was considered too far from the docks and warehouses and too remote from the old seat of government to be a desirable place of residence. When Bulfinch returned home from Europe, it was still a boy's paradise, overrun with brambles and bushes, cows and horses, and the site of a few isolated farmhouses. The first challenge to this rural scene occurred when the young dilettante replaced the fallen wooden beacon with the memorial column. A few years later, when the new State House was constructed on Hancock's former pasture, it became clear to the architect that the town's future lay among the empty stretches of Trimountain. But while Bulfinch's plan to improve the area was not carried out, a dozen houses of his design still survive on Beacon Hill as testimony to the heyday of the Federalist merchant.

Fortunately, an English watercolorist, J. R. Smith, painted the scene at just this time (*Plate 16*). Conspicuous in this view is the frame house Bulfinch designed for Dr. John Joy in 1791, the first important dwelling built on Beacon Street in three decades. It was a promising contrast to the ponderous houses strung along the upper end of the famous avenue originally known as "the way to the alms-house." The colonial mansions on Beacon Street were already historic when the Federalist experiment was launched in Boston. Old-fashioned in style and surrounded by gardens, they belonged in time and character with the Bulfinch homestead in Bowdoin Square. They were definitely not competitors to the Neo-classical houses the town's architect designed for the new Federal section of the Hill. But they were important in this period and still largely occupied by the descendants or allies of the Province House families who built them. Representing the earliest social citadel on Beacon Hill, they provided a link with the past which Bulfinch and his friends extended westward along Beacon Street and higher up on Chestnut and Mount Vernon (then Olive) streets.[1]

The most celebrated of the pre-Revolutionary houses on upper Beacon Street was begun in 1737 by John Hancock's rich uncle and benefactor, and was occupied by the flamboyant and irresolute patriot until his death two years after Joy moved to Beacon Hill. Hancock's widow, sister to the patriot Josiah Quincy, Jr., and the loyalist Samuel Quincy, lived on during this period in the splendid stone dwelling.[2] The next of the somber mansions going up Bea-

con Street in the direction of Cotton Hill was acquired by
Bulfinch's uncle, Charles Ward Apthorp, in the fateful year
1775. It was separated from Hancock's house by the "Governor's pasture," the land bought for the site of the State
House and located just east of the passage leading to the
memorial column. Since Bulfinch's uncle was a loyalist,
his house, like most of the Apthorp holdings, was confiscated by the Commonwealth after the evacuation. It was
sold in 1782 to Daniel Dennison Rogers and so passed from
the category of old Beacon Street dwellings still inhabited
by descendants of the Province House set. But the house
next door, built by James Bowdoin in 1756, remained in
possession of this important intermediary family. Bowdoin's house was a solid colonial dwelling set high off the
street and approached by a flight of stone steps, an arrangement also used in the neighboring Gardiner Greene
house.

No piece of property in the capital town was more talked
about than what became known as the Gardiner Greene
estate. The house was one of the first dwellings erected on
Beacon Street and the repository of royalist, revolutionary,
and Federalist memorabilia. Built by Edward Bromfield in
1722, it became the home of Mrs. Mary Wilkes Haley the
year Bulfinch returned from Europe. Mrs. Haley was one
of the most extraordinary of Boston's curious and eccentric
women. Unfortunately she did not remain in the town
during the whole Federal period, for with her taste in
gruff, masculine elegance, she might have become Bulfinch's most lavish patron. But she was the town's chief
subject of gossip during the years she made her home in
Boston. The widow of Alderman Haley of London and the

sister of John Wilkes, Mrs. Haley came to the New England capital to inspect the property of her deceased husband and to find a new one. These ends she promptly effected by marrying her American agent, Patrick Jeffrey. But as a memoir writer of the time put it, when "a female approaching seventy leads to the altar a bridegroom who has not seen thirty, the hours of Elysium seldom continue long."[3] Patrick Jeffrey soon renewed a bachelor's life on the estate his wife bought for him in Milton, the former country seat of the royalist governor Hutchinson where Bulfinch's aunt, the wife of the Reverend East Apthorp, spent her childhood. After her marital disaster, Mrs. Haley lingered on in Boston for a few years before returning to England, where she lived out her days in Bath playing cards in the compatible company of retired admirals and generals.

Mrs. Haley's Beacon Street house was next acquired by Gardiner Greene, who contentedly poured part of an immense fortune into improvement and adornment, especially the gardens. Gardiner Greene, whose name was singularly appropriate to one whose horticultural displays were the wonder of the town, was among the richest men in Boston. But no less interesting was Mrs. Greene. She was the daughter of John Singleton Copley and a granddaughter of a distinguished merchant of provincial Boston, Richard Clarke, who actually was too distinguished. As one to whom the East India Company consigned its excess tea, Clarke fled the town forever in the aftermath of the Boston Tea Party. But the young Greenes remained despite their loyalist background and transformed the land surrounding their house into the acknowledged showplace of Boston. Their gardens were built on a series of terraces ascending Cotton Hill, planted with flowers and fruit trees, and joined together by steps, arches, and balustrades. The effect was lavish and Italianate and surely would have stupefied the pious John Cotton for whom the hill was named.

Bulfinch's patron John Joy led the way to the sunny, southwestern slope of Trimountain known today as Beacon Hill. Joy was a fifth-generation Bostonian whose ancestry went back to the Thomas Joy who designed the original Town House. His father, a wealthy merchant loyal to the crown, departed in the British evacuation. John Joy, however, remained in Boston, having taken no part in the conflict. It was doubly necessary for him to exercise discretion since his wife was also the child of a loyalist, Joseph Green, poet and wit of the Province House set. Bulfinch's father settled Green's property when it was confiscated by the Commonwealth, and also probably helped Joy in his early professional years as an apothecary. Certainly there was great intimacy between the two families. Not only did John and Benjamin Joy together commission Bulfinch to design at least four houses on Beacon Hill, but the latter rescued the architect from one of his chronically unsuccessful ventures in Boston real estate and married his daughter to Bulfinch's son George.

Dr. Joy decided in 1791 to move his family into the country. With this in mind he purchased two acres fronting on the Common directly west of the Hancock estate for the equivalent of about four thousand dollars. When the doctor died a quarter of a century later, this property was appraised at more than six times the original cost. But when the Joys first built on the Hill no one dreamed that they were setting the fashion for the aristocratic growth of the town. "Gleaner," the pseudonym of Nathaniel Ingersoll Bowditch, records that Mrs. Joy felt "no little dismay at the prospect of living so far out . . . [and] exacted a promise from Dr. Joy that they should return to town at no distant date." The Joys never left the house Bulfinch designed for them the same year the doctor purchased his two-acre "country" property. The architect's drawing bears out Bowditch's description of the house as a "graceful wooden dwelling . . . with an imposing high-porticoed gable to the Common." The house stood until 1833 amid a box-bordered terrace at what is now 35 Beacon treet.[4]

During the decade they lived in the only Bulfinch house on Beacon Hill, Dr. Joy and his family gathered on summer evenings under the portico and looked westward over the peaceful farmlands of John Singleton Copley. The famous painter owned three houses fronting on Beacon Street surrounded by nine acres of pasture as well as ten acres of uplands on the crest of Mount Whoredom. Copley went to Europe in 1774 and never returned to his native town. But he took no part in the conflict and held on to his property because his mother remained in Boston during the Revolution. Copley's land, with its farmhouses and quiet fields, made the southwestern slope of Beacon Hill the sequestered place selected by Dr. Joy for his country seat. Very soon, however, this property became the object of tremendous interest. When the town purchased the Hancock pasture in 1795 and commissioned Bulfinch to design a new State House there, the architect and his friends, Harrison Gray Otis and Jonathan Mason, read the town's future in this direction. Along with Joseph Woodward and William Scollay, they purchased Copley's land below the Joy house and north to include the summit of Mount Whoredom. The deed to the Copley property, preserved among the Otis papers at the Society for the Preservation of New England Antiquities, gives the purchase price as "four thousand two hundred pounds lawful money of the State of Massachusetts Bay in North America." But the boundaries were sufficiently vague to accommodate years of litigation. The case was not closed until Copley's son, later Baron Lyndhurst and Lord Chancellor of England, came to America and settled the dispute according to the terms of the original agreement.[5]

Bulfinch was forced to sell his proprietary rights in 1797 to Benjamin Joy; somewhat later Scollay and Woodward sold theirs to Mrs. James Swan. The land acquired by the Mount Vernon proprietors comprised the southwestern ridge of Trimountain. This ridge, with Mount Vernon Street strung along the crest, Beacon Street at the base, and Chestnut in between, is the nucleus of the area loosely called Beacon Hill. The southern boundary was delimited by the Common and never changed. The eastern border, stretching between old Beacon and Cotton hills, and containing the new State House and the historic mansions to the east, remained fairly static during the Federal period. The area developed by Bulfinch and his associates lay along the ridge leading up to Mount Whoredom, whose name the proprietors changed about 1795 to Mount Vernon.[6] This sunny crest above the Common was the best situation in Boston; although adjacent to North Slope Village, a place of violence and disorder, it was worlds apart.

Every precaution was taken to prevent the forces of corruption from invading the southern slope of the Hill. The proprietors proposed that the mansions to be strung along Mount Vernon Street contain stables in the rear, providing a pale along Pinckney Street beyond which decency need not tread. While the proprietors' hope in respect to mansions only on Beacon Hill was short-lived, Pinckney Street did constitute an effective barrier. The North Slope Village with its steep, dark streets remained in isolated contrast to the sunny, orderly southern side. The contrast would have been even greater if Bulfinch's plan for Beacon Hill had been adopted.

In 1796, as one of the proprietors, Bulfinch naturally prepared the original site plan for the houses of the allied members of old Boston families who it was hoped would be drawn to Mount Vernon. The early development of Beacon Hill was almost entirely an undertaking of the intermediary group. The country contingent, with its grip on politics and business, was still restricted to the social periphery. The Mount Vernon proprietors were rich but not pre-eminently men of business; they were active in politics but not admitted to the ruling Essex Junto. Conscious of the present, yet deeply committed to the past, this group was never free from its Province House origins, nor did it wish to be. The proprietors decided to make a stand on Beacon Hill, to draw all of their kind together—Bulfinches, Masons, Otises, Joys, Perkinses, Swans, Phillipses —and set an unassailable example. This was perfectly understood by Bulfinch, whose plan for the development of Beacon Hill dramatized the features recommending it as an aristocratic stronghold: a lofty setting and a remoteness

encouraging exclusiveness. The scheme centered upon a
large garden square designed to dominate the ridge along
Mount Vernon Street. Really a rectangle approximately
450 by 200 feet, the square was to be planted with trees
and lawns to perpetuate the rural character of the former
Copley lands, preserve the view, and provide the right setting for the elite who were to build on Beacon Hill. As the
key to Bulfinch's plan, the garden square had a social as
well as an architectural significance. This square was inspired by the eighteenth-century proprietary squares of
London and Bath, which Bulfinch also drew on for the Tontine Crescent. But in this case the houses were not to be connected. The plan provided for streets only one dwelling
deep, with the building lots rather than houses arranged
in reference to the square. Bulfinch had in mind the creation of a bigger area of the same character as Bowdoin
Square, where his own family house and those of his relatives were set amid large gardens radiating from an open
space. The social significance of the proprietary square was
implicit in its definition: it was exactly that, private and
exclusive.[7]

The proprietors were forced to veto Bulfinch's plan because of the extravagant use of space and the necessity of
leveling the whole of Mount Vernon Street. The plan was
scrapped in favor of a practical one submitted by Mathew
Withington, a surveyor, the most disastrous aspect of
which was the total elimination of Bulfinch's garden
square. This omission was reluctantly accepted by the
proprietors, who sensed that their grand design for Beacon
Hill might not be fulfilled. The only thing resembling Bulfinch's proprietary garden was the creation, on a smaller

1. CHARLES BULFINCH IN 1786. Painting by Mather Brown, owned by Harvard University. *Courtesy of Harvard University.*

2. BOSTON BEFORE BULFINCH. Looking southeast from the site of the State House to the harbor and the hills of Dorchester and Roxbury, 1790. Engraving by Samuel Hill in the *Massachusetts Magazine*, November 1790, facing 641.

3. THE BULFINCH HOUSE IN BOWDOIN SQUARE, *c.* 1740. Drawing reproduced from Ellen Susan Bulfinch, *The Life and Letters of Charles Bulfinch, Architect* (Boston, 1896), 11.

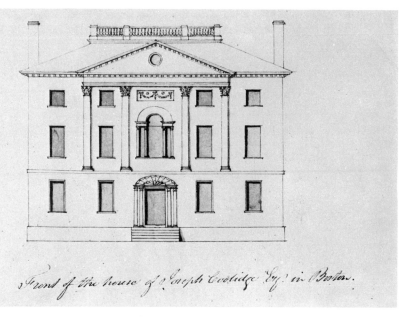

Front of the house of Joseph Coolidge Esq.: in Boston.

4. THE JOSEPH COOLIDGE, SR., HOUSE IN BOWDOIN SQUARE, 1791-92. Bulfinch's drawing in the Phelps Stokes collection of the New York Public Library. *Courtesy of the New York Public Library.*

East Elevation of the Seat of Joseph Barrell Esq. 3 Miles from Boston.

5. THE JOSEPH BARRELL HOUSE, CHARLESTOWN, 1792. Bulfinch's drawing in the Boston Athenæum. *Courtesy of the Boston Athenæum.*

6. THE HOLLIS STREET CHURCH, 1788. Bulfinch's drawing engraved for the *Columbian Magazine*, April 1788, facing 175.

7. THE FIRST BOSTON OR FEDERAL STREET THEATRE, 1793-94. Watercolor made after 1798 by an unknown artist showing the building on fire and an elevation of the reconstructed theater, owned by the Bostonian Society. *Courtesy of the Bostonian Society.*

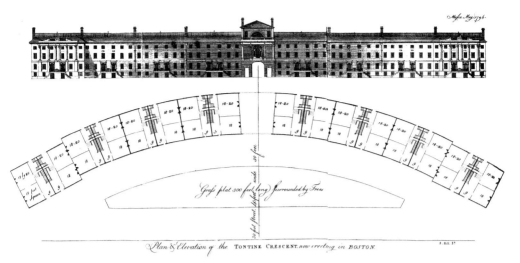

8. The Tontine Crescent in Franklin Place, 1793-95. Bulfinch's drawing engraved for the *Massachusetts Magazine*, February 1794, facing 67.

9. The Tontine Crescent and Numbers 23 and 24 Franklin Place. Painting made about 1850 by Benjamin Nutting in the Charles F. Rowley collection. *Courtesy of Charles F. Rowley*.

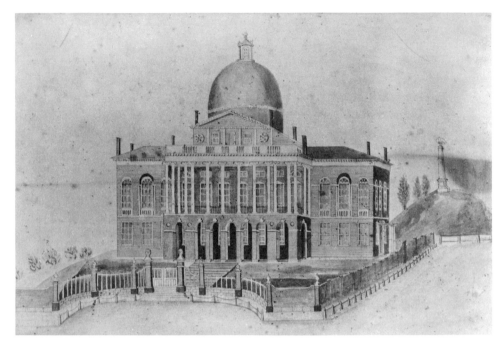

10. THE MASSACHUSETTS STATE HOUSE, 1795-98, AND THE MEMORIAL COLUMN, 1790. Watercolor made about 1805 by an unknown artist, owned by the Bostonian Society. *Courtesy of the Bostonian Society.*

11. THE ALMSHOUSE IN LEVERETT STREET, 1799-1801. Engraving by Abel Bowen reproduced from Caleb Snow, *A History of Boston* (Boston, 1825), facing 52.

12. THE MASSACHUSETTS STATE HOUSE AFTER THE RESTORATION OF 1956-61. *Photograph by Nicholas Dean.*

13. The Jonathan Mason House in Mount Vernon Street, 1801-1802. Lithograph made before 1836 by William S. Pendleton. *Courtesy of the Bostonian Society.*

14. The First Harrison Gray Otis House in Cambridge Street, 1796. *Photograph by Nicholas Dean.*

15. The Second Harrison Gray Otis House in Mount Vernon Street, 1800-1801. *Photograph by Nicholas Dean.*

16. Beacon Street and the Common, c. 1808. Left to right: John Phillips House, 1804; Thomas Perkins House, 1804-1805; John Joy House, 1791; Hancock House, 1737-40; State House, 1795-98; Thomas Amory House, 1804. Watercolor in the Boston Public Library from the original by John Rubens Smith. *Courtesy of the Directors of the Boston Public Library.*

17. TREMONT STREET, c 1800. Looking north at the corner of West Street with the Common on the left. Watercolor thought to have been painted by Lucy Knox, owned by the Boston Public Library. *Courtesy of the Directors of the Boston Public Library.*

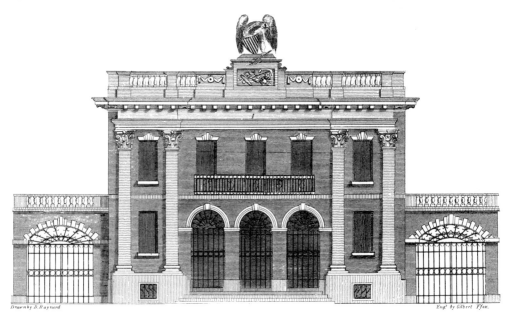

18. THE UNITED STATES BANK IN STATE STREET, 1798. Engraving from Daniel Raynerd's drawing for Raynerd and Benjamin, *The American Builder's Companion* (Boston, 1806), plate 43.

19. DETAIL FROM THE SWAN HOUSES IN CHESTNUT STREET, 1806. *Photograph by Nicholas Dean.*

20. Detail from the Third Harrison Gray Otis House in Beacon Street, 1805-1806. *Photograph by Nicholas Dean.*

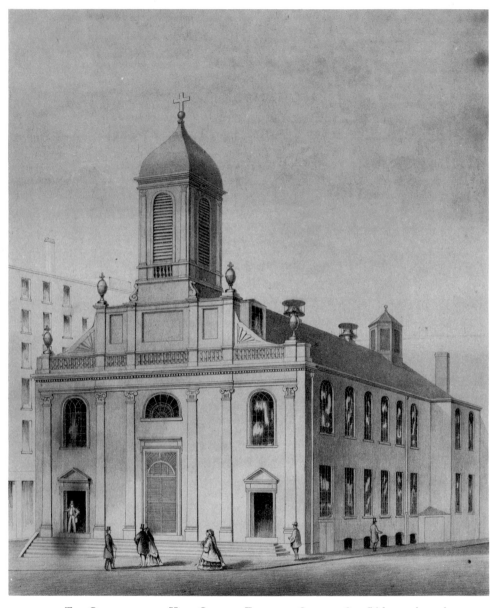

21. THE CHURCH OF THE HOLY CROSS IN FRANKLIN STREET, 1803. Lithograph made in 1859 by C. A. Evans. *Courtesy of the Boston Athenæum.*

scale, of Louisburg Square from a plan drawn in 1826. The adoption of Withington's scheme hastened the urbanization of Beacon Hill. It provided for Walnut Street to run along Dr. Joy's property between Mount Vernon and Beacon streets, ending that family's bucolic isolation. West Cedar Street was extended from North Slope Village to Chestnut Street and the newly named Mount Vernon was leveled and the earth used to lay out Charles Street. Finally, Beacon Hill was cut down and Bulfinch's memorial column destroyed. This act of official vandalism denuded Trimountain of all but one summit, Cotton Hill, which remained during the Federal period largely in the possession of Gardiner Greene as the scene of his proliferating gardens.[8]

Bulfinch was disappointed when his plan for Beacon Hill was rejected. The proprietors were also unhappy over the decision to eliminate the garden square. In order to retain some of the country charm of the old Copley farmlands, the proprietors decided to build mansions in a row on the north side of Mount Vernon Street, each house set back thirty feet from the street. In this way something of Bulfinch's original conception would be salvaged, and the proprietors would be placed in a united row along the highest street on Beacon Hill. Jonathan Mason was scheduled to build the first of these proposed mansions, followed by Benjamin Joy, Mrs. James Swan, and Harrison Gray Otis. A few years later Bulfinch recouped his financial losses and again asserted himself among this elite by buying the property below Otis. There he built a large double house but never had a chance to live in it. Nor was the proprietors' design for Mount Vernon Street realized;

checked first by Jefferson's embargo, it was finally abandoned in the War of 1812.

The first of the Mount Vernon proprietors to build a
mansion on Beacon Hill was Harrison Gray Otis. This coincided with Otis's uninhibited drive to be "first" in everything; the pacemaker for the cautious or less imaginative
newcomers. In the development of the Hill, Otis and Bulfinch were the two men most committed. And it is appropriate that their names alone survive in the general con-
text of the place. The three houses Bulfinch designed for
Otis are the most important examples of domestic Federal
architecture in Boston. Through them can be traced not
only their owner's ascent in wealth and taste but the social
tide of Boston as it moved from the established areas of
Bowdoin Square and the South End to Mount Vernon and
Beacon streets.[9]

Through all these moves shines the kind, intelligent,
and happy face of Harrison Gray Otis—the most successful
man in Bulfinch's town. Though not the best born or the
richest, he combined good breeding and sufficient wealth
with a thirst for the pleasantest ways of life. Otis not
only possessed the sense of Boston's past inherent in the
Province House descendants but had the flair and the per-
sonality to impose that group's will upon the country people. One of the chief means of this ascendancy was his
continuing patronage of Charles Bulfinch. The last house
Bulfinch designed for Otis, number 45 Beacon Street, was
also the last great house he designed in Boston (*Plate 20*).
It represented a summing up of his skill as a domestic
architect and the final expression of an age already on
the way out when the house was finished in 1806. Sur-

rounded by gardens and looking out on the Common and the waters of the Charles River, it was everything Bulfinch aimed at in his original plan for Beacon Hill.[10] But Otis's hope to maintain the rustic charm of the old Copley lands, too, was short-lived. Other houses went up around his. Ostensibly prolonging the style of the Federal period, they were really only ghosts of the English-haunted age.

But while the battle was fought, Otis stood in the thick of it. He was not as overwhelmed with old Boston antecedents and sensitivities as his life-long friend and architect. Yet his family was equally torn by the dissensions of war. Although sensationally linked to the patriotic cause, the Otises had had a foot in the Province House door. They gained prominence in Boston early in the eighteenth century, but the biggest step was made by Samuel Otis, Harrison's father, when he married a daughter of Harrison Gray, an important British official who was a conspicuous target for the Sons of Liberty. Equally embarrassing to the well-connected Samuel Otis was the behavior of his brother James and his sister Mercy—one a fire-brand of rebellion and the other the "Poetess of the Revolution." While his brother and sister were being immortalized, Samuel Otis and his immediate family suffered the hardships of a household divided by conflicting loyalties. Samuel Otis was a patriot and remained in Boston; but Harrison Gray and all his children, except Mrs. Otis, left in the British evacuation. Harrison Gray Otis's mother was torn between devotion to her husband and her departed family and died several years later of a broken heart.

Formative years passed under the shadow of family separation and divided loyalties served to unite the members of the intermediary group. They stuck together even though time reduced some, like Bulfinch, to modest circumstances and raised others, like Otis, to great wealth. Otis certainly was luckier than Bulfinch. The high hopes of his mother in naming him after her rich and influential father were fully realized. He inherited all his Uncle Jim's powers to move a crowd, as can be seen in Nathaniel Ingersoll Bowditch's remark: "There probably has never lived in Boston any individual with finer natural endowments than Mr. Otis. Possessing a noble presence, a beautifully modulated voice, great readiness and self-possession, and a cultivated intellect, he has rarely, if ever, been surpassed in the divine gift of eloquence."[11] Otis's popularity, acquired wealth, and Province House antecedents dazzled the new men. But they clipped his political wings by keeping him out of the Essex Junto; politics was Otis's one area of disappointment. He held many posts under the Federalist hierarchy yet was never offered the gubernatorial nomination. Nevertheless, he alone of the intermediary group met the new men squarely on their own terms, money, and on his own which were so much more. His manners were a legend among the "quarter-deck" milieu of the former North Shore merchants.[12]

The leaders of the intermediary group believed in the American nation and held with the new people great expectations for the future. But their obsession with Boston's past was a living, personal thing. This obsession was shared by their exiled relatives and friends who, from whatever refuge they had taken, eagerly watched the efforts of the intermediary group to transform the old colonial town under Bulfinch's leadership. They depended heavily upon letters from home. And Mrs. Thomas Bulfinch, living on in the ancestral house in Bowdoin Square, never failed in her duty to her exiled family. She wrote long and serene letters about the changing town and the unobtrusive success of her son. Here is part of one sent off to her brother East Apthorp in 1803:[13]

I am in the mansion house with my youngest daughter. I look from the window upon the houses of my other two children; they call to see me every day, and when the weather is very fine and my limbs will permit, I visit them in return. My Son, tho' he has been unfortunate, is much respected; he is president of the Selectmen, for which he receives a small salary.

These Boston exiles only knew their native place in its pre-Revolutionary state. Their knowledge of the changing Federalist town was shaped by letters such as those from Bulfinch's mother. Her concept of Boston was formed in provincial days, and she reflected the wonder of the Province House refugees when she wrote to her brother in 1804: "The town of Boston is so grown you would scarce know it for your native place; almost every spot of land is cover'd with brick buildings, and the paved streets and hackney coaches make us very noisy. The old [Apthorp] mansion house in State Street is converted into a Bank . . . The Common still remains free, and we hope always will, as we really begin to be crowded."[14]

But to their descendants it seemed as though change moved at a snail's pace. The Mount Vernon proprietors, staring over their hilly domain in the year 1804, saw little change from the earlier days when it was all merely Copley's farm and Sewell's pasture. Few of the forty lots comprising Withington's plan were sold. The proprietors' dream of a ribbon of mansions running along Mount Vernon Street did not materialize. The beginning, however, was there. Harrison Gray Otis led the way in 1801 when he moved into what is today 85 Mount Vernon Street (*Plate 15*). This house, the second Bulfinch created for Otis, retains substantially the form the architect gave it; the only important change being the relocation of the entrance porch from an original position on the western façade. Number 85 Mount Vernon Street was a departure from the colonial proportions used in the first Otis house near Bowdoin Square (*Plate 14*). It was modeled instead after Bulfinch's adaptation of the Neo-classical style in the Tontine Crescent and the double houses in Franklin Place. The architect's radical departure from colonial precedent is most evident in the modulation of window heights in relation to function, with the principal rooms clearly distinguished by full-length windows on the ground floor. The second Otis house was erected along the ridge forming the axis of Beacon Hill with a tremendous view to the west. High off the street with a lawn and driveway, it still suggests the haughty air the proprietors hoped to achieve in each of the houses proposed for their personal domain.[15]

The regal plans for Mount Vernon Street gained momentum the following year when Jonathan Mason moved out of Franklin Place into the mansion Bulfinch designed for him at the head of Walnut Street. Mason's house was completed in 1802 on a double lot and was of course set back thirty feet from the street (*Plate 13*). Approached by a circular drive and ranged about with gardens, it amply supported Bulfinch's desire to keep Beacon Hill a rural place. The house had stables in the rear fronting on Pinckney Street, a first step to seal off the beau monde of Beacon Hill from the riffraff of North Slope Village. And Mason was definitely of the beau monde. A rich member of an old Boston family, he studied law under the exiled Samuel Quincy and married Susana Powell, whose Province House ancestors included a royal governor. Like his neighbor Otis, Mason had a hand in most of the activities of Federal Boston, participating in many of the building and land schemes employing Bulfinch's talents. Mason's house was destroyed shortly after his death in 1831, and only a lithograph remains to depict that once-famous mansion. The plan, which seems to have been determined by the necessity of marrying off the five Mason girls, called for the incorporation of a ballroom in the second and third stories of the central bow front with tall windows on the second floor and blank spaces on the third. Unfortunately, Bulfinch did not here resort to the device of dummy windows in order to maintain exterior symmetry as in the earlier country house of Mrs. Swan. He also erred in placing the entrance at an awkward corner on the east side facing the first of four houses Mason built for his daughters on property ascending the hill in the direction of the memorial column. These dwellings, built in 1804 from plans apparently supplied by Bulfinch, departed from the original scheme for Mount Vernon Street. All four houses are connected without side gardens, and only the one nearest to Mason's own house (Number 57) was set back thirty feet. The other three were built flush with the sidewalk according to the precedent set in the previous year by the former Essex County merchant Stephen Higginson.[16]

[157]

The land on Mount Vernon Street above Mason's property was offered for sale by Harrison Gray Otis in 1801. At this date the proprietors still saw the future of Beacon Hill in terms of mansion houses, for an advertisement in the *Columbian Centinel* of May 27 states the site will support two "very elegant building lots." When Stephen Higginson built four houses on this land two years later, however, the set-back requirement was disregarded and the standard of architectural grandeur set by Otis and Mason abandoned.[17] The future of Beacon Hill is read in the appearance of the seven row-houses on upper Mount Vernon Street rather than in the dreams of the gentlemen proprietors. Anyway, Jefferson's embargo in 1807 was the death blow to whatever hopes existed for the development of Mount Vernon according to Bulfinch's concept. Building came to a standstill after that fatal act. Yet in the few years between the time Otis and Mason moved into their Mount Vernon Street houses and the embargo, there appeared a chance the leading Province House descendants would create an aristocratic area of Bulfinch houses amid gardens and open spaces. This hope was advanced in 1804 when Mason's brother-in-law, Thomas Perkins, began building a mansion on the corner of Mount Vernon and Joy streets (*Plate 16*).

The Perkins house was one of the most intriguing Bulfinch designed, a striking exile from the Adelphi in London. Because the location of the lot required placing the principal rooms in the rear of the house, the street front contained the entry and staircase. Upon this largely blank façade Bulfinch assembled all the Neo-classical elements he loved in a fascinating but disquieting composition. Still, the placement of the main rooms in the rear was right, since the view across Dr. Joy's garden to the Common was the famous one afforded all the original settlers on Beacon Hill. And Perkins, as anxious as his architect to preserve the country outlook, instigated a setback of fifteen to eighteen feet for all subsequent houses built below him on Joy Street in order to retain the view from the tall windows of his drawing room.[18]

Thomas Perkins is not to be confused with Thomas Handasyd Perkins, the model Federalist merchant and sometime houseowner in the Tontine Crescent. The Mount Vernon Street patron of Bulfinch was also a merchant, but his fame rests in the social role he played as an important member of the intermediary group pushing the Beacon Hill project along. He was the son of a Boston loyalist and a grandson of a royal governor of Nova Scotia. His father, James Perkins, was arrested after the evacuation but allowed to return to Boston; one of those former Province House magnates whose sole wish was to be forgotten in the post-Revolutionary era. Thomas Perkins was less repressed. His age and connections placed him in the same social group as his friends, Bulfinch and Otis, and his brother-in-law, Jonathan Mason. In many ways he was Bulfinch's most fastidious patron. He put off moving into his new house on Mount Vernon Street for two years in order to equip and furnish it in the appropriate style. The marble mantels, for example, were purchased in Italy by his brother-in-law, Thomas Appleton, American consul at Leghorn. Excerpts from an order Perkins himself placed in

London in 1805 show both the meticulous care and interest he took in his house and throw light upon a famous Bulfinch mansion that disappeared a hundred years ago:[19]

I have seen some bills of sundries purchased in your city in Mar. 1802 . . . for my Brother-in-Law Jonathan Mason . . . My motive in furnishing you with this information is for your government in the stile and cost of those I have ordered . . . On the basement story of my House is the principal Entrance the great Door opening into a square space of about 14 by 16 ft. I wish to have a very handsome Lamp adapted to it, the Height being 8 or 9 ft. will not admit of one suspended in the centre. Cannot something tasty be procured to be affixed to the side of the wall. It should be plated; must be well finished and handsome. You are not restricted in the price, suppose 7 to 8 guineas. It should have 2 Burners at least to accommodate the stairs leading to the great entry . . . One handsome Lamp or Lanthorn for Oil, for a circular entry 25 ft. in height . . . Two Grecian Lamps each 3 Burners, in handsome cut glass dishes or stands with appartus compleat, for the center of two rooms 13 ft. in height, communication with each other, to cost about £15 to £18 sterling each.

The year Perkins moved into his new house saw Bulfinch once again a property owner on Beacon Hill. No longer one of the original proprietors, he bought the lot on Mount Vernon Street next door to Otis. But it is not certain whether he planned to build a house there for himself and actually live among the elite. This was only five years after his family moved into the comfortable house in Bulfinch Street, the dwelling visible from his mother's windows in the old homestead on Bowdoin Square. At any rate, he started construction on a handsome double house set back thirty feet from the street. Half of this double house, Number 87, still stands as Bulfinch conceived it while the twin is totally altered. The bad luck that hounded Bulfinch's business enterprises forced him to sell these houses unfinished the following year. Number 87 went to Stephen Higginson of the Essex Junto, the first new man to own a Bulfinch house on Beacon Hill. But not long after this move Higginson was forced to retire to a modest house in Cambridge with a sinecure at Harvard College. The tenants of the adjoining house hardly fared better. General David Humphrey, who acquired the connecting property in 1806, died soon after moving to Mount Vernon Street; his widow married a French nobleman and suffered the same fate in respect to her second marriage as Mrs. Haley.[20]

At the time the original Mount Vernon proprietors were pushing the development of the highest ridge on Beacon Hill, Benjamin Joy was speculating in building operations of more modest dimensions in Chestnut Street. Beginning in 1799, this old friend and patron of Charles Bulfinch built a number of houses on both sides of that street above the juncture at Willow. There is great confusion regarding the participation of Bulfinch in the early building in Chestnut Street. Numbers 6 and 8, built in 1804 for Charles Paine, were certainly designed by him. So was number 29A, probably the first house built by the Mount Vernon proprietors. This charming house, facing east on a private garden, is the only surviving example of the bow front style Bulfinch used for Jonathan Mason and James Sullivan. According to Allen Chamberlain's exhaustive efforts in Beacon Hill title-searching, Benjamin Joy constructed 29A Chestnut Street late in 1799, possibly on the ruins of an earlier house.[21] Equally mysterious is the neighboring mansion built for Captain Richard Crowninshield Derby on land now occupied by the Theological School and chapel, reputed to have contained the most lavish interiors in Federal Boston.[22]

All this time the western end of Beacon Street remained largely deserted. Dr. Joy's country seat basked in rural isolation, contentedly agrarian compared with the smart, London-inspired houses looming up behind it. Joy's mansion was the only known Bulfinch house on Beacon Street until John Phillips moved into the dwelling he built on the corner of Beacon and Walnut in 1805, (*Plate 16*). For Phillips, taking possession of a Bulfinch house was a symbolic act. Seventeen years later when the old town became a city and its architect departed, John Phillips was Boston's first mayor, taking over the duties Bulfinch performed as chief selectman for almost two decades. The Phillips family was not only a pioneering one on lower Beacon Street but was also associated with the most conspicuous of the pre-Revolutionary mansions on the upper slope—the old Bromfield house. Famous as the home of the Gardiner Greenes, this colonial mansion was built by Phillips' grandfather, Edward Bromfield, and acquired by his own father, John Phillips, a dozen years before the Revolution. The house Bulfinch designed for John Phillips stands on its corner overlooking the Common but altered almost beyond recognition. The entrance, moved from Beacon to Walnut, bears no relationship to the one Bulfinch created; an indifferently reconstructed façade masks but does not completely conceal the fine proportions of the original. With the alteration of this house in the 1830's one of the authentic pieces of Federal design in Beacon Street vanished.[23]

Mrs. James Swan was the last of the Mount Vernon proprietors to build on Beacon Hill. The three identical houses Bulfinch designed for her in Chestnut Street (Numbers 13, 15, and 17) were not completed until 1807 (*Plate 19*). Mrs. Swan was born Hepsibah Clarke, a Boston heiress of pre-Revolutionary days whose fortune caught the eye of a Scottish adventurer, James Swan. After grabbing this Province House prize, Swan busied himself with the patriot cause and emerged from the War for Independence with the rank of colonel. Not the person to overlook an opportunity, Swan capitalized on his army connection with Lafayette to operate in Paris as a financier and agent for the new French republic.[24] This profitable but dangerous role terminated in a French prison in 1808, where he remained until 1830, released only a few days before his death. With the colonel incarcerated abroad, Mrs. Swan continued to live most of the year in the country house Bulfinch designed for her at Dorchester; the three houses she built in Chestnut Street were wedding presents for her daughters.[25] One of them, Sarah Swan, married Bulfinch's close friend, William Sullivan, the outspoken Federalist son of the Republican governor James Sullivan. Mrs. Swan's gift of Bulfinch houses as wedding presents was opulent but not unique. Her Beacon Hill neighbors, Mason and Perkins, together built at least six houses for prospective sons-in-law.[26]

The election of Bulfinch's patron James Sullivan as Republican governor in 1807 was a presentiment of the future. The Federalist party was on the way out, even in

Massachusetts. As a result, the Mount Vernon Proprietors' empty spaces lay unclaimed and their architect's hopes did not materialize beyond the first stage. But while his dream for Beacon Hill was never achieved, Bulfinch could feel satisfied that he had advanced Boston far along the path to good taste. Picture the scene awaiting the architect as he walked between the memorial column and the new State House down Mount Vernon Street to the intersection of Walnut, where the view widened thirty feet in front of the Mason and Otis houses: it is one of those New England winter evenings with a cold sky, and the sun, setting over the Charles River, glows on the new brick and fresh paint of more than a dozen fine houses whose good proportions are etched sharply in the clear light and set off to advantage by gardens falling away to the Common. It is a modest achievement when compared to the London model, but one reflecting both the architect's talent and the town's ambition. And in Federal America the scene was unique. With such a picture Bulfinch could be content. He might even forget the disappointments of his own life in contemplating how much he gave to his native place.

VIII

PARK STREET
AND THE COMMON

THE SOUTHERN SLOPE of Beacon Hill is still the finest sight in Boston. In the Federal period, however, the area to which Bulfinch next turned his talents, Park Street, was almost as attractive. For though Park Street was the child of Beacon Hill, an offspring of the architectural and social mood imposed by the Province House descendants on Copley's former lands, it was not a stepchild. The street commanded a superb view: the Common stretching away to the Charles River seen through a screen of English elms already old at the time Beacon Hill was reclaimed from a pasture land. These elms, the special trust of Adino Paddock, were planted before the Revolution when Park was called Sentry Street and contained the almshouse, workhouse, and granary. The town's affluent coachmaker, Paddock lived on a part of Tremont Street then known as "Long Acre." From the door of his workshop he kept a restless eye on the young trees which had survived the long voyage from England; his vigil, "Gleaner" recounts, often sending him flying across the street to berate idle lads for shaking the saplings. Paddock worried over the fate of his trees until the Revolution released him forever from that anxiety. He was a loyalist who returned in 1776 to the country where he and his trees originated.

The removal of the almshouse in 1801 and the dismantling of the workhouse and the granary signaled the development of Park Street. With these grim buildings swept away, a conspicuous property was suddenly available to Bulfinch and his friends then engaged in transforming the outskirts of the Common into the finest residential section of Boston. Park Street, or Park Place as it was called for several years, was laid out by Bulfinch in 1804 after he had secured a town ordinance restricting building there to a uniform height and style. For once Bulfinch had everything his own way. The result was a handsome avenue of related houses rivaling the architectural continuity of the Tontine Crescent. The first four dwellings were erected at the southern end of the street and became popularly known as "Bulfinch Row." Concurrently, four more houses were constructed in a similar design. But these additional houses, Numbers 5-8, ascended Park where the street climbs steeply into Beacon and the same uniformity in roof and floor levels could not be maintained. Yet even though the last four dwellings lacked the symmetry of Numbers 1-4, Park Street was wonderfully all of a kind.[1] The eight Bulfinch houses marched smartly up the hill to meet the grandest dwelling on the block, the Amory mansion at the corner of Park and Beacon (*Plate 16*).

Thomas Amory's house still stands on its enviable corner, although in a state of indifference and neglect. Built in 1804 at the height of the Federalist experiment, it was the first house constructed in Park Street and left no doubt as to origins among the neighboring intermediary family mansions on Beacon Hill. The house was designed by Bulfinch for the junior Thomas Amory, whose mother was a member of the Coffin family, which included the last Receiver-General and Cashier of British customs in Boston. This was a dangerous post to hold in the brawling years before the Revolution, and the Amory homestead, far out on the highroad to the Neck, was stoned by the Sons of Liberty. But the head of the house was actually a quiet loyalist who took no part in the conflict and arranged the terms for the British evacuation. For this service the elder Amory was allowed to remain in Boston after the exodus swept away most of his wife's family. He was always suspected of being a Tory, however, and spent the critical war years in Watertown. The son, Thomas, Jr., was not so inhibited. Like his contemporaries Thomas Perkins and Christopher Gore, whose loyalist fathers also crept unobtrusively back into Boston, Amory was prone to extravagance and went bankrupt building the house in Park Street. The wine cellar alone would have ruined almost any Federalist merchant. It contained a range of brick vaults constructed under Beacon Street, the building of which was authorized at a special meeting of the Board of Selectmen. As it was, Amory moved in and out of his mansion in rapid succession, receiving news of his bankruptcy a few hours before greeting his guests for the housewarming. If Amory's architect was present at this macabre ceremony, Bulfinch commiserated with his ruined patron from firsthand experience.[2]

The mansion passed through a number of hands following the hasty withdrawal of its original owner. In 1806 it was turned into a fashionable boarding house by Mrs.

Catherine Carter, who is said to have maintained some sixty guests, turning away twenty or thirty strangers a day. One reason for the heavy demand was the proximity of the dwelling to the new State House; during the legislative sessions the capital town was hard-pressed to supply accommodations to the lawmakers. But Mrs. Carter was not solely prejudiced in favor of politicians, one of her guests was the painter Edward Malbone. Perhaps to atone for the fiasco of the Amory housewarming several years earlier, the residents of Mrs. Carter's establishment gave an "elegant and sumptuous Ball and Supper to a number of Ladies and Gentlemen of this Town" in the spring of 1806.[3] Among the four hundred guests so honored was Admiral Isaac Coffin of the British navy, a nephew of Amory's mother and the son of a loyalist grandee who died shortly before the Revolution. It was a symptom of the English obsession of Federalist Boston that a member of an exiled family should be welcomed back as an honored guest. Equally characteristic was the setting in which the exiled hero was entertained: a Bulfinch mansion designed for a Province House descendant.

Mrs. Carter and her family of sixty-odd remained in the mansion hardly longer than the original owner. In 1807 she carried her brood away to a new abode on Howard Street, close to the Bulfinch family stronghold of Bowdoin Square. The Amory house was then enlarged and divided into four dwellings with entrances on Beacon as well as Park. The Park Street entrance was the one designed by Bulfinch, and the fine Adam porch and fan-light still remain more or less in their original form. The most desirable of the four converted dwellings faced west on the

Common and north on Beacon Street and was occupied for the last ten years of this period by the sometime Federalist politician and lawyer, Samuel Dexter. A close friend and Harvard classmate of Bulfinch, Dexter served in the Congress of the United States as a loyal representative of the Essex Junto and was John Adams's secretary of war and treasury. When Jefferson took over the White House, Dexter retired from the national scene to pursue a law practice in the more compatible air of Boston. He made one more trip to Washington, however, when he represented the merchants of Massachusetts in their attempt to have the embargo declared unconstitutional, a hopeless endeavor and just about the last task Dexter performed for the Federalists. One of the mavericks who placed nation above party during the War of 1812, he bolted Boston's sacred cause to join the Republicans. But even before this uncommon act Dexter showed his lack of stability, by Federalist standards, in departing from his old party's invariable posture—drinking—to become president of the first temperance society in Boston. His high-living cronies, men like Otis, Mason, and Gore, doubtless considered temperance as great an evil as Republicanism. The pipes of Madeira and sherry exactingly stowed away in Boston ships, often crossing many oceans before reaching Bulfinch houses on Beacon Hill and Park Street, were an inseparable part of political dinners, described by Henry Adams as occasions when "gout and plethora waited behind the chairs."[4] Such meals were generally preceded by a devastating punch served in a great bowl, a trophy of the China trade. The Federalists' hatred of Napoleon was reflected in the absence of champagne on their tables.

[169]

The course of Federalism and Madeira went unchecked in the second best of the four dwellings converted from the Amory mansion, the one next door to Dexter and running along Park Street. Utterly free of turncoats and prohibitionists, it was occupied successively by Fisher Ames, Christopher Gore, and Harrison Gray Otis's son-in-law, Andrew Ritchie. Even here, though, these early tenants seemed to live under a curse imposed by the luckless Amory. And while this portion of the house subsequently became famous as a nest of Federalists, it was first briefly the home of an old Tory, Dr. John Jeffries, who lived there less than twelve months. The next tenant, Fisher Ames, occupied the house only one year before dying in 1808. Ames's political career began at the same time Bulfinch returned from his architectural tour of Europe. A tireless worker in the formation of the Federalist party, he led the battle to get the Constitution ratified in Massachusetts. Ames served in Congress during Washington's two terms, spinning an oratorical web that ensnared even Republicans. His political star soared so high that his neighbor Samuel Dexter, himself a fantastic orator, was forced to take a back seat. It was Ames who was chosen to make the supreme Federalist gesture—the eulogy to Washington before the Massachusetts legislature. But Dexter had the last word; he delivered Ames's eulogy in 1808.[5]

Fisher Ames was followed by another twelve-month tenant, Christopher Gore. But Gore never felt at home in Park Street. He was so exaggeratedly the Beacon Hill type that only the fact he was in England during the eight years the area was developed excused him from living next door to Otis, Mason, or Perkins. He made up for this omission, however, by building a splendid country house in Waltham. Although not of the colonial aristocracy, Gore was allied to Province House families. His father was a loyalist who departed in the British evacuation and lived in exile in London for ten years. Luckier than the other Bostonians who crowded the New England Coffee House on Threadneedle Street or met weekly in the Adelphi, the senior Gore was permitted to return to the future Federalist capital, a decade before his son went to England as a commissioner to settle American claims under Jay's treaty. In the first years of his father's exile Gore remained in Boston, impoverished but ambitious. Clever and popular, he was described by his contemporary, Anna Eliot Ticknor, as "the young, beautiful, and excellent Christopher Gore."[6] Thus endowed he had little trouble getting ahead. Joining his fortunes to the Federalist party, Gore was admitted to the inner circle of the Essex Junto and was its successful candidate in the gubernatorial election of 1809.

As it turned out, Gore's penchant for splendor was too much even for Federalist Massachusetts. His acquired Province House traits, held in check during the bleak years of his father's exile, could not be suppressed forever. Added to this were eight years spent in England observing the munificence of the ruling class. Gore returned to Boston determined to live in the style of an English country gentleman. His country seat in Waltham is indubitably a grand place; its magnificence won condescending approval from the visiting British minister, Sir Augustus John Foster, who called it "a very handsome comfortable house."[7] But Gore's pride manifest in his house and appurtenances brought about his downfall. The house, isolated

amid lawns and gardens, woods and meadows, even possessing a "deer park," might have survived gossip if Governor Gore had not insisted on driving out for all the world
to see in an orange coach with footmen and out-riders in
blazing livery. This flashy equipage, which caused only
minor rumblings in the politically "safe" town of Boston,
boomeranged when the governor made a state journey
through Massachusetts with a constellation of aides and
cavalry. The wide-eyed but thinking farmers promptly
turned him out of office in the next election.

But the occupants of the Amory house and their neighbors saw nothing outrageous about the bright orange
coach so familiar a sight in Park Street. On the contrary,
they rather liked it, and some of them, or their relatives on
Beacon Hill, had carriages hardly less ostentatious. Family
connections on Beacon Hill or associations with the Amory
mansion were the key to Park Street. The crowding of relatives of Amory house occupants into the eight Bulfinch
houses below was extraordinary. Number 8 was built by
Jonathan Amory, Jr.; Number 4 was the residence of
Amory's sister, Mrs. Jonathan Davis. Two of the houses
were owned by members of the Gore family, although one
of them, 7 Park Street, was occupied by Mrs. Artemus
Ward, sister of Samuel Dexter. Another resident of the
street, William Payne, swept the gamut: his mother was
an Amory and his sister Mrs. Christopher Gore. Only one
family figured massively in the early history of Park Street
without associations in the Amory house—the Warren
family, the most distinguished residents of "Bulfinch Row."
Number 2 Park Street was the home of Dr. John Collins
Warren, son of the brillant surgeon to the Continental

troops in Boston; the neighboring house was occupied by Mrs. Arnold Wells, daughter of General Joseph Warren, the patriot hero slain at the battle of Bunker Hill.

The Warrens were the one family on Park Street who probably scoffed at the coach that carried Gore to political ruin. Somewhat good-natured scorn, though, as Mrs. John Collins Warren was a daughter of Jonathan Mason, a Mount Vernon proprietor, who did not lag behind Gore in his love of luxury. But two members of the earlier generation very much responded to the equivocal symbolism of Gore's carriage. One was old Dr. John Warren of Revolutionary fame, who lived in the house on Park Street with his son and daughter-in-law; the other was his sister-in-law, Mercy Otis Warren. Although both Dr. John and Mercy Warren lived actively through most of the Federal period, they were children of the Revolution. Neither forgot nor diminished the greatness of their respective brothers, General Joseph Warren and James Otis, even though the memory of these patriots was dimmed in an age epitomized by Gore's house and carriage. When Copley's son, the future Baron Lyndhurst, was in Boston in 1796, he wrote home: "Shall I whisper a word in your ear. The better people are all aristocrats. My father is too rank a Jacobin to live among them. Samuel Adams is superannuated, unpopular, and fast decaying in every respect."[8] Evidently he did not meet the two Warrens, Mercy and old Dr. John, both of whom sat for his father in the days when Samuel Adams's name was electrifying. These older Warrens were a cut of the same cloth; they never relinquished the beliefs their brothers shouted from the halls and taverns of colonial Boston.

The houses on Park Street backed into the Granary Burying Ground, which caused an occasional wisecrack at Dr. John Collins Warren's expense. Until the Massachusetts General Hospital was completed in 1821 from Bulfinch's design, Warren performed his operations in a room "with a well-sanded floor" on the ground story of the Park Street dwelling. Joksters suggested the proximity of burial ground and operating room was too close for comfort. Actually all the Park Street owners had gates leading from the rear of their houses into the burying ground, which they used in summer as a private park. Here the Warrens held picnics, setting up baskets, as one member records, "On the table-like structures covering the graves of families with historic names."[9] Families had entertained on the grass in the rear of "Bulfinch Row" since the first dwellings appeared on the street. One of Mrs. Carter's "family" wrote in 1806: "After the warmth of the day is over, we form animated groups. We had quite a romantic one last evening, sitting on the grass by moonlight, with the accompaniment of guitar and singing."[10] The houses backing into the burying ground were particularly pleasant and well planned. Because of the generous width of the lots (approximately forty feet), Bulfinch was able to work two rooms into the front on the principal floor. These were connected with folding doors and shared the famous view over the Common.

Today the Common is inseparably linked with the houses on Beacon Hill. But in Bulfinch's time the dwellings on Park Street had a more generous connection. They were set on its very edge and owed their fine situation to the green, open area falling away to the Charles River. Impossible as it is to think of Boston without the Common, it was only by accident that the town acquired the land in such a manner as to maintain it, at least until the last thirty years, relatively unspoiled. The site was originally reserved by William Blackstone, who before the coming of the Puritans lived in contented solitude on the slope of what is now Beacon Hill. When Winthrop and his follow-ers were encouraged to move from Charlestown to Tri-mountain, Blackstone decided, in a judicious moment rare to such dreamers, to keep fifty acres of land for himself. The Puritans took over the rest of the place, renaming it Boston after the English town where John Cotton had his church. Very soon their machinations were too much for Blackstone, who declared he had not fled "the lord-bishops" to fall before "the lord-brethren." He sold forty-five acres of his land to the town for £30 and went off once more to seek the isolation that drew him originally to Boston. The land thus acquired was public property, "After which pur-pose," states an early document, "the Town laid out the place for a trayning field, which ever since and now is used for that purpose and for the feeding of Cattell."[11]

The Common remained throughout the Federal period the preserve of cattle, a barren, hilly area where cows dis-puted with townsfolk the shade of a few elms. Captain John Bonner's map of 1722 indicates only three trees on the Common with the Great Elm in the center. The Burgis map of 1728 shows a row of thirteen new trees along the Tremont Street boundary of the Common, and the 1769 revision of Bonner's map adds sixteen more trees to this group. J. G. Hale's map of 1814 shows another six trees forming a screen east of the burial ground that impinged on the south side of the Common. The most noteworthy tree was the Great Elm, from whose limbs some gruesome objects had swung; two of the Quakers executed in the seventeenth century dangled out their lives from the branches of this solitary tree whose own life ended in 1876. Practically treeless, Blackstone's forty-five acres were in such a state of neglect that Bulfinch saw little hope of developing the actual Common. The outskirts offered greater possibilities. A double row of elms, some of them the legacy of Adino Paddock, separated the Park Street houses from the Common and was known as the "little Mall." The real Mall was a wider avenue of trees running down Tremont from the foot of Park to the southern boundary of the Common at Boylston Street. The Mall was used for military drills and promenades, and its neglect as a building site until late in the Federal period reflected the maritime character of old Boston. When Bulfinch built the Tontine Crescent, he followed tradition by locating it deep in the South End, within range of the wharves and the sea.

The development of Beacon Hill by descendants of Province House families provided a new social focus for Boston. The Bulfinch houses erected on Park and Tremont streets enlarged this focus by closing the gap between Beacon Hill and the South End. Now, having linked these social centers by the creation of Park Street, Bulfinch sought to seal the supremacy of the new area by turning the boundaries of the Common into a really attractive place. His obsession to create a promenade all around the Common originated in the optimistic days of his architectural travels in Europe. In 1786 he wrote his mother from Marseilles that every French town had one or more public walks, "shaded

with trees and kept in constant repair; these walks are usually surrounded by ye public buildings of ye place, which
are an additional beauty at the same time that they serve
as a shelter from the wind."[12] Seventeen years later Bulfinch was still trying to interest his fellow Bostonians in
the idea. In 1803 he issued an appeal for private contribu-
tions to extend Charles Street along the western boundary
of the Common so as to create "a broad and spacious Street,
which would promote the health of the Inhabitants, and
the convenience of the invalids." The surviving subscription list in Bulfinch's handwriting shows that his Mount
Vernon Street patrons, Otis and Mason, each contributed
three hundred dollars, while those on Chestnut Street,
Mrs. James Swan and Benjamin Joy, gave two hundred.[13]
The money was used to construct a promenade from Beacon Street to a point along the river where the ropewalks
commenced. This improvement was in line with a general
planting of trees along the Beacon Street boundary of the
Common by the intermediary families who owned houses
or land adjoining it. Hale's map shows a continuous range
of trees on Beacon Street extending around the bend at
Charles Street and continuing as far as the ropewalks.
Eleven of these trees were uprooted in the "Great Gale" of
1815, which claimed another thirteen along the Mall.
Among these trees was the row of elms on upper Beacon
Street whose loss was said to have affected John Hancock's
widow more than any event since her husband's death.

A town resolution of 1812 directed Bulfinch to supervise
the construction of a gravel walk six feet wide supported
by timber to run the entire length of the Charles Street
boundary of the Common. The gravel walk was to provide

protection from the river and eventually support a screen of trees hiding the ropewalks that sprawled along the mud-flats. The War of 1812, following fast on this resolution, turned the town's attention from improvement of the Common to harbor defenses. But by 1815 it was obvious Boston would be spared British raids and a balance of several thousand dollars remained on hand from funds gathered for defense. The eventual disposition of these funds is described by Bell in a letter of 1816: "What remained the subscribers generously agreed, should be laid out, under the direction of our able and ingenious Police Officer, Charles Bulfinch, Esquire, in improving the Common and Mall. The result is equally creditable to his taste and to their munificence."[14] Armed at last with a decent sum of money, Bulfinch set to work improving the southern boundary of the Common appropriately known as Frog Lane. From this marshy wilderness Boylston Street was created and a wide avenue connected the Mall and the continuation of Charles Street past the ropewalks. A gravel path was laid down along Boylston Street and the towns-folk could now walk all around the Common without worrying about sinking into the mud or being washed into the river.

Freed from these perils, the wary walker on the Common still faced the winter danger of boys on coasting sleds. While the right of Boston lads to use the Common and adjoining streets for coasting was not as ancient as that of the cows, it was more vigorously defended. When the British troops pulled down the wooden coasting slide during the occupation, the youths from the Latin School demanded its replacement. The British authorities not only capitulated, they ordered soldiers to water the slide every night to make it faster. But as the Federalist capital grew in population and decorum, coasting accidents led to an ordinance in 1813 confining boys' sleds to the Common and the Mall. The "Long Coast" was a hazardous route that began in front of the Amory house, ran down the Common as far as the West Street entrance, and continued along the Mall. Smaller boys used the "little Mall," a course extending only the length of Park Street. A cry of "Lullah" cleared the track and the sleds zoomed away into the winter scene. The exhilaration did not end when tired and breathless boys deserted the frozen track and headed for home. First they stopped off at Molly Saunders for gingerbread. "Gleaner" spoke for all the boys of Bulfinch's town when he eulogized Molly Saunders: "There have doubtless been fairer faces and more graceful forms than thine, but thy *gingerbread* was matchless . . . I have shaken hands with President Monroe, and *even* with President Pierce, but what were those glorious moments compared with one cake of thy 'buttered gingerbread—price three cents.' "[15]

Across from the "Long Coast" stood the Colonnade, a row of nineteen houses on Tremont Street designed by Charles Bulfinch in 1811. Some time later five more houses were constructed south of Mason Street in the same style by the same architect. This gave rise to the mistaken notion that "Colonnade Row" contained twenty-four dwellings. The Colonnade proper began opposite the West Street gate where the careening sleds turned out of the Common and shot down the Mall. Plate 17 shows this intersection a decade before the Colonnade was constructed, when the most prominent feature was the walled garden surrounding the old mansion of Mrs. Charles Bulfinch's grandfather, Stephen Greenleaf. The land directly across from this estate was sold by the town for building speculation in 1811. The purchasers, David Greenough and James Freeman, commissioned Bulfinch to design houses of varying size but all connected by a string of iron balconies supported by stone columns which gave the range its name. Bell, whose letters to an exiled townsman in Smyrna are among the best contemporary sources, described the row as ". . . grand, uniform, and chaste, and is surpassed by nothing of the kind, as I am informed, in the United States."[16] All that remains of this range is a pair of broken pilasters and a row of windows with dressed stone lintels at the southern end near Mason Street. But the Colonnade had a precarious beginning, too. Erected in a period of economic depression just before the War of 1812, it was more a sign of the future than the Federal age. Most of the inhabitants were "new" men in Boston even by the standards of the Essex County people, who unflatteringly referred to the Colonnade as "Cape Cod Row" in allusion to the South rather than North Shore origin of the majority of houseowners.[17]

Although the Colonnade owners were generally men of the next age who made their place in industry and had little connection with royalist or revolutionary Boston, two of them were active in the political squabbles of the Federalist capital: John Trecothic Austin at Number 5 and John Lowell at Number 19. Austin, a relative of Bulfinch, was indirectly involved in Federal Boston's only political murder. So was his neighbor Lowell, the most effective propagandist in the ranks of the Federalists. Under the ironical signature "a Boston Rebel," Lowell attacked Republicans without mercy until his premature retirement to a Roxbury estate and the more tranquilizing subject of agriculture. For like his fellow Essex Juntoites George Cabot, Stephen Higginson, and Theophilus Parsons, Lowell suffered from a lassitude of will or physical strength. And in each case the prescribed regimen was country seclusion. Not that there was anything Cincinnatus-like about these hypochondriacal statesmen from Essex County, most of whom escaped to a life they denied their hero General Washington. None of them were soldiers in the Revolution. The Republicans on the other hand were a fighting lot. Sometimes they were too much given to fighting, as in the case of Austin's young brother Charles, who was killed when he attacked a Federalist lawyer, Thomas Selfridge, with a walking stick on State Street.

The sensational trial of Selfridge for the murder of Charles Austin grew out of a comic situation on the Fourth of July, 1806. The day was observed with separate celebrations by the warring factions. The Federalists met in Faneuil Hall, which Bulfinch recently enlarged to double its original size; the Republicans marched in a procession from the State House to Copp's Hill, where they gathered under a huge tent. Benjamin Austin, father of Charles, was in charge of the festivities whose spirit fluttered in three words from a banner on top of the tent: "Hilarity, Philanthropy, Fraternity." Austin was a quarrelsome figure in this period, having earlier been involved in a dispute with John Derby that was beyond even the mediating talents of Charles Bulfinch. On the occasion in question, he arranged for the catering with the Jefferson Tavern on Salem Street, the current headquarters of the Republican party. Everything might have gone well in the big tent on Copp's Hill if the visiting Tunisian ambassador had not been invited to march in the parade. The ambassador and his retinue, in Moslem garb and flowing beards, caused near riots all along the way. Hundreds of spectators joined the marchers to stare at the exotic Easterners, and, when the parade terminated before the tent with its tempting banner, everyone, invited or not, poured in. The food supply swiftly vanished while the receipts fell hopelessly in arrears. The caterer held Austin responsible and hired Selfridge to enforce payment. Austin on the other hand accused Selfridge of initiating the lawsuit to embarrass him politically. Inevitably angry words followed. Austin's claim was false, and while he did acknowledge this, his apology was insufficient to appease Selfridge, who attacked Austin in the Federalist *Gazette* as a "coward, liar, and scoundrel." Austin replied in kind in the Republican paper, the *Chronicle*, and the stage was set for tragedy. That so trifling an incident should end in disaster was expressive both of the dizzy political feeling of the time and the growing despair of the Federalists in the face of continued Republican gains.

Even so, the situation should have remained at the routine level of swapping insults in rival newspapers. Unfortunately, Austin's eighteen-year-old son, a student at Harvard College, took up his father's defense too dramatically. Exactly one month after the July Fourth celebrations, Charles Austin came into Boston with a friend and purchased a stout cane with the obvious intention of administering a beating to Selfridge. When the two met on State Street, young Austin approached Selfridge and began striking him on the head with his cane, whereupon Selfridge drew his pistol and fired point blank at Austin. "The blows grew weaker," a witness reported, "and Austin sank dying on the pavement."[18] Selfridge was tried for manslaughter in a trial that could not possibly escape the aura of politics. He was defended by the two Federalist lawyers who lived in the Amory house, Dexter and Gore, and prosecuted by the future Republican governor and Bulfinch patron James Sullivan. Contemporaries agree Selfridge was justified in his act of defense but no one doubted that the overwhelming Federalist sentiments of the jury were more persuasive than the eloquence of Dexter and Gore.

The Colonnade was the last important group of houses Bulfinch designed around the periphery of the Common and, along with Park Street, represented the final results of his ambitions for Boston. The buildings ringing the Common were excellent. The town's principal public edifice, the State House, crowned the angle sweeping west along the tree-lined Common to the Charles River and south past the houses of Park and Tremont streets. "The finest part of the city beyond comparison," wrote Ali Bey ibn Othman in 1817, "is the Mall and the Common." This long-mysterious traveler has turned out to be the pseudonym of Samuel Lorenzo Knapp of Newburyport, who sat in the Massachusetts General Court from 1812 to 1816. But whatever its origin, Moslem or Christian, Ali Bey's description of Bulfinch's work remains the best contemporary evidence:[19]

This, tout ensemble, is a most charming view—the solemn range of trees with their dark foliage—the green field of grass swelling before the eye—the distinct water prospect opening a view of

[183]

the surrounding country—all these natural beauties with the architectural simplicity of the buildings . . . combine to render this one of the finest scenes in the world—at least I have seen nothing surpassing it in all my travels.

Bulfinch and his patrons were right in transforming this wilderness into the most attractive part of Boston. The public nature of the Common assured a perpetually open prospect; no one then dreamed the Charles River would ever do less than extend the view out across water to quiet and remote hills. The area he developed around the Common was a place in which Bulfinch could walk with tremendous pride. It attained an almost perfect state in the closing years of Federalism when the War of 1812 brought building and land speculation to a standstill. There were just enough Bulfinch houses encircling the Common to suggest the urban future, just enough neglected land to retain the rural past.

I X

FROM TOWN TO CITY

THE DEVELOPMENT of Beacon Hill and Park Street tore the town's social core away from the South and West Ends. At the same time these older areas were slowly declining as a result of the filling in of their water boundaries. Thus most of colonial Boston's contours vanished in the Federal period, even though the final blighting effects of the reclamation projects begun in Bulfinch's time came decades later. A spectacular instance was the filling in of the Mill Pond, created from the original North Cove in the first years of Puritan rule by throwing a dam across the marshes westward from Copp's Hill. By the time the Bulfinch family settled in nearby Bowdoin Square early in the eighteenth century, a number of mills churned the waters draining from the pond into the harbor through Mill Creek. Mill Creek, which then flowed southward across town under an arch at Hanover and a drawbridge at Ann Street, formed the boundary between the crowded North End and the brighter West End. The latter area, lying low along the rim of the pond with the clicking windmill on Copp's Hill in the background, retained until 1807 the appearance of a placid Dutch landscape.

The quiet scene was doomed when the idea got abroad that the pond should be filled in and used for building lots. Several groups incorporated themselves into rival companies to contest the ownership of the Mill Pond, and between 1804 and 1807 numerous town meetings and committees attempted to settle the conflicting claims. Finally a contract was completed with the proprietors of the Mill Pond Corporation, who guaranteed to fill in the pond within twenty years and give the town one-eighth of the reclaimed land. Charles Bulfinch and his Beacon Hill patron Harrison Gray Otis were involved in this scheme, Otis as chief proprietor and Bulfinch as architect. The design submitted was an equilateral triangle with the apex at Mill Creek and the base along the old dam. Into the apex of the triangle Bulfinch introduced two smaller ones which he hoped to develop as open market areas with tree-lined borders. Mill Creek was extended as a canal with streets drawn parallel to it. The design was carried out almost to the letter, a credit both to the author's skill and the sensibility of the proprietors. But planning this project was the least of Bulfinch's worries. The difficulties involved in its execution—property claims and counterclaims, bridges, underground canals, streets, sewers, and contractual disputes—demanded endless attention from the man who was architect as well as head of the selectmen to whom all grievances flowed.[1]

The Mill Pond remained throughout Bulfinch's period a shambles of "oyster shells, rubbish and street sweepings, as well as Beacon Hill gravel." Yet the proprietors promised only the latter would be used in filling in the pond. When first proposing the scheme the corporation had six of

Boston's leading physicians, including future Park Street residents John Warren and John Jeffries, attest to the healthy aspect of the project, provided pure earth or gravel was used for reclamation. But as time went by everything was thrown into the Mill Pond, including the summit of Beacon Hill. The decapitation of Trimountain's highest dome began back in 1795 when construction of the new State House took a large piece of the summit. As interest in Beacon Hill earth for land-fill mounted, more and more of the crest was eaten away. The end came in 1811 when the town sold six square rods of land on the summit, and consequently the cone-shaped dome of Beacon Hill was shorn. Mrs. Thomas Bulfinch, watching the destruction from the family homestead in Bowdoin Square, summed up the spirit of the leveling project in a letter to her exiled brother in England: "Old Beacon hill is taking down to fill up the Mill pond; as every foot of ground has become so valuable the owners of the Hill, who are the heirs of Governor Hancock, did not incline to lose the opportunity of making it useful, and have preferred interest to elegance, not a very new thing."[2]

Other thoughtful Bostonians watched the obliteration of Beacon Hill with the same sadness. One of them, Shubael Bell, wrote to his loyalist friend in far off Smyrna: "So much of this once elevated spot has been carried into the sea that the tops of the chimnies are not now so high, as the sod were over which, in your youthful days, you strolled to enjoy the richness of the surrounding scenery. Should you again visit this place, you would look in vain for that commanding eminence, Beacon Hill, once the pride of Bostonians."[3] And fifty years later "Gleaner," another chroni-

cler of old Boston, blasts the town's mean attitude in selling the top of Beacon Hill: "I regret that I cannot consigne
to deserved infamy the names of those who so disgracefully
turned an official penny by selling it. Such persons would
sell a family grave."[4] But this was only the beginning.
When Federalist Boston itself disappeared in 1817 none of
the three peaks of Trimountain would have been recogniz-
able to those who left in the evacuation of 1776.

Just as the reclamation of the Mill Pond foreshadowed
the social decline of the West End, the conversion of the
Town Cove into dry land augured the deterioration of
the garden areas of the South End. At the beginning of the
Federal period Town Cove formed a great arc extending
southward to the Battery below Fort Hill. Fort Hill, then
open country much used for promenading, stood as the eastern boundary of a chain of country houses beginning at the
old Greenleaf estate on the Common and continuing down
Summer and High streets to the sea. One of these estates
belonged to Joseph Barrell until Bulfinich purchased it for
the site of the Tontine Crescent and Franklin Place. A new
street, Arch, was then created to run from Summer
through the archway in the Crescent. Beyond this junc-
tion Summer Street merged with High in a delightful open
area dominated by the New South Church, an octagonal
structure of hammered granite completed from Bulfinch's
design in 1814.

High Street rambled away at this point to the sea. But
first it intersected Pearl and Oliver streets, the setting for
a number of important Federal mansions. One of these, the
house of Josiah Quincy, was characteristic of the miniature

estates of the South End where, as late as 1815, "there was a pasture of two acres in Summer Street and the tinkling of cow bells was by no means an unusual sound there."[5] Oliver Street ended at the crest of Fort Hill, where a wide view attracted strollers in fair weather. But this open space was curtailed when a circle of houses called Washington Place was constructed on the summit.[6] At the same time, the sleepy scene along the waterfront below, untouched since colonial days, was completely changed when Bulfinch created Front, Broad, and India streets.

Front Street was laid out in 1804 as the first step in the reclamation of nine acres of tidal land south of Beach and east of Orange streets. Orange, later Washington Street, was the last section of the many-named highroad to the Neck. Construction on Front Street was restricted to buildings set back at least ten feet from the sidewalk—the first instance of public interest in the creation of symmetrical avenues such as Bulfinch introduced a decade earlier in the Franklin Place project. Front Street was conceived in the flush period preceding Jefferson's embargo, and its planners seemed justified in their expectation of extending the thoroughfare across the Neck parallel with Washington Street. Hale's map of 1814 shows how Bulfinch laid out this area in uniform streets with a focus at the tree-lined oval of Columbia Square. This focal point (present-day Blackstone and Franklin squares) was named for the ship *Columbia*, whose epochal voyage was partly planned and financed by the Bulfinch family. The creation of Columbia Square was the architect's further attempt to endow the New England capital with the splendors of Georgian town planning. But like the earlier Tontine Crescent it was a financial failure; when the Federal period closed hardly a dozen house-owners had been attracted to the area.

Front Street ended at the narrowest portion of the Neck where the South Boston Bridge crossed the channel to Dorchester. The third span constructed since the Revolution, it represented an unsuccessful attempt to push the town limits southward. Two previous bridges, the Charles River and the West Boston, extended into areas settled as early as the capital itself. Built to relieve the geographical isolation of Boston, they made possible the movement of goods and produce in and out of town without reliance upon boats. The Charles River Bridge Company was financed through a group headed by John Hancock and empowered to collect tolls for forty years on condition it compensated Harvard College for the loss of the ferry between Boston and Charlestown. When completed in 1786, the bridge was the most important piece of engineering in the new nation. It was opened on the eleventh anniversary of the Battle of Bunker Hill in an elaborate ceremony that included a banquet at which, appropriately, thirteen toasts were downed. Bulfinch was in Europe at the time, but he wrote his father from London expressing the hope it would still be standing when he returned, "as I should like much to see it, but I am not sure whether I would venture to pass over it."[7]

Actually the bridge proved much safer than its rival, the West Boston Bridge, in the construction of which Bulfinch played a major role. He was one of the gentlemen gathered at the Bunch of Grapes tavern in January 1792 to plan a bridge between Cambridge and West Boston; he also served as one of the twelve directors who received a charter to erect the wooden span across the Charles River at the site of the present Longfellow Bridge. It is not certain whether Bulfinch aided in the design, but he was responsible for contracting the wood and other materials used in construction. The West Boston Bridge opened in 1793 with a length twice that of its Charlestown counterpart. Though the corporation had an efficient lobby and succeeded in diverting traffic by judicious road construction, the bridge proved an unfavorable financial enterprise. By 1797 extensive repairs were needed. Despite newspaper praise for "the elegance of the workmanship," the entire understructure of pine planks had to be renewed because of the destructive boring of a marine worm known as the toredo. The bridge proved a boon to the future of Boston but a mixed blessing to the West End. Its Boston approach began at Bowdoin Square in front of the Bulfinch homestead and ran along Cambridge Street, making that tree-shaded thoroughfare the main artery of travel to and from Cambridge. This disturbed the tranquility of the region and hastened the filling in of the Mill Pond, which in turn reduced the social distinction of the West End.[8]

Hardly had the ravages of the toredo been repaired when a long line of mourners advanced across the West Boston Bridge to the solemn tolling of all the bells in Boston and the surrounding countryside. The day was January 9, 1800, when Massachusetts mourned the passing of George Washington. The news reached Boston on Christmas Eve, ten days after the General's death at Mount Vernon. Newspapers at once put extras, heavily bordered in black, on the streets. The editor of the Federalist mouthpiece informed his readers Washington died as he lived: in uncomplaining pain. As the year of a presidential election was only days away, the *Centinel* could not resist a partisan hint that some of the pain sustained by the General was caused by Republican machinations. But both parties turned out in accordance with the program of public mourning prepared by Charles Bulfinch. On the appointed day the townsfolk assembled at noon in front of the State House, where their representatives then moved in a body to the Old South Meetinghouse for the eulogy delivered by George Minot. The prescribed ornaments of mourning were black arm bands for the men and similar ribbons for the women. The services at Old South concluded with an ode set to music by Oliver Holden, who composed the hymn welcoming Washington to Boston eleven years before.[9]

Two other bridges were built before the close of Bulfinch's administration, the South Boston and the Craigie or Canal span. The former touched off a bitter controversy that began with the seemingly innocent petition to the selectmen late in 1803 calling for the annexation of Dorchester Neck. As this would add 560 acres to the town tax rolls, the selectmen were naturally favorable to the plan. But suddenly it became known that all ten families then inhabiting what is now South Boston had sold their land to "a gentleman of great fortune from the West Indies" who wanted to settle there "in order to inhale the air of this more salubrious climate, and renovate a constitution which had long languished under the oppressive heat of a tropical sun." The West Indian gentleman turned out to be a combine of real estate speculators including Bulfinch's Beacon Hill patrons Harrison Gray Otis and Jonathan Mason. Otis recalled the petition at a noisy town meeting and wisely submitted the plan to the less emotional General Court, which approved it in March 1804. According to one of the lampoons of the period, approval was hastened by the presentation of "an elegant drawing of an Arch Bridge . . . to the admiring eyes of the credulous." Circumstances suggest this was the work of Bulfinch and probably followed John Soane's design for Blackfriars in London.[10]

In spite of all their efforts, the proprietors of the South Boston Corporation failed to attract settlers to the lonely and desolate Dorchester Neck. The census of 1810 showed only about 350 inhabitants. But while the townsfolk could not be lured to this area as residents, they flocked to the bridge leading to the neglected region. The South Boston Bridge offered the widest view of the town with docks and wharves, roofs and steeples, and hills and trees swinging around the water in a great half circle. The bridge immediately became one of Boston's principal promenades. Bulfinch's brother-in-law Joseph Coolidge strolled there every day from the old Bulfinch mansion in Bowdoin Square. And Josiah Quincy evoked an unsuspected Regency aspect of the Federalist capital when he wrote: "It was on this bridge I first saw the beautiful Emily Marshall . . . walking with the well-known dandy Beau Watson."[11] It was just as well South Boston continued as a quiet, deserted place demanding little commercial traffic; the Bostonians could roam the bridge and approaches without worrying about being run down by carts and wagons. For this reason the bridge became a rendezvous for lovers and was sympathetically known as the "Bridge of Sighs." Like so many of the projects begun during Bulfinch's administration, the development of Dorchester Neck prepared ground for the growth in population and building in the next age of manufacturing.

Following these unsuccessful attempts to push the town's development toward Dorchester and Roxbury, the coterie of speculators led by Harrison Gray Otis limited itself to the reclamation of that part of the Town Cove lying immediately south of Long Wharf: the Broad and India streets project began in 1803 from a plan apparently by Bulfinch.[12] Broad Street originally ran only from State to Battery March, the old division between Fort Hill and the water. India Street was laid out parallel to Broad but jutted northeastward to meet the newly created India Wharf. Battery March was deprived of its pre-Revolutionary name and designated a continuation of Broad Street. Here, facing the west end of India Wharf, was built a row of ten brick stores "according to a plan drawn by Charles Bulfinch. . . . The front of the store to be ornamented with a row of Marble ribbon."[13] Broad Street was later extended to India Wharf, also designed by Bulfinch. Half of India Wharf survived until 1962, an attenuated reminder of the Neo-classical style Bulfinch brought to his native town at a time when, as one of his contemporaries put it, commercial architecture could be both "extensive and elegant." Despite its extreme simplicity, India Wharf was closer in spirit to the Tontine Crescent than any other known Bulfinch building.[14]

Ironically, India Wharf was finished just in time for the Embargo Act. During the period of enforcement—December 1807 to March 1809—this legislation made the newly created district of Broad and India streets superfluous. The embargo was condemned at town meetings in a manner unmatched since pre-Revolutionary times, when Faneuil Hall won immortalization as the "cradle of liberty." It was fortunate Bulfinch redesigned and enlarged the hall two years before the embargo or only half the mob meeting there could have been accommodated. The original structure, a gift from Peter Faneuil, who died a few months after the building was completed in 1743 from a design by John Smibert, contained a hall accommodating about one thousand people with an open market on the ground floor. Twenty years after construction, a fire broke out in Dock Square on a winter night and roared across the street to consume the entire interior. All that remained of Smibert's building were several walls which were used when the town rebuilt the hall on the same scale. This reconstructed building was the one that figured in the saga of Revolutionary Boston.

In Bulfinch's time the inadequacy of Faneuil Hall for town meetings was notorious. And Old South Church was so constantly used as a substitute that its proprietors finally balked completely. The town then turned to her architect-administrator, who reconstructed Faneuil Hall in 1805 by doubling the width, adding a third story, and relocating the cupola at the Dock Square end of the building (*Pate 22*). Bulfinch's modest intentions are set forth in the "Description of the manner in which the Market House & Hall are to be built and finished . . . as delineated on the several drawings by Mr. Bulfinch," in which the architect records his desire "to conform with the plan

of elevation excepting the Piazza."[15] Accordingly he preserved the colonial exterior by using the original Doric
order in the first and second stories, restricting a personal
preference for the Ionic to the newly created third story.
But Bulfinch's modesty in retaining the original form of
Faneuil Hall did not prevent him from some characteristic
flourishes, such as replacing the round-headed windows on
the long façades of the third story with flat ones topped by
lunettes. This motif was repeated in the end pediments,
where framed lunettes are balanced by bull's-eye windows similar to those in the new roof.[16] As the architect's
drawing reproduced in *Plate 23* shows, Bulfinch used more
originality in the interior, where he took the opportunity
to introduce such Neo-classical refinements as swag panels, lunettes, and rondelles. The lower floor remained a
market with stalls and cellars; the second story contained
the public hall, doubled in size and greatly improved for
acoustics. Above this a huge room was constructed to accommodate the various military corps of the town. Faneuil
Hall continued to be used for the offices of the selectmen,
and on its icy steps one morning in 1813 Bulfinch slipped
and fractured his leg. He was confined to his house for
three months, suffering permanent lameness as a result of
the accident. This was almost the only time in two decades
Bulfinch did not go regularly to his small office in Faneuil
Hall from which he designed and administered Federal
Boston.

Although often opposed by the political and commercial
leaders of his town, Bulfinch was not without allies in the
struggle to create a modern city. Generally he was assisted
by Harrison Gray Otis and Uriah Cotting. Of the two, Cot-

ting was closer to Bulfinch in being primarily a builder. And like his architect colleague, Cotting paid the price of civic vision with business failure. But when solvent, he was irrepressible. His most important project, the Boston and Roxbury Milling Corporation, absolutely transformed the colonial town. The leveling of two of Trimountain's peaks and the filling in of the Mill Pond and parts of the Town Cove had already partially obliterated the outlines of the old Puritan capital. But the Boston and Roxbury Mill Corporation began a complete metamorphosis when it stretched a finger across the Charles River from the foot of the Common to Sewall's Point in Brookline. It was only a matter of time before the finger became a solid fist and there was no water left at all between Beacon Street and Roxbury. The Mill Corporation thrust another finger toward Dorchester Neck and doomed South Bay and eventually Back Bay as well.

This vast project, commenced in 1813, was part of a scheme to utilize the water surrounding Boston for manufacturing purposes. The first phase called for a dam extending westward from a point at Beacon and Charles streets and another south from Boston to the isolated shores of Dorchester Neck, recently renamed South Boston. The first dam was planned to carry a turnpike and provide a direct route to Brookline; the second would confine the tide of South Boston Bay and give access to the foundering real estate development on Dorchester peninsula. Boston Neck, lying between these two bodies of water, was to be interspersed with canals and provide the site for a string of whirling mills. It was a stupendous enterprise and barely begun when Cotting died in 1819.

Everyone, however, was not pleased by the prospect of a dam stretching across the Charles River to Brookline, especially as Cotting's original scheme for draining water off the South Boston Bay into the Charles was reversed. One outraged citizen wrote in the *Daily Advertiser* of June 10, 1814: "What think you of converting the beautiful sheet of water which skirts the Common into an empty mud-basin, reeking with filth, abhorrent to the smell, and distasteful to the eye? By every god of sea, lake, or fountain, it is incredible!" Nonetheless the project went slowly forward and was completed under the direction of Loammi Baldwin, Jr.

One of Cotting's dramatic acts involved the partial construction of a mansion on Beacon Hill, begun probably from Bulfinch's design in 1806. This house started to occupy the corner directly opposite the dwelling of John Phillips at Beacon and Walnut streets. By the time the first floor was completed, Cotting lost much of his money and unfalteringly demolished his half-finished mansion. The house remains a mystery; no plans or drawings have been discovered and contemporary references tell only that it was constructed of stone and unsurpassed in Boston for "splendor and elegance." A double house was erected on its foundations in 1816, one of whose halls is described in the reminiscences of Mary Peabody as "quite open to the roof, with circular galleries running around the three stories." The same source adds that the house was finally taken down because the glass roof made it impossible to heat.[17]

Uriah Cotting not only directed the Mill Corporation that pushed Boston's geography into undreamed-of regions, he was responsible for conspicuous changes in the heart of the old town itself. Cotting was associated with Bulfinch, Otis, Francis Cabot Lowell, Henry Jackson, and others in the development of India and Broad streets and India Wharf; he also spearheaded the construction of another important row of stores and docks, Central Wharf in 1816, which extended into the harbor from India Street equidistant between India and Long wharves. Fifty-four stores were strung down the middle of the wharf with a chapel for seafarers wedged into the center. The scars of the War of 1812 were still livid and Massachusetts was faltering between her maritime past and her manufacturing future, but Cotting had whole reservoirs of faith in Boston. The following year he completed another market area within the shadow of Faneuil Hall. Two streets, Market and Brattle, were extended and improved of Cornhill. The granite and brick stores lining the two thoroughfares became the center for femal shoppers as well as a new, most un-Bostonian type: "those loungers who have little to do but gaze." This observation comes from Shubael Bell, the hard-working mechanic and senior warden of Christ Church who spent his spare time earning something extra as turnkey in Bulfinch's new town jail on Court Street.[18]

At the same time reclamation projects were altering Boston's "island" character, Bulfinch was transforming State Street from an avenue of brick-faced shops into an imposing thoroughfare with granite banks and insurance houses. State Street had been the town's main artery in both Puritan and royalist days; in Bulfinch's period it became the symbol of Federalist power and the target of

Republican attack in the Commonwealth and the nation at large. With few exceptions, the financial houses Bulfinch designed there were controlled by the Essex Junto and represented an important source of that group's stranglehold on the economic and political life of eastern Massachusetts. When the two Adams presidents wrote of their running battles with "State Street," they referred to their squabbles with the Essex leaders who controlled the banks as well as the party. Unvaryingly the names of these leaders appeared among the directors of the banks Bulfinch designed. The Federalist leaders consciously restricted shareholders to men of their political party and tried by every means to frustrate their rivals' efforts to incorporate banking institutions. The Republicans naturally resented the Federalist financial monopoly and finally established themselves on State Street in 1811. The first president of the Republican bank (the State Bank) was the respectable shipowner William Gray, who by this time lived in the mansion Bulfinch originally designed for the late Governor Sullivan on Summer Street. Also right in the midst of the Federalist phalanx on State Street was a former hotbed of Republicanism—the old Apthorp mansion inhabited by Bulfinch's relative Perez Morton—now remodeled for the proper party's Union Bank. This renovation was publicized in the *Columbian Centinel* of August 3, 1799: "The Union Bank House is undergoing such useful and ornamental repairs, as will add much to the beauty of State Street." Bulfinch's reconstruction of a family mansion for the recently incorporated Union Bank marked the second phase in an important cycle of institutional building in Boston that began back in 1784, when his old mentor and early collaborator, Thomas Dawes, re-modeled a manufactory on the east side of Tremont Street opposite the Granary Burying Ground for the newly chartered Massachusetts Bank. Twenty-five years later, when that institution moved with the fashion to State Street, Bulfinch designed the stone-faced brick building occupied by the Massachusetts Bank until 1838.

Further down State Street stood the Boston branch of the Bank of the United States (*Plate 18*), which Bulfinch designed in 1798 and appropriately faced with Philadelphia brick. It is interesting as the only one of his many commercial structures for which a detailed record survives. Asher Benjamin reproduced Raynerd's elevation of the façade along with a section and plans in the 1806 edition of *The American Builder's Companion*. Benjamin reports the balustrade and cornice of Bath stone and the rest of the ornaments of marble; his plan shows an interior comprising a large banking room with a gallery and an arched vault. Benjamin was an appreciative follower of Bulfinch and generously designated the United States Bank "the neatest public building in the state."[19] The enormous eagle surmounting the balustrade was used by Solomon Willard as the model of one he carved twelve years later for the Boston Custom House. When Bulfinch's bank was taken down in 1824, the eagle was removed to Faneuil Hall and placed over the clock in the great assembly room.

The Essex group also controlled the three insurance companies housed in Bulfinch buildings side by side with the banks. The oldest of these, the Boston Marine, originally shared quarters with the Union Bank before moving into a new Bulfinch building in 1810. The architect earlier designed a brick structure for the Suffolk Insurance Company and a stone building for the New England Marine. Little fire or life insurance was written on State Street prior to the War of 1812, though some discerning owners of Bulfinch houses covered them as soon as completed. The first fire insurance company in Boston, the Massachusetts Mutual, insured the mansion the architect designed for Joseph Coolidge, Sr., in Bowdoin Square at the low rate of thirty-five cents per hundred dollars because it was constructed of brick. Most property owners in Bulfinch's time relied upon the ancient custom of a public appeal when their homes or places of business burned down. In such cases a subscription paper was circulated about town calling attention to the calamity and asking for assistance on the grounds that anyone might in the future suffer a similar fate. This seemingly unpredictable method actually worked; the public always responded liberally.[20]

Despite the financial and commercial projects carried out by Charles Bulfinch, a colonial flavor hung on in the town's streets, which were not yet maintained by a system of public cleaning. Street sweeping was still a private matter carried out by a battery of sweepers constantly at war with each other. Their bickering, which doubtless took violent form in the streets, was conducted through the press in a sedate manner. One sweeper characterized himself as having grown old in the service of the town and thanked his patrons for their patience while he was "under the influence of a distressing and debilitating disease." Presumably some streets went unswept during the length of this illness. Another warned his customers to beware of "several worthless characters jealous of his success" who were attempting to take over his domain.[21] Although sweeping was a private concern, the problem of keeping the streets cleared in the vicinity of the market places was a responsibility of the town's police force and a heavy weight on Bulfinch's time. Town ordinances prohibiting the choking of streets by carts, wagons, or sleds used to convey produce into Boston were sternly enforced. Also restrictive were the measures to prevent persons from setting up temporary stalls to display and sell wares other than in the designated markets. One reason was to protect people who rented space in two new marketing halls, Boylston and Parkman, completed from Bulfinch plans in 1810. Aside from the usual marketing stalls and offices, Boylston Hall contained a huge room that was used as headquarters for the Handel and Haydn Society, an organization whose success with an oratorio sung in King's Chapel in February 1815 to celebrate the Peace of Ghent brought about Boston's first permanent musical society.[22]

The farmers who brought their produce into Boston favored two lodging houses in the marketing region of Faneuil Hall—the Dock Square and Captain Palmer's. Captain Palmer's, originally the pre-Revolutionary mansion of the Codman family on Ann Street, was headquarters for the Haverhill stage and enjoyed the largest reputation among country men. More affluent businessmen, visitors, politicians, and dignitaries shied away from this rural type of inn with its too pervading odor of stage and cart horse. The luckier ones found shelter with Mrs. Carter or, after 1809, in America's first hotel, the Exchange Coffee House. This building, covering an acre of ground on Congress and State streets, was a seven-story structure of monumental disproportion. Although Bulfinch is usually given as the architect, the clumsy design belies such a choice. Yet the association is understandable; the Exchange Coffee House was the successor to a scheme he presented in September 1796 "for building a large and elegant Public Hotel, for the accommodation of strangers."[23] Having just suffered the business failure in Franklin Place, Bulfinch could not take a part in this project. The earliest published account of the building correctly assigns it to Asher Benjamin. Like Bulfinch's tontine venture, the Exchange Coffee House was a financial disaster and no attempt was made to rebuild the structure when it was destroyed by fire nine years after completion. The hotel had the best public rooms in Boston and, during its short life, superseded Faneuil Hall as the place for official celebrations and banquets. It was almost the only new building in the Federalist capital in which important visitors were welcomed by Bulfinch, as acting head of the town government, that was not designed by the chief selectman.[24]

The lengthening catalogue of new buildings in the South and West Ends helped stamp upon Boston the architectural style that came to be called Federal. As all were the work of Charles Bulfinch, or the school of Bulfinch, the town acquired a distinctive character completely absent from modern Boston. Visitors in this period marvelled at the islands of good taste created amid the hodgepodge of the old town's architecture. Elias Boudinot, who revisited Boston in the summer of 1809 after more than thirty years' absence, voiced this wonder: "I am really astonished at the appearance of Wealth magnificence & taste, thro'out the Town. Every dwelling House, Store &

Out House have an appearance of neatness or elegance, except in the old Streets, where many of the original buildings yet remain. The trading part of the Town, discovers the appearance of immense business and great wealth."[25] The projects begun in this period were not only architecturally all of a piece, they were so sophisticated by colonial standards as to seem the final word in civic and commercial development. At least Bulfinch thought so. When asked, at the end of the era, whether he had trained any of his sons as architects, he answered simply that he didn't think there was much left to do.[26]

X

ARTS AND SCIENCES

CHARLES BULFINCH MADE his last inspection tour of the town's schools late in 1816. On this occasion, a youth in the Latin School named Ralph Waldo Emerson recited a poem entitled "Eloquence." But eloquence was not the quality Emerson later assigned to the intellectual and artistic life of Bulfinch's Boston. "From 1790 to 1820," he wrote, "there was not a book, a speech, a conversation, or a thought in the State."[1] A harsh condemnation not absolutely true, it represented, nonetheless, the only judgment the next and more articulate generation could pass upon its predecessor. Excepting architecture, the Federalist stronghold was not a place of art and learning. Boston remained hostile to the movement developing elsewhere toward a national character and literature; her half-hearted effort in a cultural direction, like everything else in the town, was propelled from England. The national movement was doubly suspect in Boston. Not only was it spearheaded by Jeffersonians like Philip Freneau and Joel Barlow, but saturated with ideas of the perfectability of men totally alien to the Essex County hierarchy with its beliefs in the inequality of man. One of the Federalist party's few local poets, the lawyer Thomas Fessenden, was given the task of expressing the town's reigning spirit:[2]

> Next, every man throughout the nation
> Must be contented with his station,
> Nor think to cut a figure greater
> Than was design'd for him by nature.
>
> . . .
>
> The greatest number's greatest good
> Should, doubtless, ever be pursu'd;
> But that consists, *sans* disputation,
> In order and subordination.

The classical concept of order in nature was essential to the Bostonian's sense of society and politics. To him the romanticism of Rousseau and Madam de Staël was inexplicable. Even when the romanticists were English, like Coleridge and Byron, or became anti-French, like Wordsworth, the Federalists would have none of them. The romantic world of the Boston merchant lay far off along the trade routes of the globe; there was enough adventure and anarchy in the cold waters of the Northwest or in the hot seas of India and Africa without creating it in the home port. In his lights, the evil force in the world was France. Newton restored God to the scheme of things and the Federalists certainly would not join the Jacobins in disrupting the equilibrium. Newtonian order in Boston meant the *status quo* produced by the loyalist's forfeiture of power in 1776. That was enough of a change; democracy of the Republican brand would spoil everything. As the heirs of Cotton Mather, and of Calvin, the Federalists were rigidly conservative. Not that all their leaders were especially devoted to the old theology to which they gave lip service.

The alliance between merchant and lawyer on the one
hand and clergy on the other was political. The ministry
was marvelous in drumming up hatred against France
which was quickly transferred to hatred of Jefferson and
the Republicans.

The captivity of the clergy to the Federalist political
machine is seen in the preponderance of secular writing
during this period as against the former invincibility of
theological literature. The newspapers were the arena of
literary struggle. Most of the press reflected Federalist
sentiment, with the *Columbian Centinel* the especial
mouthpiece of the ruling party. Its editor, Benjamin Russell, was a tireless attendant to the true cause. Yet he was
a pale shadow compared to Fisher Ames, whose tirades
appeared in the *Palladium*. Ames expounded a severe Federalist view of history and politics which he admitted was
shared by less than five hundred people. But these comprised the town's economic, political, and religious leaders, and they generally succeeded in impressing their view
on the rest of the population. Ames was transfixed by fear
of France. "We listen," he warned the innocent, essentially well-behaved Bostonians of Bulfinch's time, "to the
clank of chains, and overhear the whispers of assassins.
We mark the barbarious dissonance of mingled rage and
triumph in the yell of an infuriated mob; we see the dis-
mal glare of their burnings, and scent the loathsome
steam of human victims offered in sacrifice."[3] Less neu-
rotic was Thomas Paine, the young founder of the *Federal
Orrery*, whose satires on the Jeffersonian opposition caused
him to be physically assaulted in State Street. But the Republicans waged battle in the press as well as in the street.

Their most blatant mouthpieces were the *Gazette* and the *Constitutional Telegram*. Relatively respectable was the *Chronicle*, in whose pages James Sullivan fired away at Fisher Ames.[4]

Although France was the perennial scapegoat of Federalists, the French language was considered a desirable element in the education of females. In one number of the *Columbian Centinel* in April 1809, no less than three different "professors" advertised classes in French. The most distinguished of the French teachers was the future Louis Phillipe, who was living in Boston at this time under the title of the Duc de Chartres. The newspapers also carried advertisements for French dictionaries and the works of French writers—those who predated the Revolution of course. But the old method of obtaining a reading knowledge of a foreign language through a personal translation of the New Testament was still much favored. Nathaniel Bowditch followed this course so faithfully he ended up with twenty-five copies of the New Testament translated into foreign languages. The teaching of French survived Federalist hatred of France because it was an ingrained part of the upper-class English concept of a lady's education. No such tolerance existed in the case of German. When Madame de Staël's *De l'Allemagne* appeared in translation after 1814, George Ticknor was so enthralled by her picture of Germany that he sought to learn that country's language. His project was delayed by the discovery that there was not a single book in German to be had in all of Boston or Cambridge.[5]

To those able to buy books, literature offered the widest consolation in a society where, except for church and politics, there were few outside activities. For the educated and well-to-do, reading was the undisputed pastime. One had to be well-to-do because books, even those printed in Boston, were expensive. George Ticknor's wife tells how her father, the Federalist merchant Samuel Eliot, ordered boxes of books annually from London and treasured them so that "to drop a nicely bound one troubled him almost as if it had sensation."[6] Books by Pope, Addison, Goldsmith, Richardson, Swift, as well as works on theology, science, and travel most frequently made the six weeks' journey between England and Boston. Much slower to arrive were the romantic writers already read and discussed in New York and Philadelphia. Boston booksellers were prodigious advertisers and often took over half the front page of the local newspapers. After 1800 an increasing number of notices of architectural books appeared in the press, an indication of the interest stimulated by the building projects of Charles Bulfinch. There was also a growing market for books on hot-house gardening, which seems to have been one of the few novelties taken up by Federalist gentlemen.

Sydney Smith's unfriendly remark, "Who reads an American book?", was valid in Boston, except when it came to a particularly sentimental tale. Susanna Haswell Rowson was just such an exception. Although not a native, she had a long and interesting Boston connection, arriving in the capital town in 1769 at the age of eight with her father, an officer in the British navy. Even as a child Susanna Rowson was exceptional—James Otis fondly called her "my little scholar." But he failed in his attempts to win her to the patriot side. Although her family did not leave in the loyalist exodus of '76, their property was confiscated and the father imprisoned for several years before they all returned to England. The precocious novelist brought out her first book, *Victoria,* in 1786. Among the pre-publication patrons were such diverse personalities as General John Burgoyne and Samuel Adams. A few years later she published her sensational best-seller, *Charlotte Temple,* which sent Bostonians clamoring to the bookstores for copies. This novel went through 160 editions, a record unsurpassed in America until the publication of *Uncle Tom's Cabin.* Mrs. Rowson returned in triumph in 1796 both as authoress and leading lady in the Boston (Federal Street) Theatre. Tiring of a stage career, she took a leaf from one of her own plays, *Lessons for Daughter,* and opened a school for girls. Even as a school mistress, Mrs. Rowson continued to spin her lachrymal novels. The story of the incredible twins, *Reuben and Rachel,* appeared in 1798; *Sarah* in 1804; and finally, in *Lucy Temple,* the saga of Charlotte was taken up again in the trials of that heroine's illegitimate daughter. Mrs. Rowson was as busy and as successful as any of the Federalist merchants whose daughters passed through her school or whose wives' tears washed the pages of her novels. She edited the *Boston Weekly Magazine* from 1802 to 1805, during which time she showed her total conversion to Boston ways by writing a poem with the supremely Federalist title, "America, Commerce, and Freedom."

Through a case of mistaken identity, Mrs. Rowson had a rival in the person of Mrs. Perez Morton, Bulfinch's cousin. Less equivocally known as the "Poetess of Beacon Hill" and wife of a leading Boston Republican, Mrs. Morton was long believed to be the authoress of a lurid tale, *The Power of Sympathy*. Advertised in the local papers as a true account of kidnaping, seduction, incest, rape, and suicide, the novel created such an uproar that the family of the alleged authoress stepped in and thoroughly suppressed it. Mrs. Morton's architect-cousin was particularly shocked by the scandal. Aside from ties of family and friendship, it was Bulfinch's sworn duty as chief of police to prevent the crimes the novel suggested were commonplace in Boston. The Bulfinch-Apthorp family alliance so successfully suppressed the book that almost nothing was known of it until recent research disproved Mrs. Morton's authorship.[7]

Much more important and enduring were the plays of another proper Bostonian, Royall Tyler, who served in the Revolution as aide to General John Sullivan. Returned to Boston, Tyler began the practice of law and became engaged to the daughter of John Adams. The latter project failed, but Tyler's legal talents ultimately carried him to the Vermont Supreme Court. His fame, however, rests on the writing of plays. The best of them, *The Contrast*, was produced in the middle states almost a decade before Bulfinch endowed Boston with her first theater. *The Contrast* was not popular in Federal Boston. Its theme—the superiority of a native-American type, Colonel Manly, over the affected, English-imitating Billy Dimple—could hardly endear it to the London-worshiping, anti-democratic merchants.

Tyler's contemporary fame was confined to New York, Philadelphia, and Baltimore; Bostonians found the eccentric poet James Allen far more comfortable. Unlike Tyler's

Colonel Manly, Allen mimicked certain English writers of Grub Street, appearing in ragged clothes with ruffles hanging in tatters from his neck and wrists. But this was overlooked in a member of the intermediary family group whose ancestor built one of the first houses on upper Beacon Street. This ancient stone dwelling was the weekly meeting place of the Pistareen Club, where Allen recited his poems inspired by the "West Indian Muse"—a mixture of rum, sugar, and lemon-juice.[8]

There were, fortunately, other organizations than the Pistareen Club to strengthen the town's reputation in intellectual matters. In the eighteenth century, professional men in Boston followed the progress of European science as closely as the separating ocean allowed. The provincial capital even produced a few men of science. They were mainly trained at Harvard, with important exceptions like Bulfinch's father and grandfather who held degrees from English and Scottish universities. Amateurs, too, were always a force in Boston. Their traditional patronage of science and the practical arts made the town an important intellectual center before the Revolution. Edward Bromfield, who combined a love of music and mechanical skill to construct the first organ in America, was typical of the affluent colonial amateur. But the triumph of the rigid Federalists brought the colonial penchant for arts and sciences into temporary eclipse. Salem actually acquired more notoriety for learning during this period, perhaps because her leading anti-intellectuals had moved to Boston.

Federalist hostility to political change extended to every facet of the town's life. There was only one criterion: poli-

tics. This view inhibited all new movements in thought
and led to the prosecution of eminent thinkers, such as
Joseph Priestley, under the Alien and Sedition laws. But
luckily President Adams had a higher sense of honor than
his Essex Junto critics; he did not support the indiscriminate imprisonment of every outspoken opponent of his
party. Adams did occasionally lash out at learned societies
in moments of extreme exasperation, yet basically he
agreed with Jefferson in their value and necessity. He
himself was responsible for the founding of the American
Academy of Arts and Sciences, Boston's most august
learned society, even before the Revolution was won.
While on a diplomatic mission in France, Adams was impressed with that country's esteem for the Philosophical
Society of Philadelphia founded by Franklin in 1743. He
returned to Boston determined the town would have a similar organization, and as Adams's determination was usually synonymous with accomplishment, the American
Academy of Arts and Sciences was incorporated in 1780.
The Academy was devoted to all phases of knowledge,
practical as well as esoteric. One of the early papers read
before the Academy concerned the cultivation of ginseng,
a treasured commodity in the first years of the China
trade. Bulfinch was elected a member of the Academy in
1791, vice president between 1793 and 1796, librarian,
1816-17, and a member of the council for ten years. There
is no mention of a paper ever read by the architect, although his observations on perspective should have been
given as they were the first formulated in America.[9]

The Massachusetts Historical Society was organized a
decade after the Academy by Jeremy Belknap and incor-

porated in 1794 with the future Republican governor James Sullivan as first president. Although Bulfinch did not become a member until 1801, he was associated with the society's fate from the beginning. He wrote on December 31, 1793: "In erecting the center building of the Crescent it is our intention to accommodate the Historical Society with a convenient room."[10] This room contained the large Palladian window in the central pavilion of the Tontine Crescent and was shared by the Boston Library Society. One of the tasks relegated by the Historical Society to Bulfinch in 1813 was to ascertain the original height of the three summits of Trimountain and to provide drawings and descriptions to be preserved for future use.[11] By this time two of the domes, Mount Vernon and Beacon, had become historic. These learned societies, however, were not the only source resorted to by Bostonians in pursuit of knowledge. Of equal local fame was the fortune-teller Molly Pitcher, to whose lonely house filed an endless procession of merchants, sailors, politicians, and unresourceful lovers. Like many of her customers Molly came from Essex County, the granddaughter of a fortune-teller of Marblehead. It is not known whether Bulfinch ever consulted Molly concerning his destiny, but certainly some of his patrons did.

That two of the town's leading libraries could be accommodated in a single large room above the central arch in the Tontine Crescent indicates their modest proportions. In 1817 there were less than 60,000 books in all of Boston and Cambridge. Many splendid libraries, including that of the Mathers, disappeared in the turmoil of revolution. Aside from the scarcity of books themselves, there was much duplication. The Boston Library Society was founded in 1794 specifically to provide books not obtainable in the town's private libraries or available only at great cost. By 1817, the trustees had deposited more than 5000 volumes in the Bulfinch room with the Palladian window. An additional 2000 books and manuscripts belonging to the Massachusetts Historical Society were ranged along the same shelves. And there were other important collections such as the Social Law Library and the Boston Athenæum. The latter grew out of the need of the members of the Anthology Club for a reading room to hold foreign and American periodicals subscribed to by the organization. By the end of the Federal period, the Athenæum had 10,000 volumes and served as well as depository for the American Academy of Arts and Sciences and the private library of John Quincy Adams.[12]

The Athenæum began as an offspring of Federal Boston's only really serious adventure in literature, the Anthology Club. Its spokesman, the *Monthly Anthology*, churned out quantities of good and bad material until publication was suspended in the crisis leading to the War of 1812. With the conclusion of peace in 1815, the *Monthly Anthology* reappeared as the *North American Review*, the herald of Boston's future literary triumphs. The Anthology Club variously numbered between seven and fifteen members who met one night a week to discuss the manuscripts offered for publication. Afterwards they ate and drank until the early morning hours. The force behind the *Monthly Anthology* was William Tudor, Jr., who, like his friend Charles Bulfinch, belonged to the intermediary family group that gave Federal Boston distinction in fields other than business and politics. The *Monthly Anthology* received its specific death sentence in 1811. Long before that, however, an indiscriminate policy of accepting anything publishable, "from the necessity of revelation to the purring of cats," removed it from the category of literature.[13] When Tudor revived the magazine as the *North American Review*, the old world of maritime Boston was vanishing. The publication of William Cullen Bryant's poem "Thanatopsis" two years later magnificently prefigured the new age at hand. As a boy of thirteen, back in 1808, Bryant was scribbling attacks on Jefferson; nine years later he expounded a concept of nature incomprehensible to the former rulers of Federal Boston.

The editors of the *North American Review* showed great foresight when they published "Thanatopsis" in 1817. Far less prescient was the magazine's praise in the same year of Colonel Henry Sargent's painting "The Entry of our Saviour into Jerusalem." But this mistake was moderate compared to the horrendous misjudgment of the local press in their comparison of Sargent to da Vinci and Raphael.[14] What Gilbert Stuart thought of such pronouncement is unknown—but undoubtedly it was caustic. Stuart was as unrestrained a talker and wit as that other New Englander, James Abbott McNeill Whistler, who followed him to London to make a reputation in art.[15] Eight years older than his friend Bulfinch, Stuart left Boston on one of the last ships to sail before the blockade and was soon at work in the London studio of Benjamin West. By the time the Revolution was over, Stuart was more celebrated than his master; only Reynolds and Gainsborough commanded higher prices. When it came time to return to America,

Stuart inquired into the state of the arts in Boston and wisely sailed for New York. But in 1803 Jonathan Mason persuaded him to come north and join in the artistic renaissance begun by Bulfinch. Stuart lived in Boston until his death in 1828, when the town, characteristically, rewarded his work and fame by depositing him in an unmarked grave on the Common.

Bulfinch provided the façade, domestic and public, for Federal Boston; Stuart painted the faces behind the façade. Almost everyone of the architect's patrons sat to Stuart for his portrait. He painted all the principal Mount Vernon proprietors except Bulfinch himself; he even painted Mrs. Swan's husband on one of that adventurer's few appearances in Boston between the time of his financial dealings in revolutionary France and his final incarceration in a Paris prison. Stuart painted Beacon Hill house owners Thomas Perkins and William Phillips and Park Street residents Thomas Amory, Mrs. John Gore, and Doctor John Collins Warren. The Bulfinch churchbuilders, John de Cheverus, William Ellery Channing, and Nathaniel Thayer of Lancaster, and the architect's wife's relatives, John Vaughan and James Greenleaf, were painted by Stuart. So were Bulfinch's Bowdoin Square patrons Joseph Coolidge and Samuel Parkman, and South End residents James Sullivan and William Gray. In Federal Boston only art and architecture transcended politics; Gilbert Stuart and Charles Bulfinch were conspicuous among the town's few citizens of the world.[16]

Stuart had no serious rivals in the New England capital. Washington Allston lived only one year in Boston during the Federal period; Samuel F. B. Morse came up from Yale

to Allston's studio just in time to accompany his teacher to
Europe. The Boston artist community, however, included
several competent men. One, Major John Johnston, was a
Revolutionary soldier who executed capable portraits at
prices far below the great Stuart. Another, Colonel Henry
Sargent, was also an ex-Revolutionary officer whose well-
known genre paintings are almost the only contemporary
representations of Federalist domestic life. Ethan Allen
Greenwood, unesthetically known as "Daddy" Greenwood, was another figure on the artistic scene. He had the
sense to give up a career as portrait painter, for which he
had earlier abandoned the study of law, to become an art
promoter. His exhibition in 1815 of S. F. B. Morse's "Dying
Hercules" was so successful that application was made to
the selectmen for the rental of the upper story of the old
State House as a museum. But the price of one hundred
dollars a month was too high, and Greenwood remained
in his rooms in Scollay's Building until 1817 when he
opened the New England Museum. The latter venture attempted to cut into the profitable museum operations of
Daniel Bowen, who started out early in the Federal period
with a few wax figures of Washington and Franklin as
well as some local favorites like "The Sleeping Nymph"
and "The Salem Beauty." When public rage mounted
against France, he added a tableau of Louis XVI taking
farewell of his family and a scene with a man guillotined.
His museum prospered enough by 1795 for Bowen to take
over a building in Bromfield's Lane overlooking the Granary Burying Ground and Park Street, where "Bulfinch
Row" was soon to go up. One of the great sights in Bowen's
new museum was a huge painting showing "Columbia"

mourning the ravages of war, particularly the destruction of commerce.

In talking to his Boston patrons, Gilbert Stuart often prefaced his remarks with: "When I lived in the Athens of the New World. . . ." He was referring, maliciously, to Philadelphia, for the Bostonians enjoyed comparing their town to Athens. Actually they were lucky to have had Charles Bulfinch or Philadelphia would have been ahead of them in every intellectual and cultural field, including architecture. Boston's ships, like those of ancient Athens, sailed to the reaches of the known world; but the wealth brought back was not conspicuously spent on the town's adornment. When the Philadelphia Academy paid Washington Allston $3500 for a painting in 1816, and the city of Baltimore bought another from the artist the same year, an outraged Bostonian took to the press to upbraid his townsmen for the poverty of their artistic expenditures. "What," he asks, "has been done with the riches which the commerce of half the world has for twenty years thrown into the town? The only answer that can be returned is, they have been consumed in the profusion of the table, and other luxuries equally indicating a gross and depraved taste."[17] Boston merchants paid the minimal price for the services of the town's only two great men of art, Charles Bulfinch and Gilbert Stuart.

The attitude in Boston toward the art of medicine, however, had recently undergone a tremendous change. Nothing showed this more than the wealth and social prestige bestowed upon the post-Revolutionary generation of physicians. The new attitude was remarkable in a town noted for its hatred of innovation. When Bulfinch returned to

Boston the general state of medicine was not much changed from the days when Governor Winthrop's physician prescribed a "Wilde Catt's skin on ye place grieved."[18] With a few exceptions, such as Dr. Thomas Bulfinch, the best colonial physicians left in the evacuation. Bulfinch's father was indeed an exception, unique in Boston as the second generation of European-trained physicians. The usual medical education in New England was by apprenticeship to a practicing physician. The failures in this system were appalling, especially in the science of anatomy. There was almost no way for medical students to study the structure of the body they were pledged to heal, the result of archaic training reinforced by archaic public opinion regarding dissection. When the loyalist Dr. John Jeffries attempted to defy this ancient prejudice by giving a series of lectures on anatomy, using the body of an executed criminal, a mob broke in and carried off the corpse. Lucius Manlius Sargent tells of the dilemma of judges caught between the law and the demands of science: "A poor vagabond . . . was snatched, by some of the young medical dogs, some years ago, and Judge Parsons, who tried the indictment, with a leaning to science, imposed a fine of five dollars."[19] But both doctors and students needed cadavers, and the grisly nocturnal task of "body-snatching" was widespread in Massachusetts until the legalization of dissection in 1831. Opposition extended even to the use of animals. Nevertheless, the alleys of Boston were scoured for the bodies of cats and dogs which found their way to the back door of the Medical College. Students in the Federalist stronghold were expected to learn anatomy from Vesalius or antique statuary. Shaw's contemporary description of the Massachusetts Medical College in 1816 extols the copies of the Medici Venus and Belvedere Apollo housed there for the purpose of explaining the human body.[20]

A sound inherited constitution, plenty of good water, an equally good food supply, and an unusual concern for public sanitation accounts for the health of Bostonians in Bulfinch's time. Far less credit goes to the doctors; they were mainly "bleeders" or "dosers." The senior Oliver Wendell Holmes, who grew up in the late Federal period, recalls Boston doctors bleeding their patients "like so many calves."[21] On at least one occasion a leading physician recommended the removal of three-quarters of a patient's entire blood supply. The "dosers" were amazingly modern in their approach to medical salesmanship. A Dr. Beath at South Row addressed himself to "men of pleasure, to cure the disagreeable disease so prevalent with the votaries of *Venus.*" His treatment was arbitrarily publicized as the result of twenty years' experience in China. If a gentleman resisted Dr. Beath's testimonials, he was apt to be snared by the equally well-advertised "English-cure" at the Sign of the Good Samaritan on Cornhill Street. When victims feared blood-letting, were skeptical of preparations made from crushed woodlice and beaver tails, or got no relief from the vividly publicized products of Richard Lee and Son ("Grand Restorative," "Infallible Ague and Fever Drops," "Sovereign Ointment for the Itch"), there still remained the "Calomel school" of medicine. The adherents of this cure held so high an opinion of mercury they often administered it by the pound.[22]

But not all the doctors were quacks extravagantly exploiting their wares through the newspapers. Exactly opposite to the Yankee salesman type was the town's greatest physician, John Warren. Warren was a heroic figure in the best Boston tradition: he was a patriot who served in the Revolution; balanced a large private practice with distinguished public service; lived in a Bulfinch house on Park Street; and founded a famous family. He was representative, too, in that he was a new man, although not from so far away as Essex County. The son of a Roxbury farmer, Warren received his early medical training under his brother Joseph, the patriot-physician who died at Bunker Hill. John Warren's wartime experience in the Continental Army was the critical element in his medical training. As an officer in the field, he had frequent opportunity to dissect unclaimed bodies, thereby gaining a skill in surgery unrivaled in New England. In medicine, as in every field but commerce, the act of successful revolution required the rapid attainment of a stage of maturity and an *esprit de corps* entirely absent in the colonial professions.[23]

The Revolution showed the awful inadequacy of existing medical training. John Adams estimated that professional incompetency killed ten men to every one destroyed by the enemy. As a first step in teaching Boston students a more comprehensive understanding of the body than could be obtained through the study of ancient statuary, Warren conducted a private course in anatomy during the winter of 1779-80. Aware of the earlier fate of Dr. Jeffries, the lectures were carried out at night and in secrecy at the military hospital in the West End. This step was just a beginning. Warren considered the methods of examining medical candidates and the licensing of physicians as inadequate as their training. A year after the completion of his secret lecture course, he got the Massachusetts Medical Society incorporated with authority to examine candidates for the profession and to award or withhold the testimonial letters necessary for the practice of medicine in the Commonwealth. There would be no more "Dr." John Joys, delightful as that rich apothecary was as a social ornament and Bulfinch patron. The Medical Society began with thirty-one members, eight of whom also belonged to the American Academy of Arts and Sciences. The society's *Papers* began publication in 1790 and provided a desperately needed means of communication within the profession. Concurrently, the society began accumulating a library that contained about 4,000 volumes by the time the Federal period ended.

Dr. John Warren's course of lectures in anatomy at the military hospital was the forerunner of the Massachusetts Medical College. Organized in the first year of peace, it later devolved into the Medical Institution of Harvard College. Warren was the first professor of anatomy and surgery, holding the post until his death in 1815. The desirability of housing the medical library contiguous to the college's lecture rooms and laboratory led to the erection of a new building in 1816 on Mason Street just behind the Colonnade. The building featured an octagonal "anatomical theatre" lighted by a glass dome under which the statues of Venus and Apollo were placed. In an age becoming fascinated with invention, the central heating apparatus drew the most attention. This method of supplying controlled heat to all parts of the building from a single coal-burning stove in the cellar through a system of brick flues and pipes was claimed as the invention of a local resident. Among the books in Bulfinch's library, however, is one describing a similar device used earlier in a medical building in England.

When the medical college was set up in 1783, another excellent physician, Benjamin Waterhouse, joined Warren on the faculty. Waterhouse was a Republican whose worship of Jefferson embroiled him in perpetual battle with the Essex Junto, which in Federal Boston generally meant ruin. Waterhouse was too important for the cabal to crush but he still could not exert an influence proportionate to his stature. Yet Waterhouse was responsible for the outstanding scientific achievement of Federal Boston: the introduction in 1800 of cowpox vaccination into the United States. By background Waterhouse should have been an acquiescent Federalist instead of a militant Republican. But even as a youth he avoided incipient merchants and formed a firm friendship with another colorful and outspoken misfit, Gilbert Stuart. Together they roamed the outskirts of the town hunting and fishing when those of like age were in counting houses on Long Wharf. They were not entirely idle, however, for both youths learned to draw from life by hiring a "strong-muscled blacksmith" as a model. When Waterhouse went off to England in 1775 to study, Stuart soon followed. And in later life, when fate brought Stuart back to Boston, he and Waterhouse entertained each other with jokes at the expense of the merchants one painted and the other healed.

Obviously so irrepressible a Republican as Dr. Waterhouse was no great favorite in the Federalist capital. Thus, although an original member of the faculty of the medical college, he was dropped thirty years later at the climax of the Federalist-Republican feud. His dismissal, however, did not affect his way of life. The doctor continued to live on what he called his "small but handsome seat with ten acres of land" overlooking the Cambridge Common. Dr. Oliver Wendell Holmes, who knew Waterhouse as a neighbor and by whom he was vaccinated, noted Waterhouse's aversion to tobacco and ascribes to the old Jeffersonian some lines that might have come from his own pen:[24]

> Tobacco is a filthy weed,
> That from the devil does proceed,
> It drains your purse, it burns your clothes,
> And makes a chimney of your nose.

In spite of his politics, Waterhouse's belief in cowpox vaccination had the support of the Federalist press. Sometime in 1799 he read about the success of cowpox vaccination in recent English experiments and in October of that year submitted the statistical evidence to the *Columbian Centinel*. It was very impressive: of six hundred individuals vaccinated by a single London doctor only one died and none got the disease. Waterhouse imported the first cowpox vaccine in America and in the following summer vaccinated his entire household with complete success. By that time, 30,000 persons had passed safely through vaccination in England. This was in marked contrast with the earlier and hazardous practice of inoculation, which seven years before resulted in the death of Bulfinch's eldest boys, Charles and Thomas. But while these results were sympathetically read by the nonprofessional Bostonians, the medical community remained skeptical. Ten years elapsed between the publication of Waterhouse's first article, "Something curious in the medical line," and the general acceptance of vaccination by the local doctors.[25]

By the end of the War of 1812 most of those trained in the old colonial practice were dead or inactive. Dr. Thomas Bulfinch and Dr. John Warren were gone and Dr. Waterhouse was "retired" from his post at the medical college. But oddly enough the celebrated Tory, Dr. John Jeffries, was still making his rounds. An old and close friend of Dr. Bulfinch, Jeffries enjoyed a secure place in the Province House set through a combination of Boston lineage and his post as surgeon-major to the British forces. It was he who poked among the dead at Bunker Hill to identify the body of the fallen hero, General Joseph Warren. Jeffries left in the evacuation and lived in London during the Revolution, a frequenter of those haunts of exiled Bostonians in Threadneedle Street and the Adelphi. He was more adventurous than his cronies at the New England Coffee House, however, and on one occasion shortly after the war soared away in the first balloon flight across the English Channel. Too restless to be content with passive dreams of Boston, Jeffries suddenly appeared one day in 1790 in the yellow drawing room of the Bulfinch mansion in Bowdoin Square and recounted at great length the present history of the banished Apthorp family. He resumed his Boston practice as if nothing had happened in the intervening fifteen years.

That Dr. Jeffries was a hale but ancient practioner is attested by Oliver Wendell Holmes's reference to his son as "the old doctor." The second Doctor Jeffries was a contemporary of Charles Bulfinch and typical of the post-Revolutionary physicians. By this time medicine in Boston had become something of an hereditary profession. The most respected of the second-generation physicians was Dr. John Collins Warren who, with Dr. James Jackson, was responsible for promoting the most important building project of the late Federal period, the Massachusetts General Hospital. The hospital was not built until 1818, a year after the architect left Boston. But its origin went back to the early days of Bulfinch's career. Although a number of merchants endowed the project, nothing was done until John Collins Warren and James Jackson circulated a letter in 1810 decrying the absence of a hospital to treat general diseases in Boston such as already existed in New York and Philadelphia. The War of 1812 held up developments; it was not until late in 1816 that Bulfinch was sent to the middle states to study the construction and administration of hospitals. Just as his previous trip to New York and Philadelphia provided him with the knowledge to build Boston's first theater, so now Bulfinch traveled the same route to learn how to set up Boston's first general hospital. By the time the town adopted his plan in 1818, he was permanently settled in Washington. That same year, Boston's first insane asylum, the McLean Hospital, was opened in the buildings Bulfinch devised by remodeling the estate in Charlestown he designed for Joseph Barrell almost three decades earlier.[26]

When a son of the Federalist merchant Samuel Eliot graduated from Harvard College in 1809, he discussed the problem of a future profession with his father. Young Eliot placed the practice of medicine ahead of law but below the ministry.[27] And he was right. The ministry was still the most honorable profession in Massachusetts. Commerce was the field of greatest financial opportunity, medicine was eminently respectable, and law the obvious road to politics. But the ministry! From time immemorial men and women in Boston gave it precedence over all other mortal occupations. Recalling her girlhood in this period, Mary Peabody tells how a solemn halo floated about the ministerial figure in "cloak and shovel hat." And a contemporary of hers, who sat out his childhood Sundays in the old church at Summer and High streets, remembers how respect was mixed with awe and fear.[28] That was before Bulfinch's New South Church, constructed of hammered granite, replaced this old-fashioned meetinghouse. In the earlier, yellow-painted wooden structure, the Reverend Joseph Eckley's stern demeanor and powdered headgear were the symbols of the Boston divine who exacted total deference from his congregation.

But Boston had traveled a long road in religious tolerance since Jonathan Mayhew of the neighboring West Church was decreed "fit for burning" when he came out against the Trinity in a book of sermons published in 1755. During the revolutionary crisis and the War for Independence, politics replaced religion as a subject of interest and controversy. But as often in the past, the struggle for national independence brought religious liberation as well. Ironically, the first victory was in King's Chapel, for here in 1785 reference to the Trinity was eliminated from the Episcopal prayerbook, and a new religion came to life in Boston. Like most of the ideas which convulsed Bulfinch's town, however, Unitarianism was imported from England. Its most eloquent spokesman, William Ellery Channing, was a member of a Rhode Island Federalist family and, since 1803, minister of the Federal Street Church. The Unitarian movement came to a climax two years later when Henry Ware was made Hollis Professor of Divinity at Harvard. The appointment to a theological chair at Cambridge was always a matter of intense concern to nearby Boston. This appointment was particularly significant as the college remained the last stronghold of Congregational secular power and Ware was known to be drifting toward Unitarianism. The firebrand was, then, absolutely tossed upon the altar. The Congregationalists retreated, setting up a new seminary at Andover, and young, Harvard-trained clergymen started a run on Boston churches that brought most of them into the Unitarian fold by the end of the War of 1812. From that time Unitarianism was known as the "Boston religion."

Both Channing and Unitarianism belong to the next age, the period of the New England renaissance, which Emerson dated as beginning in 1820. But even in Bulfinch's era, Channing was conspicuous for his public support of the English and French romanticists. His praise of Wordsworth and Coleridge, both of whom he visited in England, was courageous; his approval of Rousseau and Godwin was heroic. "What a writer!" Channing exclaimed after reading Rousseau's *Eloise*. Although few of his congregation had heard of *Eloise*, Channing's flair for romanticism had a response in architecture: Bulfinch designed Federal Boston's single Gothic Revival church for his friend in 1809. The contrast between medieval architecture and

Channing's increasingly liberal theology struck some contemporaries as paradoxical. William Bentley, who came from Salem to inspect the bizarre edifice within a week of dedication, observed: "We have had Gothic Theology for many generations and the style is not yet lost."[29] Altogether the Federal Street Church was an unfortunate experiment, in no sense justifying Shaw's praise of "a fine specimen of Saxon Gothic." Excepting some primitive "Gothic" decorations on the steeple and window brackets, the design was typically New England meetinghouse. Some of the interior carvings, done by Bulfinch's youthful collaborator Solomon Willard, are preserved in the Arlington Street Church and show a knowledge of Gothic architecture commensurate with the town's familiarity with romantic literature.[30]

What the Federalist gentlemen in old-fashioned clothes and powdered hair thought about romanticism in architecture or religion is more difficult to ascertain than their violently expressed views on trade and politics. Despite a high regard for the clergy, they were probably indifferent to the great schism. Deism was not popularly expressed in Boston because it was considered a symptom of Jacobinism and had adherents in Jefferson and large numbers of the lower classes. Yet the merchant politicians were often skeptics and experienced little difficulty in shifting from the orthodox to the liberal camp. Certainly few of them were as conscientious as the merchant Nicholas Ward Boylston, who returned to Boston in 1800 after visiting the Holy Lands with Bible in hand to verify the truth of that sacred volume. The conflict between the old guard and the moderates within the Congregational Church was openly waged after 1805, but four years later so intense a Presbyterian as Elias Boudinot made a tour of Boston churches and concluded: "I never heard a doctrine advanced in the Pulpit, that I could not have subscribed to."[31] The religious tolerance of the post-Revolutionary period paved the way for Unitarianism; but that movement was not characteristic of Boston's great age of maritime supremacy. Federalist pursuit of trade was never diverted by matters of the mind. The intellectual world of William Ellery Channing and the Boston Unitarians, which later so influenced the nation, was possible only after the War of 1812 released passions from the grip of partisan politics. Then, the vanished Boston of Bulfinch appeared to the new intellectuals as odd as the old Federalist gentlemen who lingered on with their powdered hair, knee-breeches, and cocked hats.

XI

THE WAR OF 1812

THE WAR OF 1812 BROUGHT the colonial world of the Federalist merchant crashing to the ground. It was not a physical debacle. Boston was not attacked by the enemy, and the town remained scornfully aloof from the fighting. In an immediate sense, the war was merely decorative: the emphasis was on fancy uniforms which never knew the dirt of battle and victory celebrations by those at sword's point with the victors and their cause. But in the wider sense of future things, the War of 1812 destroyed the old maritime character of the New England capital. It was the final act in a drama beginning back in 1787 when Charles Bulfinch returned home from Europe and joined the other newly conscripted Federalists in promoting a strong central government. Now, twenty-five years later, the central government was in the hands of Republicans, and the tide of nationalism rising in the west engulfed the Federalist party and its capital. The new nationalism required complete independence from England. This was the real issue in the War of 1812. Bulfinch's town was too divided to participate in the final severance and too isolated to make effective resistance. With the return of peace there was nothing left but to admit defeat. It was the grand old Federalist editor, Benjamin Russell who, in 1817, coined the phrase "era of good feeling." The following year William Phillips ran for lieutenant governor on the "Massachusetts Federalist-Republican" ticket. The impossible happened; the two most antithetical words in Boston's vocabulary were joined. And the parochial world of Federalist merchants in powdered hair and knee breeches ended.

The War of 1812 was full of anomalies. Allegedly fought to maintain neutral rights on the sea and the protection of American seamen, it was savagely resisted by the maritime states of New England. The merchants and their representatives in Congress voted against war while the "War Hawks" from the landlocked west supported it. The real goal, an invasion of Canada, was never mentioned; the publicized issue, American neutrality, was acknowledged by England two days before war was declared in Washington. When Madison received the news weeks later, he pushed the war ahead on the grounds of impressment. Yet the states most affected by the impressment of American sailors into the British navy were not alarmed over the issue. In the partisan squabbles over impressment, Madison, a Virginia planter, insisted there were at least 6000 cases; the General Court of Massachusetts, representing the largest shipping interest in the nation, admitted to only twelve incidents. The Republicans had a perfect opportunity to go to war over impressment five years before when the British ship *Leopard* fired on the American frigate *Chesapeake* off Virginian waters and boarded the crippled vessel to carry away four members of her crew. The Bostonians were fully aroused by this slur on the national honor and would then have supported war with England.

War was declared in Washington on June 18, 1812. Six days later the news reached Boston and the Federalist press announced THE AWFUL EVENT, describing its cause as "the inevitable effects of the infatuated policy of the Rulers of the American people."[1] The war was not fought in America because of an infatuation with Napoleon, although it was resisted in Boston because of an infatuation with England. On the other hand, the war was not staged by westerners and supported by the southern and middle states to succor New England seamen. The War of 1812 represented part of an unconscious drive to free the United States finally from the bonds of both England and France. Neutrality was not simply an issue of egress on the high seas. The slowly maturing national consciousness demanded palpable recognition, and those most capable of pressing this recognition were the young men from the west. They did not view America as a pawn in European politics. Their infatuation was with land— the indubitable factor in the New World. The term "manifest destiny" did not exist for another quarter of a century, but its nature was implicit in the issues of the War of 1812. Land meant expansion to the north, south, and west. As Boston saw it there was already too much land. Every new western state meant a diminution in New England's power. What was needed was a balance on the sea. Looking always back to London, the Federalists saw the English as the only bulwark against Jacobinism, which they read for Republicanism. By declaring war on England,

America had become an ally of the French. Boston, at least, would not join the irreligious rabble.

As the unifying effects of the war were not perceived at the time, the conflict was supported or opposed along sectional lines. The war party might triumph in Washington and even capture a renegade like John Quincy Adams, but up in Boston the newly elected Federalist governor turned a deaf ear upon Madison's requisition for artillery and infantry from the state militia. The first request was not even answered. Subsequent demands made through the war office to the military commander in Boston, General Henry Dearborn, were acknowledged and ignored. Governor Caleb Strong insisted the state militia could only be commanded by its own officers for defense against invasion. As a result the Massachusetts militia never stirred from the Commonwealth. The national government was more successful in raising recruits in Boston for the army. General Dearborn sent his recruiting sergeant out daily from the barracks in Cambridge Street with drummer and fifer at his side. Whenever there was a big enough crowd, the sergeant tossed a handful of sparkling Spanish dollars upon the head of the drum and bawled out:[2]

> If any young man should want to enlist,
> I'll give him a dollar right in his fist.
> Fall in, gentlemen, fall in.

Not many "gentlemen" fell in. The task of recruiting sons from Bulfinch houses for distant battles was a forlorn one. Yet a large number of volunteers was raised in Boston and throughout Massachusetts from among those susceptible to the promise of a discharge bonus of 160 acres of western land.[3]

Well-connected Bostonians, however, did rush to join the town's militia companies which Governor Strong promised to keep at home. The most ornamental was the Boston Hussars, formed and commanded by Josiah Quincy. Candidates were screened according to social and financial qualifications, which was wise, for the uniform and "horse furniture" alone cost $800. Captain Quincy drilled the Hussars astride a white charger and earned the sobriquet "Beau sabreur," a strange nickname for French-hating Boston. Hatred of Napoleon did not extend to things military: the uniform of the Hussars was copied from a regiment of the Imperial Guard. This un-Puritanical costume included a short jacket left unbuttoned and thrown back to reveal a brilliant waistcoat, and a square-topped hat with tassels and plume. Much more in keeping with the temper of Boston's past was the garb of the Sea Fencibles, which consisted of tarpaulin hat, short blue jacket, and white trousers. The Fencibles were characteristically armed with cutlass and pike and seemed, by newspaper accounts, to be constantly on the march. In their war exercises, as with the other fanciful companies organized in Boston during the War of 1812, the greatest interest centered in the vast dinners ending every maneuver. For this reason Medford was used by the New England Guards for target practice, since it was adjacent to the hospitable country seat of Peter Brooks. The New England Guards rivaled the Hussars in the splendor of their ceremonial attire: blue coat with gilt buttons, white waistcoat, white pantaloons, half-boots with black tassels, and round hat crowned by leather cock-ade and gilt eagle. Another smartly clad troop, the Independent Cadets, was organized as the personal escort to Governor Strong, who guided the state in a rigid policy of resistance to the war.[4]

While these meretriciously garbed soldiers were never called into battle, they did parade endlessly, wheeling about the Mall on foot or horseback with a precision thrilling to the spectators and accounting for reams of type in the local press. They marched away on many a false alarm, sometimes sounded at unpropitious moments. One member of the New England Guards rushed to a muster direct from dancing class and had to march all the way to Charlestown and back in dancing pumps. When the young soldiers were not actually at dancing classes, they attended "military academies" run on similar lines. Mr. Tromeler opened such a school on Hanover Street, where he advertised the art of fencing and "the Manuel Exercise and Military Evolution according to Steuben, or the new French method." A competitor, Mr. Hewes, offered a more cosmopolitan selection, including the "Scotch Highland Broad Sword, the French Thrust, and the Austrian Horse Sabre."[5] Hewes also advertised a course in "Cane Fighting," which was practical, as the Federalists and Republicans constantly threatened one another with mayhem. Naturally, regular army and navy personnel in Boston held the flashy militia in astounded contempt. When Commodore William Bainbridge was informed a local company was marching to the navy yard to salute him, the victor of the *Java* shouted: "Damn the Harvard-Washington Corps!"[6] Particularly painful to the regular army was the tendency of the superbly clad officers of the Boston militia to defer to the ranks for the solution of tactical problems.

The town's main defense was Fort Warren on Governor's Island and the old colonial fort on Castle Island. Castle Island, the haven to which so many royal officials fled in the days of the Sons of Liberty, had been renamed Fort Independence in keeping with the times. Less up-to-date, but also pressed into service, were the decayed fortifications at Point Shirley and Dorchester Heights. These rusting relics were indicative of Boston during the first two years of the War of 1812. Nothing happened there to disturb the mantle of passive resistance to "Mr. Madison's War." Mrs. Josiah Quincy captured the prevailing sentiment when she characterized the posting of a guard at General Dearborn's lodgings a "piece of mummery."[7] Dearborn was a distinguished hero of the Revolution who retired from the battlefield to a New England farm in the best Roman tradition. But even this could not save him from Federalist fury, for he was a Republican. Nor did he succeed in imbuing a passion for war beyond the town's fascination with its militia. Dearborn's attempts to get these troops under his control were utterly fruitless. In supporting Governor Strong's refusal to part with the command or fate of the militia, the *Columbian Centinel* assured its readers that "John Bull . . . is not so great a fool, if he intends to invade the country, to invade a part where he received so many hard knocks 37 years ago."[8] Anyway, a pleasant and profitable intercourse existed between Boston and the nation's enemy during the first two years of the war.

It was not, however, all fancy-dress parades and unreality for Charles Bulfinch. He was chief of police and directly responsible for the safety of the citizens. In August 1812 he raised the permanent watch patrol to forty-six with one hundred additional watchmen distributed according to the three geographical divisions of the town. The head of the selectmen also ordered churches to ring their bells for a half-hour in time of danger, and the townsfolk were instructed to light their front windows at the sound of alarm. An elaborate system of signals operated between Boston and the communities to warn of attack along the Essex shore. In the capital, two guns fired in quick succession and the hoisting of a red flag at the navy yard warned of danger by day, and three guns and two lanterns by night.[9] Almost two years passed before the red flag was raised in genuine alarm. Until the spring of 1814 the British blockade purposely stopped short of Rhode Island. Then, with Napoleon's first abdication, England was free to deal seriously with the American war. The blockade was extended along the entire eastern seaboard to include even the unwarlike Bostonians.

The first dangerous alarm was sounded on the morning of July 7, 1814, when the crashing of bells summoned the militia to muster. Three British barges had sneaked into the harbor and captured five lighter sloops, which had been carried away to enemy ships lying outside the Boston Light. The British offered to release the captured sloops for $100, and their owners hastened to raise the ransom— the first instance in Boston of ransoming, although it already had been practiced by the British among the less defensible seaports of Massachusetts. The initial taste of war in the home port excited rather than frightened the

Bostonians. Nothing was done to strengthen the archaic defenses until news of the fall of Washington swept the town on the last day of August. Bulfinch hurriedly issued an announcement to his worried townsmen assuring them that the militia's commanding officer, Governor Strong, had taken every necessary precaution for Boston's safety.[10]

Actually Strong did not have the situation in hand at all. Many leading Federalists, trusting to the mercy of their English friends, still insisted the town should capitulate if attacked. In a rowdy town meeting called on September 3 to adopt defensive measures, a delegation of Federalists shouted out their opposition. Among them was Harrison Gray Otis, who, since the beginning of the war, sported the uniform of captain in the Independent Light Infantry. In the midst of all the shouting, the apostate Samuel Dexter arose, denounced the Federalists for siding with the nation's enemy, and openly expressed the wish to pull Otis's nose. It looked for a few minutes as though two Bulfinch house dwellers, one from Park Street and the other from Beacon, were going to have a free-for-all while their architect looked helplessly on.[11]

The dispute over defenses was settled the next day when news was received of the capitulation of Alexandria. This Federalist town in Virginia surrendered to the English without a struggle, expecting to be treated magnanimously by fellow enemies of Napoleon. Instead, the British seized all the ships, provisions, merchandise, and tobacco in the town. After this disenchanting news, the extreme Federalists did an about-face. They suddenly showed concern over the fine target their undefended town presented to an enemy with naval superiority. A few days later an appeal was run in the press for all men under fifty to meet at the Exchange Coffee House to form corps for the town's defense. The governor also ordered thirty companies from the state militia into the capital town. The accommodation for these companies, some of whom straggled in from as far away as the Berkshires, was an extra burden on Bulfinch's time. He was already busy enough, meeting daily with committees from the twelve wards to mobilize men, matériel, and money to meet the expected attack.

All kinds of advice poured into Bulfinch's office concerning the town's defenses. While nobody paid much attention to General Dearborn's ideas, those presented by the naval hero Commodore William Bainbridge received top priority. Bainbridge recommended strong defenses at North Battery Wharf and a fortification on Noodle's Island in the harbor to protect Charlestown and Chelsea. The defenses on Noodle's Island were named Fort Strong in honor of the Commonwealth's anti-militant governor; their construction was under the supervision of Loammi Baldwin, Jr., who was assisted in the task of fortifying Boston by what Shubael Bell calls "a few other private Gentlemen."[12] These included Colonel Nehemiah Freeman, who succeeded Bulfinch as chief of police in 1817. The problem of raising money for defense so worried the chief selectman that he insisted the ward chairman report their collections daily regardless of how small the amount. Money was raised in a number of ways, including the twenty-five cent admission charge to a series of night illuminations. Although the expenses of the fortifications were modest, Bulfinch had to goad the population; the newspapers in the autumn of 1814 bristled with his urgent appeals for more volunteers and donations. The militia did most of the work on the fortification, joined from time to time by men and boys. Fort Strong was completed in less than two months and garrisoned by the Winslow Blues. In the dedication ceremony, Charles Bulfinch briefly thanked the volunteers and exhorted them to get back to work and renovate the antique defenses south of Boston.[13]

Not many more fortifications were built. Governor Strong's attempt to raise a loan of a million dollars to complete the defenses and recruit a state army was unsuccessful. The town bankers cast a cold eye on the whole proposition. But while Boston Federalists were merely unenthusiastic about digging into their pockets for the town's defenses, they were apoplectic on the subject of subscribing to national loans to keep the war going. The faithful *Columbian Centinel* defined the party's stand April 1814: "Money holders of Boston, one and all, deem it their duty not to subscribe a cent to the Loan; leaving it to be filled by those who urged the government to declare an unjust and ruinous War."[14] This attitude was more than rhetorical. Though the protesting Bostonians were ignored when war policy was debated in Washington, they had to be consulted in regard to its financing. In the first year of the war enormous amounts of specie flowed into the Commonwealth, and by 1814 Massachusetts bank deposits rose from something over one and a half million dollars to more than seven million. When the middle and southern states were sealed off by sea, New England did a booming business with her blockaded sister states as well as with the English in Canada. As a consequence, money poured into Boston and remained there. The middle states subscribed to about thirty-five million in national loans; New England raised less than three million.

The clergy of Massachusetts vigorously supported the merchants in their opposition to war loans to the federal government. In his history of the War of 1812, Benson Lossing recalls a rural divine who shouted from the pulpit: "If the rich men continue to furnish money, war will continue till the mountains are melted with blood—till every field in America is white with the bones of the people."[15] Lossing referred to the Reverend Elijah Parish of Byfield, who thundered out opposition to the war from a hamlet in Essex County. Like most of the Congregational clergy of this area, Parish opposed the war on moral grounds. But not all New England opposed the war. Henry Adams believed nearly half of the people favored it but were hamstrung by the more powerful and articulate opposition. Within the opposing party, too, there was deadlock. This was particularly true in Boston, where Timothy Pickering and the extremists in the peace party were prevented from drastic action by the moderates who balked at total treason. As a result, a general paralysis prevailed which made an offensive stand impossible. Boston would probably fight if attacked; but her leaders would not contribute to the war effort. Governor Strong expressed this policy in his Thanksgiving proclamation of 1812 calling for an end to the wicked and hopeless conflict between people who shared the same ancestors and the same gospel. Napoleon, not England, was Boston's enemy.

In a huge public gathering at the Exchange Coffee House on March 25, 1813, to celebrate Napoleon's defeat in Russia, Harrison Gray Otis reiterated the Federalist indictment of Madison's war: ". . . a war of passion and infatuation . . . without object . . . without hope."[16] On this occasion no less than twenty toasts were drunk to the victors over Napoleon, even though one of them was at war with the United States. In June the following year the town went wild when the Federalist editor Benjamin Russell announced the exile of Napoleon to Elba under the banner: GREAT AND GLORIOUS NEWS. Boston's leaders gathered in the Beacon Street mansion Bulfinch designed for William Phillips to plan a twenty-four hour celebration highlighted by a Thanksgiving Service in King's Chapel. The memorial, conducted by William Ellery Channing, was remarkably partial to the nation's enemy who was now free to concentrate all her efforts on the war in America. That night the State House blazed with two thousand lamps, hundreds of rockets burst over the Common, and far out on the Neck fireworks whirled into the summer sky.[17]

Despite such celebrations, it was an unhappy and frustrating time for Boston, caught in the most inglorious moment of her history. Still, Massachusetts was no worse than the other New England states which also refused to contribute money or militia to the war effort. Even some of the middle states restricted their militia to home territory during the first year of the war. General Stephen Van Rensselaer vainly tried to force the New York militia to cross the Niagara River and support the collapsing American attack on the heights of Queenston in October 1812. Later demands on the loyalty of New York were more successful, but the test was never renewed in New England. The government in Washington turned its back on the five states north of New York and let them go their way. Yet Boston's famous past rested unquietly on the town, evoking a stricken feeling among the less partisan inhabitants. The people were generally not as unmoved by American victories as their leaders. When young Captain James Lawrence accepted a British challenge to fight outside Boston Harbor, most of the townsfolk streamed to the hills to watch the American frigate *Chesapeake* engage the *Shannon.* But it was the citizens of Salem who saw the desperate and sad struggle end in the capture of the *Chesapeake* after its mortally wounded captain shouted, "Don't give up the ship." The people of Massachusetts mourned the naval hero, although the Federalist legislature refused a memorial vote to Captain Lawrence.

A white flag bearing the motto "Free Trade and Sailors' Rights" trailed from the ill-fated *Chesapeake* as it slipped past the Boston Light to meet the British challenger. This motto referred to the alleged causes for the War of 1812, causes unacceptable to the dominant shipping interests in New England. Nevertheless, Massachusetts was not adverse to a sea fight if there must be war. Her senior senator, James Lloyd, pleaded with Madison to supply a navy of thirty frigates which he guaranteed to man from New England within five days. The President, however, was under the influences of the western expansionists who envisaged war in the form of a swift conquest of Canada. The "War Hawks" were indifferent to the naval aspects of the conflict, although excepting the battle of New Orleans it was only on water that any notable American victories were won. Bostonians wagged their heads over the fiascos along the Canadian border but cheered the triumphs at sea.

The elaborately staged Federalist celebrations over the defeats of Napoleon could not rival the public enthusiasm for naval heroes Bainbridge, Hull, Perry, and Decatur. The sea was still the life blood of the town. Yet only a small proportion of navy personnel in the war came from Boston and none of the heroes were from Massachusetts. And for all their bluster, the Boston Federalists did not support even the naval phase of the war. Luckily for the town's reputation, William Gray had moved down from Salem and taken up residence in a Bulfinch house in Summer Street. Only his tireless support of the Administration's war policy redeemed the wholesale charge of obstruction leveled against the newcomers from Essex County. Gray personally supplied the additional money needed to get the *Constitution* to sea. Without his help, the immortal frigate never would have sailed out of Annapolis in July 1812 to meet and defeat the British ship *Guerrière* in the first American victory at sea.

After destroying the *Guerrière* off Nova Scotia, Captain Isaac Hull headed the *Constitution* toward Boston, where he arrived on August 30. This was a few days after the town received word of the surrender of Detroit by his uncle, General William Hull of Revolutionary fame. General Hull's capitulation was somewhat ignominious, and the Boston Federalists, already outraged by the folly and ineptitude of the attacks on Canada, did not conceal their scorn. Now the town was anxious to forget the black news from the west and outdid itself in welcoming the young naval hero, who sailed into the harbor with a shipload of captured seamen to retrieve the family honor. Dozens of brightly decorated boats dashed out to greet the *Consti-*

tution while the entire population applauded from the wharfs, rooftops, and hills. A great public feast, the inseparable part of every Boston celebration of this period, was attended by six hundred members of both political parties. Six months later, on a cold February day, the town again turned out en masse to watch their favorite frigate drop anchor in the harbor. The mobs along the docks roared a hero's welcome to Captain Bainbridge as he jumped onto Long Wharf to grasp the hand of Captain Hull. Bainbridge brought the *Constitution* back to Boston after a victorious battle with the *Java*. But the admiring citizens had to wait a full year before another naval victor, Oliver Hazard Perry, was marched through the streets in a cheering procession to the inevitable dinner at the Exchange Coffee House.

Every American port traded with the British in the first year of the war, and Wellington's armies in Spain and Portugal depended on this trade. United States officials and British consular officers co-operated in issuing licenses to Yankee ships with cargoes destined for Iberian ports. In 1813 half of America's native exports went directly to Spain and Portugal. The situation changed when the Peninsular War was brought to a close. But even then, with the English fleet blockading the American coast from New York to the Mississippi, New England carried on a lucrative commerce with the British armies in Canada. In fact, the blockade of all ports south of Narragansett Bay was a blessing for Massachusetts, as Boston became the principal depot for foreign goods. The town's rulers had no qualms over their good fortune; the states supporting Madison in his war deserved to suffer. Federalist merchants in New

England gave the tail an extra twist by charging all the traffic could bear.

Many New England vessels took on foreign papers, and the water between Newport and Halifax was white with the sails of newly proclaimed neutral ships. An observer in Halifax watched 20,000 barrels of flour unloaded from "Spanish" and "Swedish" vessels direct from Boston. The trade between New England and the nation's enemy in Canada and Maine really was outrageous. Late in 1813, the Governor-General of Canada estimated that two-thirds of the British army stationed there was eating beef supplied by Americans. Profits from goods available to Canada and the blockaded towns of the United States tripled the specie deposits in Massachusetts between 1812 and 1814. Yet the war had serious repercussions for the working population effected by the curtailment of shipping. Many a sea-dog or shipyard worker spent the war years unhappily digging potatoes and picking apples. The inhabitants of Bulfinch houses and their relatives and friends certainly fared better. There was enough money for hussar's horses and lavish uniforms; town houses and country seats changed hands at high prices; and the newspapers were crowded with advertisements for those luxuries irresistible to imitators of the London Whigs: Madeira wine, Holland gin, French cognac, Jamaica rum, Domingo coffee, China teas, Havana cigars.

Madison tired to prevent the contraband trade with Canada by an embargo enacted late in 1813. This legislation was so resented, however, its repeal was forced upon Madison in the following spring by commercial interests within his own party. But the Bostonians barely had time to vent their joy over repeal of the embargo when the British proclaimed a total blockade of the United States. In spite of all the toasts drunk in Faneuil Hall and the Exchange Coffee House to victories over Napoleon, the English finally turned against their friendly foe. Yet neither blockade nor subsequent raids and alarms diverted the town's fury from the Administration in Washington; England could still do no wrong. Boston clung so long to the guilty image of Madison that opposition took the form of psychosis and had to manifest itself in some terrible mistake. The mistake was the Hartford Convention.

The Hartford Convention was the bitter fruit of passive resistance; it was New England's last response to a hopeless situation. Until 1814 the way was hard but not impossible. The enemy had been indulgent. Now England was at war with Massachusetts too, and the picture appeared black from the Federalist view: the little American navy was all but vanished from the sea, the peace envoys at Ghent seemed intractable, the national treasury was empty, and a Tennessee general named Andrew Jackson was prolonging the conflict in West Florida and Louisiana. Boston awaited the attack which already placed most of the Maine towns north of the Penobscot in British hands. Obviously the national government was not going to rush to New England's defense. The dark scene was played upon by old guard Federalists to bring forward a long-considered plan to join the New England states in an united threat of separation if Madison's war was not immediately ended. Two members of the Essex Junto, Timothy Pickering and John Lowell, plumped for much more:

a declaration of New England neutrality, the suspension of the Constitution, and the elimination in one way or another of the western states. Regardless of differences as to how far New England should go in outright acts of treason, almost all the Massachusetts Federalist supported the resolution, which passed in General Court by a vote of 260 to 90. Invitations were issued by the legislature to the other New England states to convene at Hartford ten days before Christmas in 1814.

Lowell and Pickering hoped to control the Massachusetts delegation and dictate the proceedings at Hartford. Fortunately, the moderates prevailed, or the cries of treason raised in the aftermath of the convention might have had more serious and ugly effects. As it turned out, the convention and subsequent embassy to Washington was treated as an *opéra bouffe*. The situation in Massachusetts, although bleak enough, did not justify the calling of such a convention. Baltimore was attacked by combined land and sea forces a few months earlier and the inhabitants successfully defended their town in three days of fighting. It was not too much to expect Boston to do the same. As for the towns in northern Maine captured without resistance, they were territory still claimed by the British under the treaty ending the Revolution. This was not the time for a high-handed attitude on the part of pacifist New England.

Luck intervened in the appointment of George Cabot as head of the Massachusetts delegation, which assured the prudent, noncommittal character of the convention. This languid old Federalist, living in retirement on his estate in Brookline, came forward to save the convention from the grip of Pickering and Lowell. When questioned by an extremist as to the objectives of the Massachusetts delegation, Cabot replied: "We are going to keep you young hotheads from getting into mischief." [18] And they did. The delegates to Hartford were the cautious patricians of the party who guided New England in resistance to the war. It was a policy of do-nothing. The peace party in New England out-numbered the war party; in the peace party itself, the moderates out-numbered the extremists. Consequently no unanimous or positive action was possible and the original plan to present a solid front of rebellious states at Hartford collapsed. Only Massachusetts, Connecticut, and Rhode Island sent delegations sponsored by their legislatures. New Hampshire and Vermont were represented by locally elected delegates who acted without legislative authorization.

The delegates to the Hartford Convention met in the Connecticut State House designed in 1792 by Charles Bulfinch. This early public building was erected from plans drawn in the carefree days between his return from Europe and the disaster in Franklin Place. The Connecticut capitol, smaller and less grand architecturally than the Massachusetts State House, was about twenty years old when the delegates to the Hartford Convention met there late in 1814. The convention remains largely a mystery. Its sessions were held in secret and the conclusion of peace hard on the heels of adjournment prevented the testing of the resolutions. The now highly embarrassed delegates minimized the work of the convention despite the efforts of their opponents to magnify it. The old Francophile Jefferson turned the tables on the French-hating grandees of the Federalist party who journeyed to Hartford by branding them "Marats, Dantons, and Robespierres." Doubtless a good deal of treason was talked behind the correctly classical façade Bulfinch designed for the Connecticut State House. But, after all, the cornerstone of nullification was supplied sixteen years before by the Republicans themselves with the Kentucky and Virginia Resolutions. The most dangerous specific threat was the openly expressed desire for an alliance or confederation of New England states if war with England was not brought to a prompt conclusion, an obvious violation of the Constitution. The convention adjourned early in January 1815 and unwisely permitted its report to be published in the Hartford press. This was immediately taken up and circulated by newspapers and pamphleteers throughout the nation. The report stressed the rights of states to restrict their militia, to assist one another in mutual defensive measures, and offered seven amendments to the Constitution reflecting New England's sensitivity to the problems of embargo, declarations of war, the admittance of new states, and the holding of civil offices by naturalized citizens.

It would have been well if the representatives to Hartford had gone into seclusion upon the completion of their labors. Instead, one of them, Harrison Gray Otis, and two fellow Bostonians, Thomas Handasyd Perkins and William Sullivan, were sent off to Washington in an attempt to gain presidential consideration of the convention's proposals. The ambassadors innocently departed for Washington on February 3. Everything went smoothly as far as New York, where an interesting phenomenon occurred which Otis reported to his wife later in a letter from Philadelphia:[19]

We have been exceedingly amused by the circumstances of *three* black crows, constantly preceding us from New York to Philadelphia. Whenever a flock alighted which was every ten minutes, THREE of them separated from the rest and stalked over the ground, waddling and looking wise till they were frighten'd away. These are *ill omen'd* birds and in days when augury was in fashion would have been considered as sad precursors to the three Ambassadors.

And indeed they were. The ambassadors arrived in Georgetown the night of February 13, just twelve hours before the news of the signing of peace at Ghent reached Washington. The representatives of the New Englanders who convened at Hartford were in a foolish position and their opponents did not spare their feelings. They had to remain in Washington for another ten days, and were greeted everywhere with derision. The whole country exploded with mirth over the fatuous situation of the "three Ambassadors." What might have been a bitter and disastrous episode was buried in the relieved laughter of a nation once again at peace.

Harrison Gray Otis, however, was not amused; Madison understandably excluded him from White House parties. The socially accomplished Otis also missed all the festivities up in Boston where his townsmen celebrated the peace just as lustily as if they had fought in the war from the start. News of the Peace of Ghent raced through Boston on February 15, driving everyone into the streets. Strangers embraced, women wept, even Republicans and Federalists grasped one another's hands. Bulfinch announced the peace would be celebrated in Boston on February 22, the birthday of the first Federalist President. The chief selectman invited the entire town to join him that day in a public procession in honor of peace, or as he described it in his proclamation: "This interesting occasion." The celebrations began in the morning with an oratorio in King's Chapel after which the townsfolk scattered to join in the parade or to vantage points along the line of march. The most sought after places were the windows of the Colonnade, which looked directly upon the Mall where the president of the Washington Benevolent Society, Josiah Quincy, marshaled the parade. He was followed by representatives of the town's life: Bulfinch and the dignified officials, the somber clergy, the affluent merchants, the stalwart seamen, the brilliant militia, and the trades with floats showing bricklayers building a house and carpenters erecting a temple of peace. The serpentine of marchers wound for hours through the streets of the South and North Ends. There had not been such a procession in Boston since Washington visited the town in the far away days when the Federalist experiment was launched with optimism and high hopes.[20]

The parade broke up in State Street, and many of the tired marchers dropped contentedly into nearby Faneuil Hall where a huge feast awaited them. Alden Bradford, whose history of Massachusetts was published within memory of the event, noted with approval that "the citizens of Boston never have a great meeting, but they connect it with a good dinner."[21] But even more excitement was in store for the exhausted populace. Bulfinch an-

nounced that town buildings would be illuminated for
three hours after dark and a number of organizations and
private citizens added to the public glitter. Every part of
the town had fiery centers of light. Down in the South
End, where the Tontine Crescent curved along Franklin
Place, the two "firsts" Bulfinch designed for Boston
glowed in the night: the theater outlined in fireworks and
the Roman Catholic church illuminated by a blazing cross.
The colonnade of the State House held a temple and star
of peace ringed about by the Commonwealth's symbolic
pines aglow with lights. Below Beacon Hill, Bowdoin
Square glistened in reflections on the snow, and in neighboring Southack's Court, where Charles Bulfinch's family
lived through some of their worst financial years, a bright
transparency showed the lion and the eagle united. Far off
in every direction, out to Charlestown and Brookline and
Roxbury and Dorchester, bonfires roared on frozen hill-
tops and candles gleamed in hundreds of windows.

Boston's peace celebration ended the next evening in a
public ball in Concert Hall, which Bulfinch had renovated
during the war years; probably he also designed the series
of transparencies placed between the windows on this
great occasion. It was the last of the peace festivities missed
by the town's ambassadors who still remained unhappily
in the nation's capital. But Harrison Gray Otis did attend
the Washington's Birthday ball held by the Federalists of
Georgetown. He wrote home to Boston comparing it to the
ball he was not invited to attend in Washington: "The ball
here on birth night was select and genteel . . . The ball
at Washington was of a different Complexion . . . Un-
covered benches, naked walls, fiery muslins, and bloody

flags, Clerks and Clerkesses, Members of Congress, Officers of the Army."[22] The two balls were obviously worlds apart, one representing the future, the other the past.

The Federalist ladies and gentlemen gathered in Concert Hall were dancing out the past. No Jacksonian boots scarred the floor. Boots in fact were taboo at a ball in Federal Boston. Nor were gentlemen admitted without white gloves, shoe buckles, and powdered hair. A number of British officers in scarlet coats were conspicuous among the dancers moving through the decorous steps of the minuet; in Boston the waltz was not yet accepted. Most of the elderly gentlemen crowded around the huge China punch bowl wore wigs. For war or peace, though the administration be Federalist or Republican, one of the enduring sights of Bulfinch's period was the Saturday evening procession of barbers' boys carrying mountains of wig boxes through the streets for the New England sabbath. The scene at Boston's peace ball—minuets, wigs and powdered hair, silver buckles, scarlet-coated English officers—went back to the days of the Province House. It seemed everlastingly removed from the ball at Washington which the town's social arbiter so unflatteringly described. But it was not. In a few years the town almost forgot England. By 1817, when Charles Bulfinch left Boston, a new generation was as eager to express national traits as their parents had been to mimic English ones.

XII

ACHIEVEMENT

THE NEW GENERATION came of age during the War of 1812. The preceding generation, the rulers of Bulfinch's Boston, had accepted intact the provincial capital and fought every change for thirty years under the Federalist banner. But the experiment of an English-oriented American society failed. The War of 1812, not the War for Independence, worked the real revolution in Boston. And in the quiet aftermath, in the seemingly uneventful years between 1815 and 1817, the last earth was piled upon the grave of Bulfinch's town. By the time the architect left for Washington the English ideal was fully interred. The new generation was American. Something was lost, of course; not only was the model of mid-Georgian London scrapped, but so were the traditions and manners of the Province House. Boston's architecture after Bulfinch was indistinguishable from other American cities, and it was generally undistinguished. But much was gained when the old town became, at last, American. Guilt was changed to honor, and finally reverence. A new generation educated in schools Bulfinch designed and administered made Boston an American legend. The "Anglomen" of recent memory became "Yankees."

Boston ceased to go against the national grain. No one could any longer turn aside the destiny of America wonderfully disclosed by the War of 1812. The conversation among the Federalist gentlemen gathered in Concert Hall late in February 1815 to celebrate the Peace of Ghent was largely concerned with prospects of putting ships back to sea and an immediate renewal of the English connection. But there was also talk of the new venture, manufacturing, which developed so promisingly and so unexpectedly during the war. Back in 1813, when the coast below Narragansett was blockaded and the middle and southern states hard pressed for goods, the *Connecticut Herald* described the situation in New England: "Wheels roll, spindles whirl, shuttles fly."[1] This busy but monotonously landlocked scene steadily became more representative of Massachusetts than adventures on the high seas. Boys would still run away to the China trade and the sleek clipper was yet to be designed; nonetheless, manufacturing was the key to Boston's place in the American system. The merchants who convened at Hartford and published their objections to foreign-born citizens were soon advertising in Europe for workers in mills constructed outside Boston from profits earned in commerce.

Francis Cabot Lowell and Patrick Tracy Jackson set up the first complete cotton factory in Waltham in 1813. Originally from Essex County, they now joined other former North Shore residents and their children in instituting a new pattern, the founding of factory towns along the rivers to the north, west, and south of the capital town.[2] Although the center of activity moved inland, maritime pursuits naturally commenced again. Immediately after news of the Peace of Ghent, the newspapers took up the cry of seamen pouring into Boston from Massachusetts farms anxious "to be once more ploughing the ocean." Every port on the eastern seaboard sent their ships out before the wind; Europe was hungering for the two American harvests the blockade kept from its shores. But Boston's share in the soaring exports was niggardly compared to the southern states: two-thirds of American exports in 1815 were in cotton, tobacco, and rice. Foreign commerce absorbed less and less of Boston's capital and interest. The new manufacturers won their victory over the die-hard merchants on the issue of tariff even before Bulfinch left the town in 1817.

Boston traditionally supported a number of industries associated with maritime pursuits, such as rope, rum, and duck cloth. Blockades, embargoes, and counterblockades strengthened the idea of manufacturing among the more flexible merchants. This changing attitude was reflected in the Boston press, which after 1813 featured advertisements for local products that previously competed unfavorably or not at all with imports: cotton and woolen goods, needles, ink, wire, books, hats, clothing, furniture. Shubael Bell, writing to his loyalist friend in Smyrna, tells of the new manufacturing undreamed of in the Province House days. "You know, it has become a proverb, that 'Boston folks are full of Notions.' We have cucumber slicers, potato and Apple parers, coffee roasters . . . to say nothing of our inventions to lessen the labours of the other sex, in washing, ironing, crimping. . . . You may smile perhaps when I tell you we have a machine to teach grammar!"[3] The manufacturer and purveyor of "Notions" emerges as the image of the new generation coming of age in Boston during the War of 1812. One of them was Charles Bulfinch, Jr., who did not become a gentleman-architect like his father, or a physician like his colonial grandfather and great-grandfather. Charles Bulfinch, Jr., bent to the changing times and threw in his lot with the future: he opened a hardware store on Dock Square and prospered.[4]

The future was the new city of Boston, the manufacturing capital that superseded the old maritime town. Although some irreconcilable Federalists dreamed of restoring the traditional supremacy of the merchant, they faced a virile, overpowering rival in the manufacturer. An indication of the large amounts of capital drifting into manufacturing during the last year of the war could be seen in the passage of twenty-four bills of incorporation for textile companies in a single session of the General Court meeting in January 1815. With peace restored, this money could not sensibly be withdrawn. Federalist merchants initially invested in manufacturing as a temporary adjunct to foreign trade, as a means of employing idle capital piling up in Boston strong-boxes. They never dreamed the economic life of Massachusetts was on the verge of a revolution. But as the war dragged on, and more factories were built, and profits were good, it appeared obvious that manufacturing had arrived permanently. Not that the economic revolution occurred over night. Many uncompromising Federalists opposed industry as avidly as they fought every new movement. Discredited in the nation's capital, holding the

Commonwealth in a precarious grip, the old guard Federalists still retained great power in Boston. Wildly conservative, they dreaded the changes an industrial society would bring. Indubitably it would increase the power of the Republicans. When a Boston merchant lost two dozen Merino sheep in 1810 through an attack by dogs, the Republican press charged the Federalists with destroying their own sheep to prevent competition with the English woolen industry. Such an accusation was impossible five years later. Federalist capital not only financed the new textile industry in eastern Massachusetts but was responsible for the breeding of the controversial Merino sheep as well. Still, for a number of years following the peace, obdurate Federalists longed to revive the days and ways before Jefferson's embargo and Madison's war.

They were willing to fall again into English hands. And Old England accommodated by doing everything possible to put New England back as a carrier rather than competitor of manufactured goods. The British planned to sink the infant American industries by flooding the market with goods priced absurdly low. As usual, however, England failed to understand the changes taking place in the United States. When the wave of cheap English goods struck the eastern coast, the New England manufacturers set up a cry of alarm. The states north from Connecticut, so conspicuous for their defiance of national authority during the war, now appealed to Washington. And their petitions to Congress for a protective tariff were sympathetically received. The Republicans came forward as protectionists. The newly self-conscious Americans would not let the old enemy destroy their budding industries even before the ink was dry on the Treaty of Ghent; the westerners and "War Hawks" flew to New England's rescue. The wheel made a full turn. Jefferson, who froze at Hamilton's concern for manufacturing in the almost forgotten days when Federalists held the nation's capital under Washington and Adams, eloquently took up the cause of tariff. But Josiah Quincy, a merchant-politician of Federalist Boston, and the man who as mayor from 1823 to 1829 was to lead the city into a prosperous era of manufacturing, violently opposed it. Another legendary figure of the next age, Daniel Webster, also fought the tariff on the floor of Congress in 1816. But the tariff passed over their objections. In the benign years after peace, the Republicans buried the axe and helped the Federalist outcasts into the future. The Republicans could afford to be magnanimous; they had won everything.

After 1815 a great feeling of unity existed among the previously divided sections of the country. America finally became a nation. The prolonged differences dividing the two factions, later parties, at the time Bulfinch returned from Europe disappeared except among the extremists. The Republicans gradually adopted most of Hamilton's principles. They evolved from advocates of loose unity to solid nationalism. And the measures the Federalists particularly opposed—embargo, the Louisiana Purchase, war in 1812—all strengthened the federal concept. Ironically, the Federalists' steady retreat from advocacy of strong central government to the sectionalism of the early Jeffersonians accelerated union. The transition from commerce to manufacturing was the final path along which Boston returned to the national fold.

The new generation, and the more compromising of their elders, felt the exhilaration of going forward. The war left the middle, southern, and western states exhausted but full of expectancy for the future. And prosperity returned to them in a rush. Federal Boston was exhausted too, but it was the exhaustion of frustration and despair. And it took the town longer to recover. Yet everyone in America wanted to forget destructive differences and divisions; a new generation of Bostonians turned with relief to the nation developing around them. Nation took the place of party. In May 1817 the leading Boston Federalist newspaper complimented a speech by Governor Wolcott of Connecticut because "its language breathes a zeal for the public good and . . . does not contain a single expression which appears to be dedicated by party spirit."[5] With such extraordinary changes taking place in the old Federalist strongholds, President Monroe set out on a peacemaking tour into New England.

Even the weather was conciliatory on the second day in July 1817 when President Monroe arrived in Boston. It was a splendid summer morning, exactly the time for banishing old hatreds and looking ahead to a new era. Boston responded trustingly to Monroe's gesture of good will; the entire populace was packed along the route he traveled from Dedham to quarters in the Exchange Coffee House. The President entered Boston astride a white charger as had Washington three decades earlier. He was officially welcomed by Charles Bulfinch, who occupied first place in the two miles of carriages and horses trailing away in the President's wake. The vast entourage wound along Orange Street and passed down Boylston Street beside the

Common amid an avenue of 4,000 children. The boys wore blue coats and white trousers reminiscent of the uniform of the Sea Fencibles Monroe and his predecessor never could get pressed into the nation's service; the girls carried emblems symbolizing the union of the parties. Every window and doorway along the route was jammed with smiling faces, and the rooftops were alive with people. It was a sincere demonstration of loyalty and atonement which Monroe accepted as sufficient repentance for the guilt of the war years.

The following morning the President was out early on a tour of the town. Bulfinch undoubtedly accompanied him on this occasion, although the architect's modesty prevented him from elaborating on his role excepting to note: "My duty as Chairman led me to be almost constantly in company with the President during his visit of about a week."[6] Bulfinch's son, Stephen Greenleaf, was not so reticent. In a letter written to his daughter forty years after the event, he noted that the President was not only delighted with his reception but "was pleased with the public buildings . . . and found that the architect of them was the gentleman at his side."[7] Bulfinch and Monroe were not strangers to one another. They had met six months earlier when the Bostonian was touring the country's medical establishments prior to submitting his design for the Massachusetts General Hospital. Bulfinch's town, hitherto unknown to the President, never looked better. All the architect's improvements were at their prime: the trees planted along Boylston, Beacon, and Charles streets were in full leaf; the gravel paths bordering the Common were freshly raked; the red or painted brick fronts of the

Beacon Hill mansions glowed among the summer gardens
lying between the river and the State House. Beyond the
Colonnade, at the head of the Common, Summer Street
stretched away to the Tontine Crescent and Franklin
Place. No matter how self-effacing Bulfinch was by nature, he could not conceal from the observant President
the enormous part he played in the plan and architecture
of Federal Boston. To a visitor seeing it all for the first
time, Bulfinch's work was staggering.[8]

Monroe's presence intensified the ceremonies observed
with general good will by the town on the Fourth of July.
There were no rival Federalist and Republican celebrations such as the one leading to the shooting of young
Charles Austin in the uncompromising year 1806. The official oration delivered by Edward T. Channing in Faneuil
Hall was absolutely mollifying, all Federalist clichés were
omitted. In rhetorical anticipation of the future, Channing
praised the lack of partisanship in Monroe's Administration and extolled the manner by which Boston was to become great: ". . . the development of the mind, the
achievements of genius, by the arts."[9] All the things, except for architecture, depressingly absent in the Federalist
capital.

The climax of President Monroe's visit was a ball given
in the Beacon Street mansion of Harrison Gray Otis, the
third house Bulfinch designed for him within a single decade. The Otis ball was a social indication of Boston's acceptance of the new American age and the swan song of
the intermediary families who kept alive the traditions of
the Province House. The people whose ancestors had
scanned the harbor from the hills and cupolas of pre-Revo-

lutionary Boston largely disappeared as a social force in the next decade. The Essex County families who imitated them from the time of the loyalist exodus were more adaptable; they flourished in the coming age of mill and factory. A few irrepressible social lions like Otis held out, but the milieu of their ancestors was gone. Even in mid-1817, with the coming age only hovering in sight, changes were enormous. When Otis threw open the doors of his oval drawing room and announced: "Ladies and gentlemen, the President of the United States," a protégé of the hated Jefferson unassumingly entered.[10] Every guest in the room remembered a few years back when Republicans—even Republican gentlemen living in Bulfinch houses—were *persona non grata*. The Federalist experiment had clearly ended in a rout. Monroe, however, was a wise pacifier. He drove out to Quincy the following day to visit John Adams, whose son was the Secretary of State. The old President walked the new chief executive over to see his neighbor, Josiah Quincy, who had voted against nearly every Republican bill during his years in Congress. The "era of good feeling" was firmly begun.

Bulfinch almost missed the chance to be Monroe's constant companion during the President's goodwill tour of Boston. At the annual town meeting in March 1815, he was not re-elected to the Board of Selectmen. The meeting adjourned in a storm of protest and reconvened four days later when all nine selectmen resigned in a demonstration against the architect's exclusion. In the intervening days the subject of Bulfinch's defeat dominated the capital; the meeting of the town held to draw up a new slate for selectmen had the largest attendance ever recorded for the month of March. Bulfinch was elected in this balloting by a vote of 1354 to 1186. There obviously was considerable opposition, the nature of which he designated in a speech delivered the following day. A public vindication of a quarter of a century devoted to the life of his town was something Bulfinch had not hitherto contemplated. Boston's lack of appreciation was a fact the architect took for granted, and his sense of neglect was only expressed in the bosom of his family. But Bulfinch was fighting for his livelihood; he needed the salary accruing from his services as Boston's chief public officer. The aroused head of selectmen began his defense with a sentence summing up his contribution to Boston: "Twenty-four years have elapsed since I was first chosen to this board; and I have ever since . . . served the town with all the talents which I was possessed of." He told his fellow citizens how he sometimes came into conflict with private interests in the discharge of these duties, specifically mentioning the hostility encountered in straightening and widening streets and in attempting to control vice and lawlessness in North Slope Village on the dark side of Beacon Hill. Those gathered in Faneuil Hall on March 17 listened for once in appreciation of the man who had done so much for their town and had asked and got so little in return. When the speech was completed, they unanimously voted to have it published in all Boston newspapers.[11]

Bulfinch's defeat and re-election emphasized the defects in Boston's municipal system and hastened the change from town to city government. Until 1822, when Boston was incorporated and elected her first mayor, all important matters were discussed in town meeting in Faneuil

Hall. Everyone had the right to speak. And, according to Ali Bey, too many townsmen exercised the privilege: "After a great deal of speechifying, they did not come to any practical results at all, but everything was said to gain applause, which in truth was dealt out to them very liberally, by clapping hands, stamping, huzzaing, etc."[12] Town government was one of the last colonial heritages the people of Boston surrendered to the changing times. It had been under steady attack since 1791, when the young Charles Bulfinch was appointed to a committee formed to propose changes in the municipal structure. The committee's recommendations, however, were not popular. Old radicals like Samuel Adams and Mercy Otis Warren opposed any tampering with the ancient ways and were supported by a majority of the town. But when Federalist control of the boards which performed the business of the town was complete, the Republicans gradually came around to favor an incorporated city. Although Bulfinch referred to specific enemies in his vindication speech, it seems likely his defeat and the closeness of his re-election resulted from general Republican resentment with so long and unbroken a tenure. The time was ripe for change. Boston's population in 1817 was 40,000, only a fraction of which could fit into Faneuil Hall for town meetings. The hall was also the only polling station in Boston. Voters entering the building were given printed or written ballots by representatives of the two parties lining the steps. There was no secrecy in the balloting. The Federalist, with an economic stranglehold on the town, had the greater advantage. Many a Jeffersonian stayed at home rather than run the gauntlet of unforgetful Federalist eyes.

By the time of Monroe's visit, watchful Republican eyes had become important too. The Federalist stronghold was quietly crumbling, and Bulfinch was lucky to leave before the final collapse. The first serious indication for him was temporary defeat in 1815. He was given two years' reprieve, but it is doubtful the Federalists could have kept him in office after 1817. Early in that year he had to relinquish his post as chief of police, although the salary from this office was switched to him as head of selectmen. But that could not go on much longer. Bulfinch's future in Boston loomed bleakly ahead. The town was moving into a period of prosperity yet almost no building was undertaken. Nor had he any longer a monopoly in what his mother once described as "the architectural line."

Just at this unpromising moment, as the year 1817 drew to a close, fortune sought the man she so long ignored. President Monroe offered Bulfinch the appointment of Architect to the Capitol with a salary of $2500 a year and expenses to move his family to Washington. It must have seemed unbelievable. Not only was the salary double what he received in Boston, but he was to begin an exciting and important work: the completion of the wings and construction of the central portion and dome of the Capitol from designs already prepared. Bulfinch understood his task perfectly. "I shall not have credit for invention," he wrote early in 1818, "but must be content to follow in a prescribed path."[13] And excepting the colonnade on the west front, which is reminiscent of the Massachusetts State House, he largely followed the lines laid out by previous architects. Bulfinch's achievements in Washington were

[270]

diplomatic rather than architectural. The devotion, good taste, experience, patience, and tact which enabled him to make Boston the most beautiful of Federal cities were now put to the nation's service, and, after more than forty years of indecision, the Capitol was completed under his supervision.

Years later Bulfinch recalled the time he spent in the nation's capital: "I love Washington, I passed there twelve of the happiest years of my life in pursuits congenial to my taste, and where my labors were well received."[14] Bulfinch loved Boston too. And while the years he worked as architect and administrator of the Federalist capital were not always happy, they were marvelously productive. He rarely allowed personal disappointments and failures to color his sense of devotion to Boston. Occasionally, however, bitterness did creep into his meager reminiscence. At the annual meeting of the town in 1818 a vote of thanks was rendered the architect by the same body that three years earlier had sought to crush him. Bulfinch was contentedly living in Washington and felt secure for the first time in many years. The uncomplaining ex-servant could relax a little. And so he noted under the date March 16, 1818, a letter from the town clerk of Boston, ". . . presenting a vote of the Town, expressing their thanks for my long and faithful services—the cheap rewards of republics, for which, however, I am grateful."[15] With a new job and a salary commensurate with his talents, he could afford a little bravado.

It was only that. Bulfinch had always utilized every opportunity to serve his town. He was head of selectmen, chief of police, designer and inspector of schools, prisons, streets, and civic buildings; the architect of its churches, houses, halls, markets, wharves, stores, banks, and warehouses; the beautifier of its Common and hills. Of course he was sometimes stung by the lack of appreciation, sometimes by the lack of any monetary payment at all for his time and ability. But he never lost the love for Boston that impelled him as a young man to ruin himself over the Tontine Crescent. And in the end he fulfilled his youthful dream. He returned from Europe in 1787 to a provincial capital lagging far behind New York and Philadelphia in style and improvement; when he left thirty years later Boston was the most perfect architectural city in the nation. The town could not possibly thank or pay him adequately. His labors were their own reward.

In 1829 Bulfinch returned to Boston, where he lived in retirement until his death in 1844, "occupied with his books, and cheered by the society of his wife and children."[16] But he designed nothing more for his native place. The architect's usefulness ended when the colonial town became an American city. Charles and Hannah Bulfinch lingered on in the homestead in Bowdoin Square. Each Sunday morning the two elderly gentlefolk went up from the West End to sit in the family pew in King's Chapel, the stone church built almost a century earlier with money donated by their grandfather. What changes the old couple had seen. Born in provincial days, reared during the Revolution, maturing in the Federal period, they passed unobtrusively away in the American age. At King's Chapel the Anglican service was replaced by the Unitarian. And there were no longer British officers in scarlet coats or merchants in wigs and silver-buckled shoes. The London-haunted town whose architecture Bulfinch created, whose social life his family and friends prolonged, and whose affairs he administered, vanished in the new age of manufacturing.

BIBLIOGRAPHICAL NOTES

I : RETURN TO BOSTON

1. Ellen Susan Bulfinch, *The Life and Letters of Charles Bulfinch, Architect* (Boston, 1896), 56; cited hereafter as Bulfinch. Miss Bulfinch's life of her grandfather remains the major source for family letters, memoirs, and memorabilia. It is based on the architect's "Autobiographical Note" and letters; the correspondence and journal of Mrs. Charles Bulfinch; an extract of family papers made shortly before Bulfinch's death by his son Thomas; the memorial and reminiscences of another son, Stephen Greenleaf; the memoir of Mrs. Susan B. Lyman; and the letters of Mrs. Thomas Bulfinch to her exiled relatives in England.

2. James Bowdoin to Benjamin Franklin, Boston, June 4, 1785, Massachusetts Historical Society *Proceedings*, XII (1897-99), 143. The Mather Brown portrait was presented to Harvard University by the late Francis Vaughan Bulfinch and hangs in University Hall, designed by Charles Bulfinch in 1812.

3. Hannah Apthorp Bulfinch described her husband's nature as of a "temperate, philosophick turn." From "a fragment, found among our mother's papers" in the manuscript notebook of Thomas Bulfinch, 1841, 18, in the Bulfinch family papers; cited hereafter as Thomas Bulfinch *MS.*

4. Contemporary accounts of Boston at the time of Bulfinch's return from Europe are in *Columbian Magazine*, I (December 1787), 789-90; Thomas Pemberton, "A Topographical and Historical Description of Boston," Massachusetts Historical Society *Collections*, III (1794), 241-304; cited hereafter as Pemberton; *Connecticut Maga-*

zine, I (February, 1801), 80-82; Edmund Quincy, *Life of Josiah Quincy* (Boston, 1868), 36-7.

5. Excepting the much restored Revere House, little remains of seventeenth-century Boston. James H. Stark, *Antique Views of ye Towne of Boston* (Boston, 1901); and *Memorial History of Boston.* Justin Winsor, ed. (Boston, 1880-81) give the best pictorial representation of the old town. The Boston Athenæum collection of architectural views is discussed in Walter Muir Whitehill, *Eye to Eye: Bulletin of the Graphic History Society of America*, 4 (March 1954), 12.

6. Walter Muir Whitehill, *Boston: A Topographical History* (Cambridge, Mass., 1959), 5-7; cited hereafter as Whitehill.

7. Jean Pierre Brissot de Warville, *New Travels in the United States.* Translated by Charles Brockden Brown (London, 1794), I, 70-71.

8. Henry Cabot Lodge, *Boston* (Boston, 1891), 167.

9. Quoted in Samuel Eliot Morison, *Life and Letters of Harrison Gray Otis, Federalist, 1765-1848* (Boston, 1913), I, 49.

10. *Journal and Letters of Samuel Curwin.* G. A. Ward, ed. (New York, 1842), 234. A friend of Bulfinch's proscribed relatives, Curwin gives a first-hand account of the New England Club in the Adelphi, London.

11. Quoted in Carl Bridenbaugh, *Mitre and Sceptre* (New York, 1962), 226.

12. The authorship of Apthorp House is discussed in Wendell D. Garrett, *Apthorp House: 1760-1960* (Cambridge, Mass., 1960), 26-7; and Fiske Kimball, *Domestic Architecture of the American Colonies and of the Early Republic* (New York, 1922), 278. See also Carl Bridenbaugh, *Cities in Revolt* (New York, 1955), 339.

13. This union took place November 20, 1788, and is described by Hannah Bulfinch: "I was by this event united to a man of high attainments, of strict moral worth . . . his fortune equal to my own, and his family the same." Thomas Bulfinch *MS.*, 10.

14. Quoted in James H. Stark, *The Loyalists of Massachusetts* (Boston, 1910), 352. Commander Charles Bulfinch, the architect's great, great grandson, is a partner in the architectural firm of Shepley Bulfinch Richardson & Abbott.

15. Bulfinch, 42.

II : NEO-CLASSICISM

1. The influence of European architectural books on American building in the eighteenth and early nineteenth centuries is discussed in Kimball, *Domestic Architecture*, chapters 2 and 3; and Hugh Morrision, *Early American Architecture* (New York, 1952), especially chapters 9 and 17.

2. Boston *News Letter*, March 10, 1768.

3. The best brief discussion of English Neo-classicism is John Summerson, *Architecture in Britain: 1530-1830* (Penguin Books, 1954), 247-90. Christopher Hussey, *English Country Houses: Mid Georgian, 1760-1800* (London, 1956), is useful for the lesser known architects who influenced Bulfinch and for its many splendid photographs.

4. The houses Bulfinch designed for the two Joseph Coolidges had been the subject of much confusion until clarified by Abbott Lowell Cummings in his study, "Charles Bulfinch and Boston's Vanishing West End," *Old-Time New England*, LII (October-December 1961), 31-49. Bulfinch's original design for the house of Joseph Coolidge is in the Phelps Stokes Collection of the New York Public Library; that of Joseph Coolidge, Jr., is in the Boston Athenæum. Contemporary descriptions of the houses are in Mary J. Peabody, *Old Boston for Young Eyes* (Boston, 1880), 7-8; cited hereafter as Peabody; and Nathaniel Ingersoll Bowditch's "Gleaner" articles published in the Boston *Transcript*, July 2, 1855-January 11, 1856, and reprinted in *Fifth Report of the Record Commissioners*, 1880, 66-8; cited hereafter as *B.R.C.*, V.

5. Boston *Advertiser*, February 20, 1869.

6. Bulfinch certainly had access to Dawes's important architectural library, twelve volumes of which passed to the Boston Athenæum upon the builder's death in 1809. Dawes's Brattle Street Church, for example, influenced Bulfinch's designs for the meetinghouses at Taunton and Pittsfield, built between 1790 and 1793. Dawes's architectural work is discussed in *Publications of the Colonial Society of Massachusetss*, 21 (1919), 419.

7. Helen Park, "A List of Architectural Books Available in America before the Revolution," *Journal Society of Architectural Historians*, XX (October 1961), 115-30. A catalogue of architectural books in

Jefferson's library is in Fiske Kimball, *Thomas Jefferson, Architect* (Boston, 1916), 90-101; Harrison's books are noted in Carl Bridenbaugh, *Peter Harrision, First American Architect* (Chapel Hill, 1949), 168-70.

8. Bulfinch, 83.

9. Charles Bulfinch to James Cutler, Boston, May 2, 1791. Amory Collection, Massachusetts Historical Society.

10. Other architectural books remaining in the Bulfinch family are a 1794 edition of John Plaw, *Rural Architecture*, and W. F. Pocock, *Designs for Churches and Chapels* (London, 1819).

11. Columbian Centinel, August 13, 1808.

12. Bulfinch's studies in perspective are in the Library of Congress. A possible source for this pioneering work is discussed in Dirk Jan Struik, *Yankee Science in the Making* (Boston, 1948), 79.

13. The card is among the Bulfinch papers in the Massachusetts Historical Society.

14. Bulfinch, 82.

15. Ibid. 147.

16. As late as 1808, Bulfinch received only forty dollars for his design of the Massachusetts Bank in Boston. See note 19, Chapter IX.

17. John Summerson, *Georgian London* (Penguin Books, 1962), 129.

18. It is uncertain that even the Brimmer house was actually faced with stucco. A photograph in the Bostonian Society taken when the dwelling was razed shows only the brick structure and no indication of the simulated masonry prescribed in Bulfinch's drawing in the architectural library at Massachusetts Institute of Technology.

19. This is admittedly untrustworthy evidence. Another painting in the Bostonian Society of about 1815 shows the State House house red, and an English visitor before 1811 reports the same, E. Mackenzie, *View of the United States of America* (Newcastle, 1819), 103-4. Some time in the first quarter of the nineteenth century the brick was painted yellow and it remained such for a hundred years.

20. An oil painting of Franklin Place made in about 1830 in the Bostonian Society shows one of the double houses painted gray and another painted yellow; Benjamin Nutting's painting of the Tontine Crescent, made twenty years later, portrays the houses painted white. Miss Bulfinch describes her grandfather's brick house in Bulfinch Place as white also, Bulfinch, 142. The highly porous condition of locally made brick in the Federal period suggests there was practical as well as esthetic reason for painting the surface of Boston houses. The question is discussed by John Alden in a letter to the authors, Boston, May 15, 1962.

21. Perez Morton's country house in Roxbury is illustrated in John Mead Howells, *Lost Examples of Colonial Architecture* (New York, 1931), plates 162, 164; cited hereafter as Howells.

22. Pemberton, 253; Jeremy Belknap to the Hon. G. R. Minot, June 30, 1795, Massachusetts Historical Society *Collections*, IV (1795), 190.

23. Shubael Bell, "An Account of the Town of Boston Written in 1817," *Bostonian Soc. Pub.*, III (1919), 15-65, gives perhaps the best contemporary picture of local building techniques and materials; cited hereafter as Bell.

24. Fisk Kimball assumed that Jefferson planned Bulfinch's architectural journey in France and Italy, *American Architecture* (Indianapolis, 1928), 77. Bulfinch's French passport, given by Jefferson in Paris, August 16, 1786, remains in the Bulfinch family.

25. A photograph and plan of Mrs. Swan's Dorchester house are in Kimball, *Domestic Architecture*, 162-3. The house is described by Mrs. Swan's granddaughter, Mrs. E. S. Oakey, "Recollections of American Society," *Scribner's Monthly*, XXI, 3 (January 1881), 419; and by another visitor, Nathaniel Ingersoll Bowditch, *B.R.C.*, V, 218-19. See also William Dana Orcutt, *Good Old Dorchester* (Cambridge, 1893), 394-9; Francis S. Drake, *The Town of Roxbury* (Boston, 1905), 135-6.

26. Bulfinch's drawing of the Barrell house is in the Boston Athenæum; a floor plan made by Ogden Codman is in Kimball, *Domestic Architecture*, 279. The house is recalled by Mr. Barrell's granddaughter, Anna Eliot Ticknor, *Memoir of Samuel Eliot* (Boston, 1869), 15-16; cited hereafter as Ticknor. Other contemporary sources are the *Memoir of the Life of Eliza S. M. Quincy* (Boston, 1861), 62; Bell, 24-5; *Columbian Centinel*, December 19, 1792; *Massachusetts Magazine*, VI (November 1794), 693. A detailed study made of the structure prior to demolition is in Massachusetts Historical Society *Proceedings*, 10 (1895-96), 550-51. Frank Chouteau Brown summarized recent investigations in *Old-Time New England*, XXXVIII (January 1948), 153-62. The double staircase and several soapstone mantelpieces are in the Somerville Historical Society.

27. Bulfinch's famous spiral staircases inspired the novelist Michael Foster to a panegyric: ". . . which soared cool and sweet as a young girl's voice." *American Dream*, New York, 1937), 76.

28. Photographs of the interiors of Bulfinch houses subsequently destroyed or altered are in Howells, plates 198, 203, 207, 208, 210, 222, 230.

29. Bulfinch's plan for the rebuilding of "Oakley" is in the Harrison Gray Otis papers in the Society for the Preservation of New England Antiquities. The architect's association with this house is discussed by George G. Bulfinch, Jr. in a paper read June 11, 1933, at the dedication of a tablet in commemoration of the "History of the Mansion now the Clubhouse of the Oakley Country Club." The authors are indebted to Commander Charles Bulfinch for a copy of the address.

30. For the extraordinary notion that the house was designed by John Soane, see Ralph E. Carpenter, Jr., *The Fifty Best Historic American Houses: Colonial and Federal* (New York, 1955), 49. The authorship is discussed in Philip Dana Orcutt, "Gore Place, Waltham, Massachusetts," *American Architect*, 150 (June 1937), 67-74. For a late interpretation see Allen Gowans, *Images of American Living* (Philadelphia, 1964), 234-6.

31. Bulfinch's Salem commissions, as well as his influence on Samuel McIntire, are discussed in Fiske Kimball, *Mr. Samuel McIntire, Carver: The Architect of Salem* (Essex Institute, Salem, 1940), 11-13, 30 ff.

32. *Memorial History of Boston*, IV, 476.

33. Asher Benjamin began practicing in Boston in 1803. Peter Banner, an Englishman, is first listed as an architect in the Boston Directory of 1806; he worked for Bulfinch on at least one project, as witness the indenture dated November 6, 1812, in the Harrison Gray Otis papers in the Society for the Preservation of New England Antiquities. Alexander Parris's first Boston commission was apparently given by David Sears in 1816—the year he appears in the town Directory as "architect Poplar street." Solomon Willard entered the field in 1810. William W. Wheildon, *Memoir of Solomon Willard* (Boston, 1865), 33. The relationship of Parris and Willard to Bulfinch is treated in Walter H. Kilham, *Boston after Bulfinch* (Cambridge, Mass., 1946), 23-30.

34. Parris's rendering of Bulfinch's plans and elevations for the Massachusetts General Hospital is in the Boston Athenæum; some of

Willard's carvings for the Federal Street Church are preserved in the Arlington Street Church.

35. See especially *Columbian Centinel*, January 4 and 8, 1817.

36. *The Rules of Work of the Carpenters, in the Town of Boston* (Boston, 1800). The whereabouts of Bulfinch's copy of this work, with amended notes and measurements of buildings, is not known. See Bulfinch, 84.

37. *Columbian Centinel*, December 22, 1792.

38. Published in Boston, 1833. Bulfinch's copy is inscribed: "Presented to Charles Bulfinch, Esq., with the respects of the Author."

III : CHALLENGE AND FAILURE

1. *Columbian Magazine*, II (April 1788), 178. The *Columbian Magazine* became the *Massachusetts Magazine* in 1789 and was published in Boston from January of that year until December 1796.

2. The Hollis Street Church was rebuilt in East Braintree in 1810 and destroyed by fire in 1897. Relics of the building are preserved in the Bostonian Society. Contemporary sources are *Massachusetts Magazine*, IV (December 1793), 707-8; Pemberton, 253; Charles Shaw, *A Topographical and Historical Description of Boston* (Boston, 1817), 253; cited hereafter as Shaw. The design was used six years later by Caleb Ormsbee for the First Congregational Church in Providence, Rhode Island (destroyed 1814); pictured in Antoinette Forrester Downing, *Early Houses of Rhode Island* (Richmond, Virginia, 1937), 314.

3. Quoted in *Memorial History of Boston*, IV, 196.

4. Henry Cabot Lodge, *Life and Letters of George Cabot* (Boston, 1877), 19. This attitude was also shared at one time by Charles Bulfinch, who in 1786 wrote to his friend and future brother-in-law, George Storer: "theatrical exhibitions corrupt the manners of a people." Bulfinch, 50.

5. Quoted in William T. W. Ball, "The Old Federal Street Theatre," *Bostonian Soc. Pub.*, 8 (1911), 45.

6. Bulfinch, 77.

7. Quoted in Merl Curti, *The Growth of American Thought* (New

York, 1943), 139. The theater in Board Alley is described in *Recollections of Samuel Breck*. H. E. Scudder, ed. (Philadelphia, 1877), 82.

8. Pemberton, 255.

9. Harold Kirker, "The New Theater, Philadelphia, 1791-92," *Journal Society of Architectural Historians*, XXII (March 1963), 36-7.

10. *Columbian Centinel*, February 9, 1794.

11. The medal is reproduced in Charles A. Place, *Charles Bulfinch, Architect and Citizen* (Boston, 1925), 61; cited hereafter as Place. The medal, which remains in the Bulfinch family, may be the work of Paul Revere, as it bears a remarkable likeness to the engraving of the theater on a silver urn presented in 1796 to General Henry Jackson by the proprietors and now in the Boston Museum of Fine Arts.

12. The records of the theater are in the Boston Public Library; John Alden's abstract of this material is in the American Antiquarian Society *Proceedings*, 65 (1955), 9-74.

13. A representation of the second Boston Theatre is in Caleb Snow, *A History of Boston* (Boston, 1825), opp. 334; cited hereafter as Snow. See also *Columbian Centinel*, October 27, 1798; Ashton R. Willard, "Charles Bulfinch, the Architect," *New England Magazine*, III (November 1890), 291-2; cited hereafter as Willard. Frank Chouteau Brown discusses the architectural differences between the first and second theaters in *Old-Time New England*, XXXVI (July 1945), 6-7. The second Boston Theatre was destroyed in 1872.

14. General Henry Jackson to General Henry Knox, Boston, April 13, 1794. Massachusetts Historical Society Collections.

15. The tontine craze was at its height in Boston in the summer of 1792. See especially *Columbian Centinel*, June 16, July 4, August 11, 1792.

16. The Crescent was the most discussed of any Bulfinch building excepting the Massachusetts State House. Contemporary descriptions are in the *Columbian Centinel*, July 6, July 31, November 23, December 4, 1793; *Massachusetts Magazine*, VI (February 1794), 67; Boston Directory, 1796, 6; Pemberton, 250; Shaw, 199; Thomas C. Amory, *Life of James Sullivan* (Boston, 1859), I, 357-8. The Crescent was demolished in 1858.

17. See Charles D. K. McLanathan's Harvard thesis "Charles Bulfinch and the Maine State House," 1951. The Maine commissions are pictured in Place, 132, 270-72.

18. Asher Benjamin, *Practice of Architecture* (Boston, 1833), Preface; *Massachusetts Magazine, VI* (February 1794), 67.

19. Bulfinch, 99. This quotation is from the journal of Mrs. Charles Bulfinch, the present whereabouts of which is not known. A comparison of Miss Bulfinch's published extracts in the *Life and Letters of Charles Bulfinch* with those in the manuscript notebook of Thomas Bulfinch reveals numerous discrepancies, mostly syntactical. Thomas Bulfinch made his copy of the journal more than fifty years before Miss Bulfinch prepared her manuscript for publication, and he submitted his work to his father for verification. Despite this, and the many and important errors of fact in the *Life and Letters,* we have accepted Miss Bulfinch's rendering of the journal in most instances when there is a duplication of entry.

20. The origin of the urn, erroneously thought to have been brought to Boston by Bulfinch himself, is discussed by W. F. Spaulding in the Boston *Evening Transcript,* April 30, 1890. A photograph of the urn is on the cover of *Old-Time New England,* XXXVI (July 1945).

21. Massachusetts Historical Society *Proceedings,* I (1791-1835), 58.

22. The Lancaster church was completed in 1816 and is the only Bulfinch church to remain substantially unchanged. *Columbian Centinel,* January 4, 1817; Willard, 279. Charles A. Place, formerly minister of the Church of Christ, Lancaster, discusses this building in *Old-Time New England,* XIV (July 1923), 18-20.

23. *Columbian Centinel,* January 26, 1791.

24. Breck, *Recollections,* 117.

25. Ibid. For a picture of Bulfinch's friend of more than a quarter-century see Walter Muir Whitehill, *A Memorial to Bishop Cheverus* (Boston, 1951).

26. Bell, 39. For other contemporary observations by Boston Protestants see *Proc. Bostonian Soc.* (1898), 47; and Thomas Wentworth Higginson, *Life and Times of Stephen Higginson* (Boston, 1907), 234.

27. *Columbian Centinel,* October 1, 1803; Shaw, 256; *Bostonian Soc. Pub.,* II (1905), 31 ff. A lithograph of the interior of Holy Cross by William Pendelton is in the American Antiquarian Society Collections.

28. Like many Bulfinch buildings, St. Stephen's had design and construction faults. In this case the pitch of the roof was too slight and serious leakage developed, a condition corrected only by the construc-

tion of an entirely new roof of imported slate. It is gratifying to note that the restoration of St. Stephen's has been authorized by Cardinal Cushing. Boston *Traveler*, September 17, 1963. Ephraim Eliot, *Historical Notes of the New North Religious Society* (Boston, 1822), 40.
29. The coffee urn presented by the Catholics of Boston to the architect was made in Paris by Mathieu de Machy and is in the Boston Museum of Fine Arts.

IV : THE GREAT SELECTMAN

1. Bulfinch, 108.

2. Ibid., 142. The Bulfinch house was destroyed in an urban renewal project in 1962 after undergoing drastic alterations almost a century earlier. See Abbott Lowell Cummings, "Charles Bulfinch and Boston's Vanishing West End." 31-49. The Society for the Preservation of New England Antiquities has a conjectural floor plan of the house made in 1920 by Professor George B. Brigham, Jr. of the University of Michigan, and also one of the wooden swag panels from the house.

3. Hannah Bulfinch to Thomas Bulfinch, Boston, July 15, 1817, in the Bulfinch family papers.

4. Bulfinch, 107-9, 142, 190.

5. Joseph Blackburn's portrait of Mrs. Thomas Bulfinch hangs in the Boston Museum of Fine Arts.

6. Funeral Sermons, Preached at King's Chapel, Boston, Occasioned by the Death of Mrs. Susan Bulfinch, Relict of Thomas Bulfinch, M.D. (Boston, 1820), 21.

7. Annie Haven Thwing, *The Crooked and Narrow Streets of the Town of Boston* (Boston, 1920), 211-12.

8. Photographic copies of two colored drawings of the Kirk Boott house are in the Bostonian Society. See *Proceedings* of that society for 1922, opp. 10. For a contemporary description see *B.R.C.*, V., 68-9.

9. Massachusetts Historical Society *Collections*, III, Fifth Series, 233-4. Early descriptions of the column are found in *Columbian Centinel*, June 18, 1791; *Port Folio*, 17 (November, 1811), 409-12; Mackenzie, *View of the United States*, 103; Shaw, 117; *B.R.C.*, V, 153; *Memoir of Eliza Quincy*, 86; William W. Wheildon, *Sentry, or Beacon*

Hill; the Beacon and the Monument of 1635 and 1790 (Concord, Mass., 1877), 69-80.

10. Not all contemporary sources are favorable. In a diary entry for November 1790, William Bentley judged it "too small." *Diary of William Bentley, D.D.* (Essex Institute, Salem, 1905-14), I, 211. Two years later Nathaniel Cutting lampooned "the ridiculous Obelisk, if such the thing may be called." Quoted in Wheildon, *Sentry, or Beacon Hill,* 66.

11. Shaw, 117.

12. The authorization for this work, given on March 26, 1802, by Governor Caleb Strong to Charles Bulfinch, Thomas Dawes, and Edward Robbins, is in the possession of Mr. William B. Osgood of Boston.

13. Place, 90.

14. Elias Boudinot's Journey to Boston in 1809. Milton H. Thomas, ed. (Princeton, New Jersey, 1955), 44; cited hereafter as Boudinot. Contemporary descriptions are in *Columbian Centinel,* January 10 and 13, 1798; Shaw, 214-17; Snow, 323. Bulfinch's "Elevation and plan of the principal Story of the State House in Boston" is in the Phelps Stokes Collection of the New York Public Library. The authenticity of Plate 10 is established by comparison with contemporary drawings of Abel Bowen and William Thackara.

15. Quoted in *Memoir of Eliza Quincy,* 86.

16. Boston Town Records, 1784-1796 (Boston, 1903), 253. See also *Boston Town Records, 1796-1813* (Boston, 1905); *Boston Town Records, 1814-1822* (Boston, 1906); *Selectmen's Minutes, 1787-1798* (Boston, 1896); *Minutes of the Selectmen's Meetings, 1799-1810* (Boston, 1904); *Minutes of the Selectmen's Meetings, 1811* to 1817, *and Part of 1818* (Boston, 1908). Unless otherwise noted, subsequent references to town affairs are from these sources and will not be individually documented.

17. Columbian Centinel, March 15, 1815.

18. Thomas Bulfinch *MS.,* 10.

19. In his capacity as chief of police, Bulfinch published in 1801 *The By-Laws and Orders of the Town of Boston,* from which most of the ordinances cited in this chapter are taken. A copy of the publication with the architect's annotations is preserved in the Bulfinch family.

20. John Tucker Prince, "Reminiscences of an Old School-Boy," *Bostonian Soc. Pub.,* III (1906), 86.

21. The view was painted by Joseph Stubbs. G. Bernard Hughes, "American Views on Staffordshire Blue," *Country Life* (February 8, 1962), 270-71.

22. Columbian Centinel, August 14, 1790.

23. Ibid. March 15, 1800.

24. Bulfinch, 128. An account of Bulfinch's administration as chief of police is given in Edward H. Savage, *A Chronological History of the Boston Watch and Police, 1631-1865* (Boston, 1865), 53 ff.

25. J. F. Hunnewell, *A Century of Town Life: A History of Charlestown* (Boston, 1888), 84.

26. Bulfinch, 154.

27. Thomas Hamilton, *Men and Manners in America* (Edinburgh, 1833), 97-8. For Bulfinch's own views on penology see the pamphlet written in June 1829 and presented to President Andrew Jackson as ". . . A Concise Statement of the construction and of the physical and moral effects of penitentiary prisons, on the Auburn Principle: compiled from authentic documents in the possession of his humble servant, Charles Bulfinch, Present Architect Capitol Washington," 7-8.

28. Savage, *Chronological History,* 41.

29. Breck, *Recollections,* 36-7.

30. Proc. Bostonian Soc. (1896), 27.

31. Bulfinch, 189-90.

32. Shaw, 227.

33. John T. Apthorp to Charles Jackson and Samuel P. Gardner, Boston, May 5, 1818. Bulfinch's note is dated July 15, 1806. All in the Francis Cabot Lowell papers in the possession of Mrs. Harriet Ropes Cabot and cited with her permission. This loan is especially interesting when it is known that a month earlier Bulfinch, in his capacity as chief of police, was called upon to order Mr. Lowell to cease drawing an excessive quantity of water from the well of his distillery on Chambers Street, with the result that the business was suspended and eventually sold. Letter of Charles Bulfinch to Francis Cabot Lowell, Boston, June 19, 1806.

34. Bulfinch, 188.

35. Columbian Centinel, September 6, 1800; Snow, 209-10; *Memorial History of Boston,* IV, 241; Russel B. Nye, *The Cultural Life of the New Nation: 1776-1830* (New York, 1960), 160.

36. The Hawkins Street building (Mayhew School) was replaced in 1847 by a new structure and converted to a stable. J. Smith Homans, *History of Boston, From 1630 to 1856* (Boston, 1856), 213.

37. Nathaniel B. Shurtleff, *A Topographical and Historical Description of Boston* (Boston, 1872), 309-10; hereafter cited as Shurtleff.

38. Bell, 19-20; Shaw, 218; Snow, 324.

39. Boston *Advertiser*, February 20, 1869.

40. Mackenzie, *View of the United States*, 104.

41. Columbian Centinel, June 10, 1801.

42. Bulfinch, 58. An example of Bulfinch's "giving gratuitous advice in Architecture" was a request in 1791 to referee a property dispute in Salem between his friends Benjamin Austin and Captain John Derby. Benjamin Austin to John Derby, Boston, April 14, 1791; John Derby to C. Davis, Salem, April 16, 1791. C. Davis Collection, Massachusetts Historical Society.

43. The sketch was made two years before Bulfinch's death by Alvan Clark and is reproduced in Bulfinch, frontispiece.

44. Josiah Quincy, *A Municipal History of the Town and City of Boston, during Two Centuries* (Boston, 1852), 26-7.

V : POLITICS

1. Pictured in *Massachusetts Magazine,* II (January 1790) opp. 1. The controversy over the Washington Arch is discussed in Amory, *Life of Sullivan*, I, 254.

2. Massachusetts Magazine, II (January 1790), 3.

3. Ibid. I (October 1789), 659.

4. John Hancock's use of gout as a political weapon was notorious. See Brissot de Warville, 94; and W. V. Wells, *The Life and Public Service of Samuel Adams* (Boston, 1865), III, 258.

5. Massachusetts Magazine, I (October 1789), 331-3. The drawing was used by James Hoban for the capitol of South Carolina and Bulfinch himself used it when he designed the capitols of Connecticut, Massachusetts, and Maine.

6. Bulfinch, 78.

7. Perhaps the best brief description of a Boston Federalist is given in Higginson, *Life and Times of Stephen Higginson*, 279.

8. The horror which these events aroused in even the most liberal Bostonians is told in the *Memoir of William Ellery Channing.* William Henry Channing, ed. Boston, 1848), I, 60.

9. Quincy, *Josiah Quincy,* 362.

10. Fisher Ames, *Works.* Seth Ames, ed. (Boston, 1854), I, 334.

11. Lodge, *George Cabot,* 21.

12. Quoted in Quincy, *Josiah Quincy,* 64.

13. Pictured in Howells, plate 76. See also Amory, *Sullivan,* I, 267, 292.

14. Theophilus Parsons, Jr., *Memoir of Theophilus Parsons* (Boston, 1859), 108.

15. Bulfinch, 158.

16. Story, who represented Salem in Congress, was held by Jefferson as chiefly responsible for the embargo's repeal and was cast out of the inner circles of his party with the epithet, "Pseudo-republican." William W. Story, *Life and Letters of Joseph Story* (Boston, 1851), I, 185.

17. Henry Cabot Lodge cites the loss of shipping in Boston alone in 1807 as equal to 40 per cent of the national tonnage. *Boston,* 185.

VI : COMMERCE

1. Samuel Eliot Morison, *The Maritime History of Massachusetts, 1783-1860* (Boston, 1921), 164. Morison gives one of the earliest serious studies of the architecture of Charles Bulfinch as well as a superb picture of the Boston merchant in the Federal period.

2. Quoted in *Memorial History of Boston,* IV, 203.

3. The *Columbian* medal is reproduced in Massachusetts Historical Society *Collections,* 79 (1941), 162.

4. Charles Bulfinch to Francis Vaughan Bulfinch, Roxbury, July 24, 1838, in the Bulfinch family papers.

5. Foster Rhea Dulles, *The Old China Trade* (Boston, 1930), 46-7.

6. Henry F. Bond, "Old Summer Street, Boston," *New England Magazine,* XIX (November 1898), 350.

7. Morison, *Maritime History,* 64-6.

8. For the sometimes tragic end of the youthful sailors see Harriet

Ropes Cabot, "The Early Years of William Ropes & Company in St. Petersburg," *The American Neptune*, XXIII (April 1963), 131-2.

9. Both Nathaniel Silsbee and Richard Cleveland were born in Salem and moved to Boston; one as a director of the Boston branch of the United States Bank and the other in the Boston Custom House. Richard Cleveland's *A Narrative of Voyages and Commercial Enterprise* (Boston, 1842), is perhaps the most celebrated first-hand account of Federal maritime experience.

10. Quoted in Morison, *Maritime History*, 57.

11. Memoir of Thomas Handasyd Perkins. Thomas G. Cary, ed. (Boston, 1856), 295.

12. See note 31, Chapter II and note 22, Chapter VII.

13. Lucius Manlius Sargent, *Dealings with the Dead* (Boston, 1856), 351. This remarkable collection of erudition, wit, and nonsense is important chiefly as an indication of the dawning spirit of humanitarianism in the late Federal period.

14. The best picture of the merchant's day is given in Morison, *Maritime History*, 129-33. See also Ticknor, 166-7; Bond, "Old Summer Street," 350; *Proc. Bostonian Soc.* (1896), 25.

15. Ticknor, 142.

16. Bulfinch's friend, Henry Sargent, painted such a scene in his own house in Franklin Place in about 1816. The painting, "The Dinner Party," hangs in the Boston Museum of Fine Arts.

VII : BEACON HILL

1. Although Olive Street did not become Mount Vernon Street until 1832, it is hereafter designated by its present-day name. *A Record of the Streets, Alleys, Places, Etc., in the City of Boston* (Boston, 1910), 349.

2. The Hancock house was finished in 1740 and demolished 123 years later amid a storm of protest. A replica was built in 1926 at Ticonderoga to house the New York State Historical Association.

3. Breck, *Recollections*, 109.

4. Quotations are from *B.R.C.*, V, 170. Bulfinch's elevation and floor plan of the Joy house are in the Boston Athenæum.

5. Copley's conflict with the Mount Vernon Proprietors over his fa-

ther's estate is discussed by the artist's granddaughter, Martha Babcock Amory, *Domestic and Artistic Life of John Singleton Copley* (Boston, 1882), chapters VIII and IX.

6. The designation Mount Whoredom was probably dropped sometime in 1795. Nevertheless, Nathaniel Ingersoll Bowditch recalled in 1855 having seen "a very large and accurate plan in the possession of the Mount Vernon Proprietors, made 60 or 70 years ago, which was entitled by the surveyor in large and elaborate letters, a plan of 'Mount Hoardam.' " *B.R.C.*, V, 152-3.

7. Bulfinch's projected plan for Beacon Hill, superimposed upon Withington's executed scheme, is given in Allen Chamberlain, *Beacon Hill* (Boston, 1925), opp. 70; cited hereafter as Chamberlain.

8. Carl J. Weinhardt, "The Domestic Architecture of Beacon Hill 1800-1850," *Proc. Bostonian Soc.* (1958), 13-14.

9. The first Harrison Gray Otis house was designed by Bulfinch in 1795 and is presently headquarters of the Society for the Preservation of New England Antiquities. It closely resembles the William Bingham mansion in Philadelphia, which Bulfinch visited in 1789. For a detailed description of the Otis house see *Bulletin* of the Society for the Preservation of New England Antiquities, VIII (March 1917), *passim;* the floor plan is given in Fern Ingraham, "A Visit to the Harrison Gray Otis House," *Old-Time New England,* XXIX (July 1938), 21-31.

10. The third Harrison Gray Otis house is headquarters for the American Meteorological Society, and with the exception of the granite basement is unchanged on the exterior.

11. B. R. C., V., 212.

12. See the anecdote told by an unnamed friend of Harrison Gray Otis in *Proc. Bostonian Soc.* (1896), 40.

13. Bulfinch, 146-7.

14. Ibid. 150-51.

15. The second Harrison Gray Otis house is privately owned and the interior has been altered. See Morison, *Life and Letters of Harrison Gray Otis,* I, 229; Place, 163-4; Marjorie Drake Ross, *The Book of Boston: The Federal Period, 1775-1837* (New York, 1961), 103-4; cited hereafter as Ross.

16. Three deeds dating between 1799 and 1803 relating to the Mason property on Mount Vernon Street are among the Harrison Gray Otis papers in the Society for the Preservation of New England Antiquities. One of Mason's row houses, No. 55, remains substantially unchanged. It is Mr. Abbott Lowell Cummings's belief that this house is the work of Asher Benjamin; on the other hand, the late Mr. William James assigned it to Bulfinch in a letter to the authors, Tuscon, Arizona, January 18, 1961.

17. Number 49 suggests the probably appearance of all the Higginson houses built in 1803 on upper Mount Vernon Street.

18. The house of Thomas Perkins was demolished in 1853; it is pictured in Howells, plates 74 and 75. Bowditch described it from memory as "a fine brick dwelling-house of large and elegant proportions." *B.R.C.*, V, 183.

19. Quoted in Chamberlain, 111.

20. Number 87 Mount Vernon Street is occupied by the Colonial Society of Massachusetts. See *B.R.C.*, V, 206; Ross, 110-11.

21. Chamberlain thinks the bow front dates from alterations made after 1817 by Charles R. Codman. *Beacon Hill*, 164.

22. A description of Captain Richard Crowninshield Derby's house is given in Peabody, 14.

23. Samuel Adams Drake, *Old Landmarks and Historic Personages of Boston* (Boston, 1901), 337; cited hereafter as Drake.

24. It was while acting in this capacity that Colonel James Swan sent home the furniture that is now in the Boston Museum of Fine Arts. Howard C. Rice, Jr., *Bulletin of the Museum of Fine Arts*, 38 (June 1940), 43-8; Ross, 138.

25. See note 25, Chapter II.

26. Chamberlain, 168; Ross, 111-12.

VIII : PARK STREET AND THE COMMON

1. The earliest account of the architecture of "Bulfinch Row" seems to be Bell, 23. The plan and elevation of the first four houses are in the Massachusetts Historical Society.

2. Kimball, *Domestic Architecture*, 275; Drake, 353. For the background of this and other Park Street houses see Robert M. Lawrence, *Old Park Street and Its Vicinity* (Boston, 1922); cited hereafter as Lawrence.

3. Columbian Centinel, May 10, 1806.

4. Henry Adams, *History of the United States* (New York, 1889-1891), I, 92.

5. Ames's eulogy to Washington is given in Ames, *Works*, II, 71-88.

6. Ticknor, 119. A fine description of Gore is given by his friend William Sullivan, *Familiar Letters on Public Characters and Public Events, 1783-1815* (Boston, 1834), 370-71.

7. Jeffersonian America: Notes on the United States of America Collected in the Years 1805-6-7 and 11-12 by Sir Augustus John Foster, Bart. Richard Beale Davis, ed. (Huntington Library, 1954), 329.

8. Quoted in Stark, *Loyalists*, 219.

9. Quoted in Lawrence, 103.

10. Ibid. 82.

11. Memorial History of Boston, I, 85.

12. Bulfinch, 51.

13. Printed proclamation, Boston, July 1803, in Harrison Gray Otis papers in the Society for the Preservation of New England Antiquities.

14. Bell, 26. Bulfinch's appeal to the townsmen to join him in making this "the most extensive and beautiful public walk in any city of the United States" is in *Columbian Centinel*, November 16, 1816. See also Shaw, 310; Mary Farwell Ayer, *Early Days on Boston Common* (Boston, 1910), 44.

15. B.R.C., V, 31.

16. Bell, 24. Photographs of the Colonnade are in Howells, plate 72; and Whitehill, 68. See also Samuel Arthur Bent, "Colonnade Row," *Bostonian Soc. Pub.*, XL (1914), 9-57; Shurtleff, 308; Drake, 316; Frank Chouteau Brown, "The First Residential Row Houses in Boston," *Old-Time New England*, XXXVII (January 1947), 60-69.

17. Drake, 316. Colonnade Row was also called "Codfish Row."

18. Amory, *Sullivan*, II, 162-86.

19. Samuel Knapp, *Extracts from a Journal of Travel in North America, . . .* (Boston, 1818), 56-7.

IX : FROM TOWN TO CITY

1. Bulfinch's plan for the Mill Pond is reproduced in Whitehill, 80. Among the Harrison Gray Otis papers in the Society for the Preservation of New England Antiquities are more than a dozen relating to the Mill Pond project, several of them in Bulfinch's hand.

2. Bulfinch, 174.

3. Bell, 22.

4. *B.R.C.*,V, 141.

5. Drake, 381. The country-like atmosphere of old Fort Hill is described in *Eliza Quincy Memoir, 72.*

6. Bulfinch's project for the development of Fort Hill was announced in the *Columbian Centinel,* November 14, 1801.

7. Bulfinch, 48, See Frederick L. Oliver, "The Bridges of the Charles," *Proc. Bostonian Soc.* (1952), 33-47. The Charles River Bridge was designed by Major Samuel Sewall, *Massachusetts Magazine,* III (March 1790), 143.

8. *Columbian Centinel,* January 7, March 24, April 11, 1792.

9. Bulfinch's proclamation is in the *Columbian Centinel,* January 1, 1800. The funeral is discussed in *Bostonian Soc. Pub.,* IV (1907), 138-45.

10. The petition of the Selectmen dated December 27, 1803, the remonstrance circulated by Edward Tuckerman in 1804, and other pamphlets relating to the South Boston Bridge controversy are in the Houghton Library.

11. Josiah Quincy, *Figures of the Past* (Boston, 1883), 334.

12. Harrison Gray Otis papers, Society for the Preservation of New England Antiquities.

13. Bulfinch's authorship of the Broad Street project is established in a draft for masonry work in 1806 among the Harrison Gray Otis papers in the Massachusetts Historical Society and in the many works agreements in the Francis Cabot Lowell papers, some of which are cited in Abbott Lowell Cummings, "The Beginnings of India Wharf," *Proc. Bostonian Soc.* (1962), 17-24. The stores were destroyed in 1952.

14. An English visitor described India Wharf in about 1810 as "An extensive range of lofty warehouses . . . built of red brick, with much neatness and uniformity." Mackenzie, *View of the United States,* 104. The Bostonian Society has a photographic record of the project.

15. Bulfinch's plans, elevations, and specifications for rebuilding Faneuil Hall are in the Boston Public Library.

16. Bulfinch's modesty is testified to in some lines composed by a

friend and included in Stephen Greenleaf Bulfinch's memorial to his
father in the Boston *Advertiser,* February 20, 1869:

> A wonder in our days, my friend—
> An artist I have known,
> Who never slandered others' works,
> Nor ever praised his own.

17. Peabody, 13-14; *B.R.C.,* V, 176.

18. Bell, 29-31.

19. Asher Benjamin, *The American Builder's Companion* (Boston,
1806), 66 and plates 43 and 44. Two years later Benjamin lost out to
Bulfinch in a competition for the Massachusetts Bank, erected in 1809
at 64 State Street. The financial rewards were negligible: $40 to the
one and $25 to the other. *The First National Bank of Boston* (Boston,
1934), 37.

20. Little is known of the three insurance offices Bulfinch designed
for State Street other than what is given in the architect's list of buildings in Bulfinch, Appendix.

21. Columbian Centinel, January 3, 1816.

22. A photograph of Boylston Market and Hall taken before demolition in 1888 is in Howells, plate 12; the *Columbian Centinel,* May 24,
1809, reported the cornerstone laid by John Quincy Adams. The
cupola, one of the finest Bulfinch designed, is now on the Calvary
Methodist Church in Arlington. Parkman's Market was apparently
similar in design to Boylston Hall, Snow, 332. Sometime before 1806
Bulfinch designed a large double house for Samuel Parkman that subsequently was erected of Chelmsford granite in Bowdoin Square. It
was razed in 1902. Kimball, *Domestic Architecture,* 277; Place, 218
and 220.

23. Columbian Centinel, September 14, 1796: "A subscription is filling for building a large and elegant Public HOTEL . . . from a plan
lately presented by CHARLES BULFINCH, Esq."

24. Harold Kirker, "The Boston Exchange Coffee House," *Old-Time
New England,* LII (Summer 1961), 11-13.

25. Boudinot, 34.

26. As told by the Reverend Dr. Edward J. Young, Massachusetts
Historical Society *Proceedings,* VII (1891-92), 455. This observation
was seconded by Bulfinch's friend, the surveyor John G. Hale, *Survey
of Boston and Its Vicinity* . . . (Boston, 1821), 20-23.

X : ARTS AND SCIENCES

1. Journal of Ralph Waldo Emerson. Edward Waldo Emerson and Waldo Emerson Forbes, eds. (Boston, 1909-14.), VIII, 339.

2. Quoted in Curti, *Growth of American Thought,* 193.

3. Ames, *Works,* II, 354.

4. Henry Adams's observation that the Boston newspapers failed "to instruct the public in any useful purpose" is applicable to magazines as well. The only "foreign" periodical much read was Joseph Dennie's violently anti-Republican *Port Folio,* published in Philadelphia by a former Bostonian. The Boston press in the Federal period is discussed in Shaw, 282.

5. Struik, *Yankee Science,* 66; Adams, *History,* I, 94.

6. Ticknor, 149.

7. Nye, *Cultural Life of the New Nation,* 253.

8. Breck, *Recollections,* 190-91.

9. Kimball, *McIntire,* 78.

10. Place, 71-2. At a special meeting of the society on July 13, 1801, Bulfinch was elected a resident member, and it was noted "That in consideration of the generous donation of the Library room . . . he be exempted from paying eight dollars on his admission, and also from the annual payments of two dollars." Massachusetts Historical Society *Proceedings,* I (1791-1835), 143-4.

11. Ibid. 236.

12. Shaw, 278.

13. Lewis P. Simpson, *The Federalist Mind: Selections from the Monthly Anthology and Boston Review, 1803-1811* (Baton Rouge, Louisiana, 1962), 12.

14. North American Review, 4 (January 1817), 286; "Peregrinus" in Massachusetts Historical Society *Collections,* III (1815), 229.

15. According to an anecdote told by an English visitor, Stuart's wit was sufficient to charm even the taciturn General Washington. *The Aristocratic Journey, Being the Outspoken Letters of Mrs. Basil Hall, Written during a Fourteen Months' Sojourn in America, 1827-1828.* Una Pope-Hennessy, ed. (New York, 1931) 32-3.

16. But even in this area Boston's isolation was so complete that when in 1834 William Dunlap brought out his pioneering *History of the Rise and Progress of the Arts of Design in the United States,* Charles

Bullfinch (sic) was alloted only two and one-half lines in the appendix of the second volume. Thirty years earlier the Reverend William Bentley called him "the most eminent architect of our Country." *Diary*, II, 417.

17. *Columbian Centinel*, April 10, 1816.

18. Quoted in Maurice Bear Gordon, *Aesculapius Comes to the Colonies* (Ventnor, New Jersey, 1949), 65.

19. Sargent, *Dealings with the Dead*, 26.

20. Shaw, 218-19. The Massachusetts Medical College was designed by a builder knows only as Jacob Guild. It is pictured and briefly described in Walter L. Burrage, *History of the Massachusetts Medical Society* (Norwood, Mass., 1923), 100, 128.

21. Quoted in *Memorial History of Boston*, IV, 559.

22. For typical medical advertisements see *Columbian Centinel*, January 26, 1806, and February 17, 1816.

23. John Warren's role in Revolutionary medicine is discussed in Brooke Hindle, *The Pursuit of Science in Revolutionary America* (Chapel Hill, 1956), 289-91.

24. Quoted in Struik, *Yankee Science*, 157. The poem was not included in Dr. Waterhouse's popular tract, *Cautions to Young Persons Concerning Health . . .* (Cambridge, Mass., 1805).

25. *Columbian Centinel*, March 16, 1799.

26. Excepting additions to the original wings made about 1820, the exterior of the Bulfinch Pavilion of Massachusetts General Hospital remains substantially unchanged.

27. Ticknor, 171.

28. Peabody, 18-19; *Proc. Bostonian Soc.* (1896), 33.

29. Bentley, *Diary*, III, 482.

30. Shaw, 251. A drawing of the Federal Street Church is in Abel Bowen's *Picture of Boston* (Boston, 1829), opp. 153. See also Ezra S. Gannett, *A Memorial of the Federal-Street Meeting-House* (Boston, 1860), 79. Bulfinch's only other executed work in the Gothic style is the spire of the first building at Kenyon College, Gambier, Ohio. See Richard G. Solomon, "Philander Chase, Norman Nash & Charles Bulfinch: A Study in the Origins of Old Kenyon," *Historical Magazine of the Episcopal Church*, XV (1946), 209-31. The connection between Bulfinch and Bishop Chase is noted in Bulfinch, 260.

31. Boudinot, 51.

XI : THE WAR OF 1812

1. Columbian Centinel, June 24, 1812.

2. Prince, "Reminiscences of an Old School-Boy," 91.

3. Massachusetts supplied more volunteers for the regular army in the War of 1812 than any state but New York. Adams, *History,* VIII, 235-6.

4. James B. Gardner, "New England Guards," *Bostonian Soc. Pub.,* IV (1907), 9-53; *Proc. Bostonian Soc.* (1949), 34.

5. Columbian Centinel, September 26, 1812.

6. The authors are unable to locate the source of this quotation, which is thought to have come from General H. A. S. Dearborn's *Life of William Bainbridge, Esq. . . .* It is not included in James Barnes's edition of that work published by Princeton University Press in 1931.

7. Eliza Quincy Memoir, 157.

8. Columbian Centinel, January 2, 1813.

9. See Note 16, Chapter V; also Savage, *Chronological History,* 54.

10. Columbian Centinel, August 31, 1814.

11. Morison, *Life and Letters of Harrison Gray Otis,* II, 12.

12. Bell, 28.

13. Columbian Centinel, October 1, 1814; Walter Kendall Watkins, "The Defence of Boston in the War of 1812," *Proc. Bostonian Soc.* (1899), 35-74.

14. Columbian Centinel, April 16, 1814.

15. Benson J. Lossing, *The Pictorial Field-Book of the War of 1812* (New York, 1868), 1009.

16. Sketch of the Church Solemnities at the Stone Chapel, and Festival at the Exchange, Thursday, March 25, 1813 . . . (Boston, 1813), 34.

17. Channing, *Memoir,* II, 99-100.

18. Lodge, *George Cabot,* 519.

19. Quoted in Morison, *Life and Letters of Harrison Gray Otis,* II, 163.

20. Columbian Centinel, February 22, 1815; *The Articulate Sisters.* M. A. DeWolfe Howe, ed. (Cambridge, Mass., 1946), 12-4; *Proc. Bostonian Soc.* (1896), 33-4.

21. Alden Bradford, *History of Massachusetts, From the Year 1790, to 1820* (Boston, 1829), III, 230.

22. Quoted in Morison, *Life and Letters of Harrison Gray Otis*, II, 168-9.

XII : ACHIEVEMENT

1. Quoted in Adams, *History*, VIII, 14.
2. The rise of industry in Massachusetts, with emphasis upon architecture, is told in John Coolidge, *Mill and Mansion* (New York, 1942), especially 9-72.
3. Bell, 62-3.
4. *Columbian Centinel*, March 20, 1816.
5. Ibid. May 21, 1817.
6. Bulfinch, 192.
7. Stephen Greenleaf Bulfinch to Maria Harriet Bulfinch, Boston, January 7, 1857, in Bulfinch family papers.
8. An English traveler in Boston at the time of President's Monroe's visit described Bulfinch's transformation of the Common as the equal to anything in London. Mackenzie, *View of the United States*, 154.
9. *An Oration Delivered July 4, 1817 at the Request of the Selectmen of Boston* (Boston, 1817).
10. Eliza Quincy gives a picture of the interior of a Bulfinch house in her account of the ball, *Memoir*, 19-20.
11. The *Columbian Centinel* carried Bulfinch's speech in the issue of March 18, 1815.
12. Knapp, 40-41.
13. Bulfinch, 214.
14. Place, 279.
15. Ibid. 206.
16. Manuscript memoir prepared by Stephen Greenleaf Bulfinch for his daughter, Maria Harriet, Jamaica Plains, November 6, 1864, in the Bulfinch family papers.

Index

INDEX

Massachusetts General Hospital, 51, 228, 265
Massachusetts Historical Society, 70, 214-15
Massachusetts Medical Society, 224
Massachusetts State House (new), 33, 81-3, 142, 147, 148, PLATES 10, 12
Massachusetts State Prison, 41, 92
Mather, Rev. Cotton, 55, 207
Mather, Rev. Increase, 7, 8
Matignon, Abbé François, 72
Mayhew, Rev. Jonathan, 25, 229
Medicine, 220-27
Memorial Column, 80-82, 151, PLATE 10
Mill Creek, 185, 186
Mill Pond, 11, 185, 186, 191
Mill Pond Corporation, 186
Miller, John, 44
Minot, George, 192
Mitchell, Robert, 44
Monroe, James, 37, 264, 265, 266, 267, 270
Morison, Samuel Eliot, 128, 131
Morse, Samuel F. B., 218
Morton, Perez, 41, 116, 119, 139, 200
Morton, Mrs. Perez, 40, 211-12
Morton, Perez, house (Boston), 116
Morton, Perez, house (Roxbury), 40, 47, 49
Mount Vernon, 14, 148, 149, 158, 215
Mount Vernon Proprietors, 148, 149, 150, 151, 152, 155, 158, 161
Mount Vernon (Olive) Street, 143, 148, 150, 151, 152, 157, 158, 160, 164
Mount Whoredom, 11, 14, 84, 147, 148
Mylne, Robert, 44

New England Guards, 237, 238
New England Marine Insurance Company, 202

New North Church (St. Stephen's), 74, PLATE 24
New South Church, 41, 188, 229
North End, 11-12
North Slope Village, 14, 137, 148, 149, 151, 157, 268
North Square, 12, 13

Olive (Mount Vernon) Street, 143, 148, 150, 151, 152, 157, 158, 160, 164
Oliver Street, 188, 189
Otis, James, 16, 153, 154, 173, 210
Otis, Harrison Gray, 17, 111, 115, 116, 137, 147, 151, 152-4, 156, 157, 158, 169, 177, 186, 193, 194, 196, 199, 241, 244, 253, 254, 256, 257, 266, 267
Otis, Harrison Gray, house (No. 1), 46, 47, 156, PLATE 14
Otis, Harrison Gray, house (No. 2), 41, 156, 164, PLATE 15
Otis, Harrison Gray, house (No. 3), 41, 48, 152, 266, PLATE 20
Otis, Harrison Gray, house (Waltham), 49
Otis, Samuel, 153
Otis, Mrs. Samuel, 153

Paddock, Adion, 165
Pain, William and James, 36
Paine, Charles, houses, 161
Paine, Thomas, 208
Palladio, Andrea, 30, 31, 46
Parish, Rev. Elijah, 244
Park Street, 165-6, 183
Parkman Market, 203
Parkman, Samuel, 68
Parris, Alexander, 51
Parsons, Theophilius, 23, 111, 115, 117, 181
Payne, William, 68, 172
Peabody, Mary, 198, 229
Pemberton, Thomas, 40, 59
Perkins, James, 159

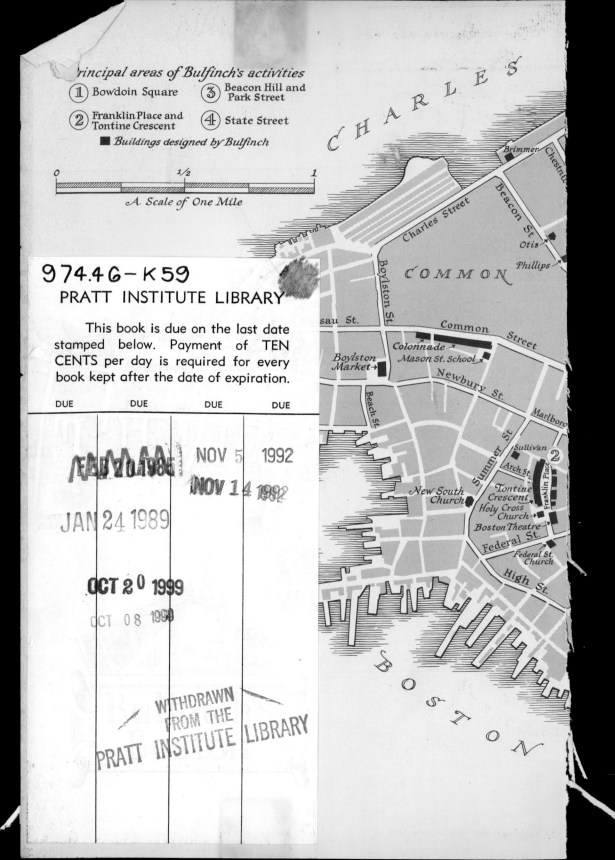

Principal areas of Bulfinch's activities

① Bowdoin Square   ③ Beacon Hill and Park Street
② Franklin Place and Tontine Crescent   ④ State Street
■ Buildings designed by Bulfinch

0   ½   1

A Scale of One Mile

CHARLES

Brimmer
Chestnut
Beacon St.
Charles Street
Otis
Phillips
Boylston St.
COMMON
Nassau St.
Common Street
Colonnade
Mason St. School
Boylston Market
Newbury St.
Beach St.
Marlboro
Summer St.
Sullivan
Arch St.
Franklin Place
New South Church
Tontine Crescent
Holy Cross Church
Boston Theatre
Federal St.
Federal St. Church
High St.

BOSTON